Marketing, Morality and the Natural Environment

Andrew Crane

London and New York

First published 2000
by Routledge
2 Park Square, Milton Park, Abingdon, Oxon OX14 4RN

Simultaneously published in the USA and Canada
by Routledge
270 Madison Ave, New York NY 10016

Routledge is an imprint of the Taylor & Francis Group

Transferred to Digital Printing 2007

Typeset in Baskerville by
Keystroke, Jacaranda Lodge, Wolverhampton

British Library Cataloguing in Publication Data
A catalogue record for this book is available from the British Library

Library of Congress Cataloging in Publication Data
Crane, Andrew, 1968–
    Marketing, morality and the natural environment / Andrew Crane.
        p. cm. – (Routledge advances in management and business studies)
    Includes bibliographical references and index.
    1. Green marketing—Moral and ethical aspects. I. Title. II. Series.
    HF5413.C73 2000
    658.8–dc21   00-035310

ISBN10: 0–415–21382–7 (hbk)
ISBN10: 0–415–43961–2 (pbk)

ISBN13: 978–0–415–21382–0 (hbk)
ISBN13: 978–0–415–43961–9 (pbk)

Printed and bound by CPI Antony Rowe, Eastbourne

To my mother and father

Contents

Preface

This book is the product of some six years research and reflection on issues of morality and how they relate to marketing and the natural environment. Its main basis comes from my doctoral research, carried out at the University of Nottingham between 1994 and 1998. This research represented an attempt on my part to address a number of issues concerning morality in organizations that had preoccupied me for some time. In particular I was fascinated by questions of how organizations shaped the morality as felt, experienced, exercised and communicated by their members, particularly in the area of marketing. I was also curious to learn how this might affect or mediate the organization's and the individual's relationship with the natural environment. Whilst enrolling as a doctoral student gave me a new language and a scholarly frame of reference with which to approach these questions, I remained dissatisfied with much of the literature that ostensibly addressed issues of marketing, morality and the natural environment. I felt that a new approach was needed, one that sought to get to the heart of *moral meaning* in the organization. Whereas most of the literature seemed to be mainly concerned with describing or judging the decisions made by people whilst at work, I was more interested in understanding the moral lenses through which they viewed their roles, their organizations, and their relationships and responsibilities to wider society. My subsequent research sought, as far as possible, to unravel these issues, and over the next few years I spent a significant portion of my time building up case studies and interviewing managers and employees in the seven organizations detailed in this book.

The data presented in the book then relate back primarily to 1995 and 1996 when the bulk of my fieldwork was carried out. As an example of inductive research, the analysis, findings and theoretical propositions presented in the book have been developed from this fieldwork, and are thus firmly 'grounded' in the data. As far as possible, I have attempted to present my analysis of my informants' experiences in a way that is sympathetic to the context in which they operated. But clearly this is very much my interpretation of the situation, as I perceived it, albeit filtered through their perceptions and descriptions.

Having completed my doctorate in 1998, I have since had time to revisit and rethink this work, and in many parts of the book, my original analysis has been strengthened, developed and enhanced. The final result, I believe, makes for a much stronger and more insightful explication. The format and style of the book is that of a fairly traditional research monograph. The opening three chapters introduce the issues, assess the literature and make a case for the research agenda and method. The central part of the book reports the empirical work, with Chapters 4, 5 and 6 covering in turn three different organizational contexts. The final part of the book consists of three chapters which discuss these findings, theorize about them, and draw out implications and conclusions.

Of course, as with any piece of research, I owe a considerable debt to a number of people. First of all I should like to thank my supervisors, Professors Christine Ennew and Ken Starkey from the University of Nottingham. Their support, encouragement and in particular their willingness to let me go my own way with the research project have been invaluable. A number of other colleagues have also shaped and coloured my thinking about many of the issues discussed in this book. In particular, I would like to acknowledge the insightful and illuminating comments of Mick Rowlinson, Andrea Prothero, Pierre McDonagh, John Desmond, Ken Peattie, and last but by no means least, the examiners of my doctoral thesis, David Knights and Mike Saren. Finally, this work would also not have been possible without the time and information provided by the various respondents whose reflections and opinions illuminate the text, and bring to life *Marketing, Morality and the Natural Environment*. My sincere thanks then to all of the individuals and organizations that offered to assist with the study in any way.

1 Introduction

The practice of marketing[1] has, in its long history, never really been free for long from the critical, and reproachful, gaze of society's moral custodians. From Christ's attempts to drive buyers and sellers from the temple courts in Jerusalem, to the burgeoning consumer movement of the last century, marketers and their actions have continued to be attacked, abused and condemned. Many writers on marketing ethics have highlighted the lack of public trust in the advertising and sales professions (e.g. Laczniak and Murphy 1993; Assael 1995; Desmond 1998), and marketing is often argued to be perceived as the least ethical of all the business functions (Baumhart 1961; Tsalikis and Fritzsche 1989). The emergence of environmentalism has added further impetus to these criticisms, primarily by identifying marketing as the ringmaster of ever-increasing consumption, and thus firmly implicating it in the attendant problems of resource depletion, pollution, species destruction and climate change. Hence, the public antipathy for marketing seems to be little changed in the thirty-odd years since Farmer (1967) rhetorically asked: 'Would You Want Your Daughter to Marry a Marketing Man?' Indeed, even to the most casual observer, the moral criticisms of marketing, rather than showing any signs of abating, if anything appear to be intensifying.

At the same time of course, as a cornerstone of capitalism, marketing has also played a key role in precipitating the enormous rise in living standards and material wealth which have been a feature of many developed economies over the last two centuries. Moreover, as a source of brand identities, advertising and other promotional communications, marketing can be said to have been a chief producer of some of the twentieth century's most powerful artefacts and icons of popular culture (see Barthes 1973). Now, with the advent of companies such as the Body Shop and Ben & Jerry's, who promote their corporate ethics and environmental responsibilities in order to enhance market share, the interconnections between marketing and morality have become ever more complex. The moral position of marketing is thus a difficult one to establish, and as a discipline and as a profession, marketing remains both venerated and vilified.

It is not surprising then to observe that the academic study of marketing has been increasingly concerned with the subject of morality. Various different strands to the literature have emerged, in particular: societal marketing, marketing ethics, ethical consumerism and green marketing. This then is an extraordinarily rich vein of research, but as Desmond (1998) notes, this plurality of approaches represents a fragmented response, and might more accurately be discussed in terms of 'marketings' rather than a unified academic literature. However, each of these strands makes an important contribution to our understanding of marketing and morality, and throughout this book I shall draw on all of these in order to provide deeper understanding of this area.

My reason for not focusing on any one of these areas alone is, however, an important one, and indeed, it is this more than anything which is at the very heart of this book. I firmly believe that these parallel, and at times overlapping, projects have been rather limited in epistemological terms. I am particularly uneasy with the way in which the very idea of morality tends to be constructed within such projects as societal marketing, green marketing and the like. When it is not simply ignored, or else merely left implicit, the marketing literature usually views morality through the lens of either ethics or social responsibility, both of which tend to be used in a highly prescriptive and objective fashion. That is, there are implicit assumptions that: (i) there is a consensus regarding which marketing activities are open to moral consideration, and (ii) that 'good' and 'bad' can be in some way unilaterally applied to these activities and decisions providing the right ethical theories are invoked. In this book however, I take the position that the denotation by a social group that any given subject is 'moral' in nature can be seen as a process of social construction (Berger and Luckmann 1966; Phillips 1991; Parker 1997). Hence, rather than moral status being viewed as concrete and real, it should be regarded as fluid, subjective and contestable. Accordingly, for the moral dimension of marketing to be understood in any meaningful way, it is necessary to suspend any external definitions, or judgements from above, of the ethics of specific activities, and to seek instead to understand how morality is given, or denied, meaning inside the social group itself (Parker 1997). My intention therefore is not to be prescriptive about how marketing should be conducted; nor is it my intention to sit in judgement of the behaviour of marketing practitioners; rather, I am seeking to explore the morality embedded in every-day behaviours, the moral meaning applied, communicated and interpreted in relation to marketing. I aim to understand and analyse rather than judge.

This book then attempts to explore how those involved in marketing deal with morality in their work. The core thesis of the book is fashioned from extensive fieldwork that I conducted in and around a number of UK organizations between 1995 and 1997. This involved talking with senior executives, middle managers and shop floor employees about marketing, about their jobs, and about environ-mental issues, and attempting to identify where *moral meaning* played a role, and what kind of role this was. I was seeking to explore how morality was construed, experienced, felt, and communicated during the marketing process. As it happens, much of what I found related to how morality was *denied* meaning and expression – a phenomenon that I refer to as *amoralization*. In the latter part of the book, I describe this process of amoralization in considerable detail: its foundations, its context, its dynamics and its consequences. I also explore the opposite process, *moralization*, i.e. how moral meaning can be interjected, or put back in, to marketing. These, I might suggest, are the central themes of the book.

I imagine that some readers will already be wondering what all this has to do with the natural environment. The answer to that is simple: my investigation of moral meaning in marketing is primarily focused on one particular form of marketing, namely *green marketing*. What I mean by green marketing is marketing which, in one way or another, explicitly concerns or considers the natural environment.[2,3] The reasoning behind this focus on marketing and the natural environment is as follows. First, from a purely practical perspective, the need to develop empirical work appropriate for the study of moral meaning in marketing meant that the broad scope of marketing had to be reduced to a more manageable scale. Hence, I chose one specific area of marketing – green marketing – rather than all marketing phenomena. Second, I wanted an issue that was intrinsically 'social' in nature. That is, it had to be one that pertained to marketing's impact on society. The environment again served this purpose well. Third, given the contemporary relevance of green marketing, and its obvious moralistic overtones, I figured that a focus here would yield empirical findings of a particularly inter-esting and vivid nature. And finally, given that existing theories and practices of green marketing suggested very little understanding or consensus regarding the role that morality should, could, or even does have, I felt that an impor-tant contribution to this literature could be readily made. Of course, in order to provide such a contribution, my fieldwork had to examine contemporary green marketing practice in some detail. An additional claim for the book I should like to make then is that it provides new and important empirical insights into green marketing theory.

Before proceeding further, I feel that a brief note on terminology is called for. As I have said, one of the key points of departure for this study was a posited distinction between the moral content of marketing or the moral experience of organizational members (how they think and feel about morality; how notions of morality impinge upon behaviour; how a sense of morality is recognized and expressed, etc.) and the means by which those thoughts, feelings and behaviours can be judged, and decisions reached. Over the course of the book, I shall use 'morality' to refer to the former, i.e. any distinction between right and wrong, good and evil, either in thought, feeling or behaviour; 'ethics' I shall use to refer to the latter, i.e. a moral code, or system of rules, through which judgements of right and wrong, etc. can be made. Parker (1997: 3), in a sharp criticism of the business ethics project, makes a strong case for the possibility of such a distinction:

> Another way to justify this suspension of judgement about judgement is (what philosophers sometimes call) 'descriptive' as opposed to 'prescriptive' 'Ethics'. This is also sometimes framed as morals – mores, norms, values – as opposed to ethics – codes, rules, tablets from the mountain . . . I suppose this is to 'sociologise' the 'Ethical', to draw it down from its supposed lofty place into the flow of the ordinary . . . It means refusing to accept a division of labour that distinguishes the 'Ethical' from the other things that people do in

particular times and places . . . So if we accept this social construction of the 'Ethical' . . . then this effectively presses upon us a suspension of our judgement, an attempt to go beyond good and evil, a gesture at relativism in the interests of a thicker description.

This move into descriptive ethics is important for the contribution I am hoping to make with this book. It also feeds into (and draws upon) contemporary debates regarding the possibility that formalized ethical codes may actually disturb, and even corrupt, a true sense or feeling of morality (see Bauman 1989, 1993). Desmond (1998) for example has argued that the codification of 'good' or 'right' or 'ethical' behaviour in marketing has done little to redress its moral culpability, or to improve the already tarnished reputation of marketers.

There are however, as Parker notes, certain aspects of moral relativism[4] implicit in the approach I wish to adopt. If I wish to avoid judgements, then I am also leaving myself open to the charge that I am therefore tolerating any particular moral behaviours, norms or codes that I observe, whatever implications they might suggest. Whilst I agree that this could potentially be problematic, it would be clearly inappropriate to engage in judgement before reaching understanding – and understanding is certainly something that is lacking at present regarding marketing, morality and the natural environment. Moreover, simply by making a 'gesture' at relativism, as Parker puts it, it does not mean that relativism is being wholly and unreservedly embraced. It has been necessary for me merely to acknowledge that moral norms and ethical codes other than my own exist, and that they are worthy of examination. Given the impact of marketing on society and on the natural environment, it would be extremely difficult to deny that the morality of those who work in it is indeed a critical area for investigation.

But how to approach the area in order to develop new and interesting insight? Given my doubts regarding theoretical development in this area in marketing, the approach adopted here is very much an interdisciplinary one. Obviously by identifying an area of study such as 'marketing, morality and the natural environment' the academic range is almost by definition beyond any single literature. The book thus spans the three literatures of marketing, business ethics and green business that are home to the main subjects under investigation. Critically, however, this is also very much a study of organizations, of their management, and of the individuals who work in them. Therefore, by the very nature of my engagement with the research area, this book also draws heavily on the organization studies and management literatures. More specifically, the introduction of environmental considerations into the marketing process is addressed in terms of issue selling (e.g. Dutton and Ashford 1993; Ashford *et al.* 1998) and product/policy championing (e.g. Chakrabarti 1974; Drumwright 1994). It is principally through tracing the individual and organizational sense-making activities (Weick 1995) attending the issue selling process, and the impression management activities (Gardner and Martinko 1988; Ashford *et al.* 1998) of green protagonists that the themes of amoralization and moralization are explored.

Aspects of organizational culture feature quite heavily here, and during the course of the book the role of culture in supporting moralization and amoralization in marketing is often returned to and elaborated on. Although there is considerable debate regarding the concept of organizational culture, it is regarded here as being concerned with a broad range of phenomena: various artefacts such as behaviours, stories, myths, symbols, language, etc.; cognitive beliefs, values, attitudes and codes; and basic, taken-for-granted assumptions (Schein 1992). These are the basic contents of the culture concept. Indeed, the phenomenon of amoralization is principally set out in the book in terms of the symbolic activity (Pfeffer 1981a), language (Watson 1994a) and narratives (Wilkins 1983) which champions use to support and facilitate the introduction and institutionalization of green marketing practices. Further organizational culture concepts, such as the shared values and beliefs of organizational members, are also explored in order to make sense of the moral dimension of marketing. Acknowledging the importance of cultural context in shaping the moral construction of greening (Drumwright 1994; Fineman 1996), the study explores moral meaning in three very diverse organizational types, namely *conventional companies, social mission companies* and *business–NGO collaboration*. These will be defined in more detail in Chapter 3, but basically these refer, respectively, to those with economic goals clearly prominent, those with social goals clearly prominent, and those involving partnership between profit-making and not-for-profit organizations.

Essentially then, culture is used here as an epistemological device with which to frame the social terrain of the organization – what Smircich (1983) identifies as a 'culture as root metaphor' approach. That is not to say however, that when I claimed this to be an inter-disciplinary study, I meant simply one crossing the subdisciplines which fall under the rubric of what might be more generally termed management or organizational studies. Whilst these might be the main influences on the book, the reader will no doubt also recognize influences from fields as disparate as philosophy (e.g. Baudrillard 1981, 1997), economics (e.g. Galbraith 1977), politics (e.g. Gorz 1980), cultural studies (e.g. Williamson 1978), even literature (e.g. Unsworth 1992) and film (e.g. *Wall Street*). All of these, and others too, have made contributions to my understanding and examination of various aspects of marketing, morality and the natural environment.

The rest of the book is set out as follows. In the next chapter, marketing is explored as a moral domain. The main concepts and theories which have been brought to bear on the study of marketing and morality are discussed and analysed. A case for more insight regarding moral meaning in marketing is developed, and the basic principles for such an investigation are introduced. In Chapter 3, I set out the philosophical perspective of the study, and the research method employed during the fieldwork. My interpretive approach is explained, the comparative case study methodology is justified, and the particular case organizations studied are introduced. Here too, I explain and justify my decision to focus the study mainly on green marketing.

In Chapters 4 to 6 I present the main results of the empirical study which forms the main basis of the book. Each chapter relates to a different organizational type, with conventional organizations, social mission companies and business–NGO collaboration being the respective subjects. Whilst the format of these chapters differs somewhat in order to explore the particular issues arising during data analysis of each case, a basic framework is used to maintain some degree of consistency. Therefore, during all of these chapters, the general approaches to green marketing in the case organizations are explained, and the relationship of green marketing with notions of social responsibility examined. The largest part of each chapter however is given over to describing the cultural dynamics of green marketing observed in the case organizations, and analysing the implications for moral meaning and for morality generally.

In Chapters 7 to 9, the findings of the study are discussed, their implications examined and conclusions reached. Chapter 7 deals specifically with green marketing as observed in the case organizations. In the first half of the chapter, the results from Chapters 4 to 6 are compared, contrasted and integrated, such that an extensive, empirically based examination of contemporary green marketing practice is presented. This is then used as a basis for exploring possible theoretical development. In the second half of the chapter, the moral dimension of green marketing as observed in the case organizations is set out. In Chapter 8, the discussion is extended to examine in detail some of the principal findings of the study, namely the phenomena of amoralization and moralization. These are described in some depth and possible explanations and consequences are explored. This discussion is then used as a basis to explore the likely implications for the management of morality in marketing. Finally, in Chapter 9, I summarize the main contributions of the book and present some conclusions regarding marketing, morality and the natural environment.

2 Marketing and morality

Perspectives and issues

Introduction

Consideration of the moral dimension of marketing has increased significantly in recent years. Areas of literature such as marketing ethics and green marketing have experienced rapid development since their emergence (or re-emergence) in the 1980s; new forms of behaviour such as ethical consumerism and ethical branding have opened up entirely new areas of literature; and various concepts and theories such as macromarketing, social marketing and the societal marketing concept have become firmly established constituents of marketing thought. It would be wrong, however, to assume that these new areas of interest represent the beginning of the marketing discipline's consideration of morality. There is evidence of moral issues entering marketing thought for as long as marketing has existed as a distinct field in itself, and since then there have been a number of waves of interest in morality. Marketing is therefore an extraordinarily rich field in which to study morality. In this chapter, I examine the various strands of the literature. The main aims are to illustrate the diversity of this literature, its contribution to our understanding of marketing and morality, and also some of its shortcomings in this respect. My ultimate intention though is to be in position to make a case for the study of moral meaning in marketing in Chapter 3; it is after all on this that my claims for the contribution of this book principally rest.

Robin and Reidenbach (1993) have shown that there are two broad areas in which moral questions can arise in marketing. First, we have macromarketing questions, which relate to the morality of marketing as a discipline, function or process in itself. Second, we have narrower micromarketing questions, which question morality in relation to the specific actions of individual marketers, marketing organizations and marketing industries. We might therefore ask either, 'What is morally relevant about marketing itself?' or, 'What is morally relevant about particular marketing practices?'. These two questions have occupied marketing scholars and various critics of marketing throughout the development of marketing thought and practice. Here, I shall discuss both, including not only the moral criticisms of marketing, but also the various lines of moral defence that have been forthcoming from marketing practitioners and academics.

Marketing as a moral subject

Although discussion of the moral standing of marketing is not overly prominent in the contemporary, mainstream marketing literature, there is a considerable history of academic debate in this area. Desmond (1998) claims that moral concerns featured at the very beginning of marketing thought. Utilizing Jones and Monieson's (1990) historical analysis of the academic roots of marketing, he points to two US schools of economic thought in the late nineteenth century which competed for pre-eminence in charting the moral course of marketing theory. The first was a 'reformist' group located at the University of Wisconsin. This school maintained that marketers should principally work in the overall interests of society by aiding in the state regulation of the marketplace. In this way marketers could ensure fair play between buyers and sellers and ensure equitable distribution of goods. The second school, based at Harvard University, subscribed to a more 'managerialist' orientation. Informed by *laissez-faire* economics, the Harvard school contended that morality should be entrusted to the individual self-interest of buyers and sellers acting through the market. Marketing was hence seen as a quasi-science, primarily aimed at achieving efficiencies in distribution.

As Desmond (1998) suggests, the Harvard model has become dominant in academic marketing. There is now an accepted moral basis for marketing enshrined in the utilitarian ideology of the market-based, economic model of capitalism (Galbraith 1977; Gaski 1985; Robin and Reidenbach 1987). The role of marketing in society is assumed to be essentially a distributive one, such that consumers can find and purchase the goods that satisfy their needs and thereby increase their material satisfaction. Essentially then, marketing has traditionally been ethically justified from a consequentialist position – i.e. by facilitating the satisfaction of consumer needs, it maximizes consumer welfare. Hence, the invisible hand of the market ensures both material welfare and just distribution.

Effective functioning of this marketing system is based upon the assumed primacy of consumer demand. This is reflected in the notion of *consumer sovereignty* – an analogy based on the premise that the economy is ruled and directed by the customer. It is this concept which forms the underlying rationale for capitalism,[1] and hence provides an ideological basis for marketing (Smith 1990). Galbraith (1972) refers to this as the 'accepted sequence', i.e. needs originate within the consumer, these are translated into a demand for products, and this demand duly activates a response from firms in the form of products that satisfy the consumer's needs. The dominant model of marketing assumes then that the role of the marketing function is technical rather than moral in nature – its purpose is to translate demand into production, not to legislate on what demand or products might be 'good'. Firms may be expected to maximize profits so long as they remain within the law (see Friedman 1970). This means that marketing has no explicit role to account for its impact on society or to protect the consumer in any way. Indeed, the conventional marketing maxim of *caveat emptor* suggests that providing it is legal to sell a product, it is the buyer's own responsibility to look out for their interests, not the marketer's (Smith 1995).

There has however been a constant stream of criticisms of this classic marketing model, much of which has focused on questions of morality in order to examine the legitimacy of the marketing project. I shall move on now to discuss these criticisms before turning to the subsequent developments in marketing thought that have been introduced in an attempt to restore credibility and legitimacy for the traditional marketing model.

Moral criticisms of marketing

As I have already suggested, there have long been moral criticisms of marketing, even from before marketing came into being as a field of study. As an academic enquiry, however, these criticisms began to be formalized in the late 1950s, and since the 1960s their development has become more sophisticated and extensive. I should like to analyse this literature by dividing the criticisms into three main groups. First, we have those that question the functioning of the marketing system, i.e. they seek to throw doubt upon the consumer sovereignty model of marketing. Second, there are those that question the impact of marketing on society, i.e. they seek to illustrate the socially undesirable results of marketing. And third, there are those criticisms that explore incidences of unethical marketing, i.e. they question the actual manner in which marketing is conducted. In this section, I shall discuss each of these themes in turn, and in this way build up a picture of how morality has been used to explore the problems and pitfalls of marketing theory and practice.

Functioning of the marketing system

As I have said, the moral basis of marketing theory is based upon the notion of the sovereign consumer, and it is perhaps unsurprising that both marketing theory and practice are replete with the discourse of consumer sovereignty (Dixon 1992; Knights *et al.* 1994; Christensen 1995). Most common definitions of marketing and the marketing concept tend to be predicated on the consumer sovereignty model, with emphasis firmly placed on the need for 'customer orientation', 'customer focus', 'customer-driven strategies', or some such version of what is essentially an 'outside-in perspective'. The following, taken from one popular textbook (Kotler *et al.* 1996), is indicative of most definitions of the marketing concept, and is explicit in its promotion of Gailbraith's (1972) accepted sequence:

> The marketing concept holds that achieving organizational goals depends on determining the needs and wants of target markets and delivering the desired satisfactions more effectively and efficiently than competitors do.
>
> (Kotler *et al.* 1996: 15)

The discourse of consumer sovereignty has by now permeated beyond marketing into a broad range of theoretical and practical arenas of management in contemporary organizations and organizational theory (Du Gay and Salaman 1992). It is, however, based on two critical assumptions: (i) that needs originate from the consumer; and (ii) that firms identify and act upon these needs when translated into consumer demand (Galbraith 1972; Dixon 1992; Knights *et al.* 1994). As we shall see, both of these have been criticized as empirically inaccurate.

With the publication of *The Affluent Society* in 1958, Galbraith (1977) provided an early, important and influential moral critique of marketing. He famously argued that firms *generate* rather than satisfy consumer needs, claiming that the industrial system had assumed sufficient size and power to render the consumer helpless in deciding what and how much is produced. To Galbraith this represented the 'revised sequence' – a categorical denial of the 'accepted sequence' of consumer sovereignty which accords power in the economic system to the individual. Galbraith's contention was that modern industrialized countries were effectively planned economies, ruled over by large self-serving corporations with little regard for the public interest. The massive expenditures on marketing were in fact cited by Galbraith as evidence for want creation on a huge scale. Also in the late 1950s, Packard's (1957) populist work, *The Hidden Persuaders*, brought moral concerns about the manipulation of consumer need through marketing to a still wider audience. With his stylistic mixture of conspiracy theory and 'pop' psychology, Packard sought to reveal how the 'depth men' of consumer research callously turned the hidden urges and frustrations of innocent consumers into blind desires for unnecessary and unwanted products.

In his early work Baudrillard[2] (1981, 1997) develops these ideas, claiming too that 'the freedom and sovereignty of the consumer are mystification pure and simple,' (1997: 72). Where he departs from Galbraith, however, is in his denial that if consumer needs are created by marketing, they can be categorized as 'false' or 'artificial', compared with underlying 'real' or 'natural' needs. He posits that, in terms of the activities of consumption, there can be no distinction, because consumers do not consume for use value or exchange value, but for *sign value*. Hence, all consumption is driven by a single basic force which is 'the logic of social differentiation', i.e. the need to distinguish oneself through the purchase and use of consumer goods. Indeed, Baudrillard (1997: 73) condemns Galbraith's 'moralizing idealism' and his depiction of the individual as a passive victim of the system.[3] For Baudrillard (1981, 1997) the important unit of analysis is not individual need, but the *system of needs*; and it is the system of needs that is the product of the system of production.

Marketing then might not so much be regarded as creating need for individual products, but rather, in aggregate, as contributing to the capitalist culture which emphasizes and rewards material accumulation (Baudrillard 1981, 1997; Featherstone 1991). I shall return to this issue shortly, as part of a broader discussion of the impacts of marketing in society. In terms of consumer sovereignty though, the question of the origin of consumer need remains problematic (Knights *et al.* 1994) – a point occasionally, though rarely, acknowledged in marketing textbooks (Dixon 1992). However, even if it could be argued that needs were objective and existing prior to consumption, for consumer sovereignty to be upheld, they would have to be duly acted upon by companies (Smith 1990; Dixon 1992; Knights *et al.* 1994). Smith (1990) however sets out the position that only under perfect competition will firms be passive to the demands of consumers. In practice, he suggests, this assumption clearly does not hold and therefore firms are likely to have discretionary power within the market (see also Galbraith 1977). It is this then which perverts the connection between consumer sovereignty and the marketing concept: consumer sovereignty presupposes the firm as passive whereas the marketing concept presupposes an active, strategic role for the firm (Smith 1990; Dixon 1992). Leading marketing academics such as Kotler explicitly acknowledge that marketing involves the firm not so much in responding to demand but in managing it:

> Marketing management seeks to affect the level, timing and nature of demand in a way that helps the organization achieve its objectives. Simply put, marketing management is demand management.
>
> (Kotler *et al.* 1996: 12)

Knights *et al.* (1994) have analysed the financial services market to illustrate how profit and cost concerns can channel as well as limit the attention accorded to consumer need. Moreover, they argue that consumer indifference can prompt firms to create rather than follow demand, such as through 'informing' and 'educating' customers of new technologies, beliefs and ways of behaving. Indeed, the creation of new markets that do not yet exist, and of going beyond what the customer thinks s/he wants, is being increasingly touted as the pre-eminent marketing strategy of successful, forward-thinking companies (see Hamel and Prahalad 1991, 1994; Martin 1995). Overall then, as Smith (1990) contends, we might regard *absolute* consumer sovereignty as more grounded in ideology than in empirical fact. However, he does suggest that it can, in some circumstances, exist to reasonably significant *degrees*. More recently (Smith 1995), he has set out the necessary criteria for such degrees of consumer sovereignty in terms of consumer capability, information provision and consumer choice.

Impact of marketing on society

Even if it could be argued that the consumer was fully sovereign in the economy, this would not necessarily provide a moral justification for traditional marketing theory. The marketing concept is concerned with marrying individual customer satisfaction with firm profitability. As Dixon (1992) argues though, this does not necessarily mean that *social* good is maximized. The consumption decision is an inherently individual one, where we seek to satisfy our own immediate needs and desires. For the most part, social concerns are not a significant force in our consumption decisions, since these are essentially about long-term, shared aspects of our lives. We might then distinguish between our concerns as consumers (what we want for ourselves) and our concerns as citizens (what we want for everyone); we are as Sagoff (1986) puts it, essentially schizophrenic. The justification for marketing therefore may be argued to be morally hollow when viewed socially. There is no reason to suggest why consumers acting upon their own self-interest will act in the interests of society as a whole. Marketing may help to sustain economic growth but it does not *a priori* promote quality of life and social welfare (Dixon 1992).

A second major issue, as I have already suggested, is that marketing in aggregate socializes and conditions consumers into a general state of perceived need and 'enforced' materialism. Kangun's (1972) book *Society and Marketing* makes one of the earliest contributions to the debate from within the marketing discipline, and his thoughts, set out in the book's preface (p. xiv), serve as a useful introduction:

> Marketing activities have a formidable influence on the ethical and social values of society. Although it may be reasonably argued that such institutions as education, religion and government have a significant influence on shaping this country's values, only marketing commands the tremendous resources that are used to convey a single message, 'consume'.

In this respect, the role of advertising has been particularly open to critique, with arguments emerging since the 1960s from a range of subfields such as business ethics (Chryssides and Kaler 1993; Phillips 1997), marketing (Greyser 1972; Pollay 1986) and cultural studies (Williamson 1978; Davidson 1992; Baudrillard 1997). Pollay (1986) provides a comprehensive summary and evaluation of many of the pertinent arguments. Central to the criticisms of advertising, he argues, has been the identification of its role in the generation and perpetuation of ideologies of consumption, and more broadly in instituting in society an identification of consumption with happiness. Advertising can create deep social unease by instituting a perpetual desire for what one does not have, and by depicting the (unattainable) possibility of a life enriched by material goods. Moreover, advertising is said to romanticize and fetishize goods, encouraging individuals to transfer their emotions and sense of self and identity away from people and spiritual matters onto objects. Greyser (1972) suggests that many of these moral attacks and defences are inherently ideological in nature, rendering few conclusions value free. This though is hardly surprising given, as Pollay (1986) wryly observes, that advertising is in itself so value laden. None the less, he regards these as important moral concerns and as such remain in need of further consideration and research.

Phillips (1997) however argues that the question is itself mis-specified; it is neither advertising nor marketing that should be open to such moral debate, but rather capitalism itself. Baudrillard (1997) too depicts the culture of consumption as a logical result of the system of production. Indeed, to some extent the debate over the ethics of marketing's propagation of materialist values has been largely undermined by the recognition that consumer society, or consumer culture, are pre-eminent in modern capitalist economies. This has shifted attention towards the (largely postmodernist) project of identifying and describing the morality (or moralities, or amorality) of consumer culture (e.g. Featherstone 1991). Indeed, the recognition that consumption might have its own morality has opened up a whole new conceptual space for scholarly enquiry in this respect – a point that the marketing ethics literature has yet to fully recognize.[4]

Since the 1960s, two more issues can be said to have constituted the moral critique of marketing's social impact. First, and of most interest in the context of this book, the ecological impact of marketing has come under considerable scrutiny. To some extent this has reflected cycles of social concern regarding the natural environment within industrialized countries, with bursts of activity occurring in the late 1960s/early 1970s and again in the late 1980s/early 1990s. Marketing is clearly implicated by most ecological critiques of business (see Fisk 1973, 1974; Irvine and Ponton 1988; Peattie 1992). The promotion of ever-increasing consumption has helped to destroy natural resources and habitats, decimate entire species, create severe waste management problems and con- tribute to alarming levels of air and water pollution. Not only this but marketing can also be seen to have further contributed to environmental deterioration through its reliance on enormous quantities of packaging, the creation of out-of- town shopping centres and the resource-sapping movement of consumer goods across the globe. The demands of the grocery and fast food industries for standardization and predictability in food products in the name of customer satisfaction has also led to myriad ecological problems associated with the use of agrochemicals, industrial pesticides and genetically modified crops. However, as modern marketing has advanced, specialized, outsourced and globalized, the distance between consumers and producers has widened (Bauman 1989; Desmond 1998). This has increasingly left customers (perhaps wilfully) unaware of the social and ecological costs of their purchases, be it rainforest destruction in Brazil, the erosion of traditional community lifestyles in Papua New Guinea or the growth in child labour in the sweatshops of Manila. Recent exposés regarding labour standards in the developing world associated with leading brands such as Marks & Spencer, Nike, Levi's and Manchester United, as well as attempts from various quarters to develop 'fair trade' or 'ethical' sourcing arrangements have ensured that these issues are currently very much on the corporate agenda in many developed countries (Strong 1996; Crane 2000).

The second outstanding issue is that of ideological stereotyping – once more an issue that has particular resonance for advertising. The main thrust of the moral criticism here is that advertising can perpetuate socially undesirable stereotypes of certain categories of person and lifestyle. For example: women become either housewives or sex objects; certain body shapes become associated with health, beauty and happiness; nuclear families become associated with 'normality'; and racial minorities, handicapped people and homosexuality become excluded from the picture of 'normal' life (e.g. Pollay 1986; Chryssides and Kaler 1993). In defence of such depictions, it is commonly argued that marketers do no more than reflect the social norms of target audiences, and that the brevity and directness of marketing messages leaves no scope for social reform (Greyser 1972; Advertising Association 1993). This 'cultural mirror' argument is criticized by Pollay (1986) who documents important arguments regarding the distorting effects that advertising can have on the culture that spawns it. He summarizes the main criticisms regarding stereotypes thus (1986: 27):

> Simplistic, symbolic stereotypes, chosen for their clarity and conciseness, serve as poor models and inhibit sympathetic understanding of individual differences. This position has been articulated in detail regarding the portrayal of women, but the problem is universal, as ads can reinforce stereotypes for not just the sexes, but also for races, ages, occupations, family relations. To the extent that these images are disrespectful or unworthy of emulation, they are socially divisive.

Such arguments have by now been well rehearsed in the extant literature, and to some extent, the debate has now moved on. Commentators have pointed to the increasing 'de-massification' and fragmentation of society into a profusion of diverse cultural groupings and identities (Featherstone 1991). Also, marketing practitioners have been entreated to increasingly offer specific marketing mixes to ever narrower market segments, even to the point of 'mass customization' (Kotha 1995). This means that previously excluded and misrepresented groups of consumers have been directly targeted by firms, suggesting that their particular tastes, styles and interests might be better researched and represented. This of course brings with it additional moral questions. For example, there is the possibility of simply replacing one undesirable set of stereotypes – e.g. that women are either housewives or sex objects – with another – e.g. that women should 'have it all' and be a housewife *and* sex object *and* successful businesswoman (Williamson 1986). Indeed, the expansion of professional marketing into hitherto ignored lifestyles is in itself a cause for concern for some critics. Featherstone (1991) for example points to how the need for stylistic individuality leads the modern consumer to construct a particular lifestyle as part of a calculated life project of conspicuous consumption. Baudrillard (1983) warns of the loss of reality as 'real' lives, 'real' people and 'real' sex become submerged under the saturating torrent of superficiality, signs and signification that constitute the world of advertising.

All these are serious issues to be addressed. Indeed, marketing academics, and the various apologists for the marketing discipline, have not been silent in the face of these criticisms. However, before I go on to discuss their response, it is necessary to deal with one last area of criticism. As I mentioned at the beginning of this chapter, there has also been considerable interest in morality in relation to micromarketing practices – essentially specific incidences of 'unethical' marketing.

Unethical marketing

There is a long history of concern over the questionable practices of marketers. The sale and purchase of goods has always brought with it questions of fairness

(Levy and Zaltman 1975), and there is ample evidence of the problems faced by customers in the nineteenth century and before with unsafe, inefficacious, over-priced or misrepresented products (see Bonner 1961; Nadel 1971). Numerous consumer co-operatives, and later regulatory agencies and consumer organiza-ions, subsequently emerged with the aim of protecting consumers from the more nscrupulous activities of marketers. This institutionalized consumer protection is continued and expanded throughout the twentieth century, and since the '60s, the momentum of the consumer movement has gathered pace yet further abriel and Lang 1995: 152–172). Perhaps this high level of attention afforded to ethical marketing practices is due to the visibility of the marketing function in role as interface between the organization and its environment. Since we all isume, we are all affected by such problems. And the unyielding attentions of media to marketing practices has meant that many of the most renowned and imous examples of corporate ethical abuse over the years have concerned the vities of the marketing department (Murphy and Laczniak 1981; Laczniak and rphy 1993). Indeed, it is true to some extent to say that most marketing isions are likely to have moral content of some form or another (Laczniak and rphy 1993). Academic literature in this area, however, has only emerged in quantity in the latter part of the twentieth century, partly as a response to the r reputation enjoyed by the marketing profession. In the main, this has fallen in the 'marketing ethics' field – essentially a subdiscipline within business cs. These normative studies of marketing ethics have basically been concerned a assessing which marketing decisions are supposedly 'ethical', and which are . These questions have been principally posed with respect to the exchange lf, or any of the decisions and practices associated with the marketing process. ny, if not all, of these areas have been examined in one way or another in the iting literature, with coverage of issues at present expanding, particularly as v concerns and practices arise (Laczniak 1993).

3eauchamp and Bowie (1997) argue that the ethics of marketing exchanges are icipally centred on two key issues: freedom of choice in entering transactions, the consequences of making those transactions. In terms of the first issue, George (1990) claims that any market transaction might be considered fair thical if both parties have adequate and appropriate information and both r the transaction willingly and without coercion. Conversely, freedom to choose can be said to have been restricted when there is evidence of undue influence, such as coercive behaviour or excessive manipulation, or informational irregularities, such as misleading or untrue claims, on the part of one of the agents of exchange. Clearly there are degrees of persuasion, and whilst some degree of persuasion may be acceptable, and clear cases of fraud may be illegitimate, difficulties arise in making ethical judgements in more questionable areas such as deception and puffery (De George 1990). Issues concerning the legitimacy of promotional tactics such as over-claiming, misrepresentation and misleading claims have thus received considerable coverage in both the marketing literature (Murphy and Laczniak 1981; Chonko and Hunt 1985) and the business ethics literature (Beauchamp and Bowie 1997; De George 1999). Ethical concerns related to freedom of choice have also been considered in relation to pricing and distribution decisions (see Smith and Quelch 1993; Laczniak and Murphy 1993).

In terms of the second issue, consideration of the outcomes of individual marketing transactions principally concerns issues such as product safety and fitness for purpose (Beauchamp and Bowie 1997). Research investigating ethical issues in this sense has tended to focus on the harmful consequences of transactions, and in particular on analysing specific high profile cases such as the Ford *Pinto*, Proctor and Gamble's *Rely* tampon, and Nestlé infant formula (e.g. Beauchamp and Bowie 1997; Beauchamp 1989). Whilst ethical concerns of this type have focused on the consequences to the individual of the marketing transaction, increasing social and environmental awareness has prompted investigation regarding the broader consequences of the exchange. For example, the environmental impact of products does not directly affect the individual consumer involved in the exchange, but rather affects society as a whole (Prothero 1990).

In addition to this literature related directly to the marketing exchange, other studies of unethical marketing have focused on decisions and practices in the broader marketing process. This includes analyses of ethical issues relating to the basic 'four P's' of the marketing mix – product, promotion, pricing and place decisions (for reviews see Laczniak and Murphy 1993; Smith and Quelch 1993) – as well as market research techniques (e.g. Akaah and Riordan 1989). Increasing fragmentation of markets has also seen greater attention afforded to unethical targeting practices, and in particular the targeting of 'vulnerable' groups such as children, ethnic minorities and patients (Beauchamp 1989; Sharp Paine 1993; Smith 1995; Smith and Cooper-Martin 1997; Rittenburg and Parthasarathy 1997).

This normative marketing ethics literature has predominantly featured the 'grand narratives' of ethical theory – most notably, deontology, utilitarianism and, to a lesser extent, virtue ethics (Robin and Reidenbach 1993).[5] Overall, it would appear that academics have been largely successful in mobilizing these theories to analyse and condemn the moral deficiencies of various marketing practices. They have shown which decisions can be supposedly regarded as ethical or unethical, and using various ethical theories, have explained why this should be so. Moreover, for incidences of unethical marketing, they have also indicated the path that managers 'should' have followed in order to be ethical. None the less, the continued and unabated incidence of questionable marketing practices suggests that the marketing discipline has been less successful in prescribing a useful and practicable model of ethical marketing, or at least in effecting any significant change in the moral rectitude of marketing practitioners. Whilst this prescriptive project is clearly a more challenging one than the normative project, it has often been claimed that improvements in marketing practice are one of the key driving forces behind much of the work in this area. Authors such as Robin and Reidenbach (1987), Smith (1995) and Desmond (1998) have argued (though not necessarily always for the same reasons) that there are problems in applying ethical theories meaningfully to marketing problems, particularly when doing so from outside the arena in which they occur and are experienced. This has the effect not only of distancing the 'ethical' from the commonplace realities of marketing practice, but privileges the perspective and discourse of the judge over that of the judged (Parker 1997). As I suggested in the introduction to this book, I believe it is important for theoretical development to move away from such ethical judgements drawn from a lofty philosophical plane, and move more towards an understanding of morality located more directly in marketing practice. As I turn to look now at the response of the marketing discipline to this and the other moral criticisms identified during this chapter, I wish to show how the failure of prescriptive marketing ethics is principally due to a misunderstanding of how marketing is manifested and made meaningful within the organization. In particular, I wish to show how the well-meaning attempts by marketing academics to interject morality into marketing thought through reformed and reconstructed theory are based upon a fundamental misconception of the moral terrain of marketing. This then is a problem of descriptive ethics more than it is one of prescriptive ethics. The ontological premises on which these prescriptions are based are, I suggest, highly problematic.

Changing models of marketing and morality

Moral criticisms of marketing have never gone totally unheeded in marketing thought, and new, ostensibly more enlightened, models of marketing began to emerge as a response by the academic discipline to the criticisms and counter-cultures of the 1960s (Arnold and Fischer 1996). It is possible to identify three initial strands of this response, labelled by Arnold and Fischer (1996) as the *apologist*, the *social marketer*, and the *reconstructionist* paradigm. Whilst interest in these areas has waxed and waned over the years, more recently, two more strands have emerged, labelled here the *ethical consumerism* and the *ethical decision-making* paradigms. I shall discuss each of these in turn and in doing so assess their role in developing a more moral conception of marketing.

The apologists

In many ways, mainstream marketing thought has changed little in the face of the criticisms outlined above. Notions of consumer sovereignty and the marketing concept have very much continued to dominate marketing theory (Dixon 1992). As Arnold and Fischer (1996) argue, marketing academics have largely rejected any moral criticisms that have been aimed at the subject and have focused instead on reaffirming the intrinsic social contribution of marketing. This has included claims regarding its role in ensuring the smooth functioning of the economy, its contribution to economic growth, and its role in facilitating material wealth. Hence, for the apologists, the profit motive is itself seen as a suitable social tool, and rather than marketing bearing any additional social responsibility, its role should be to ensure that any social value desired by customers is delivered efficiently.

This denial that marketing, and indeed business generally, is in need of any significant moral change has been made a number of times in the literature (e.g.

Levitt 1958; Friedman 1970; Greyser 1972; Gaski 1985). The arguments are by now fairly well rehearsed, therefore, and include a variety of quite significant assertions. Friedman (1970) has famously argued how the development of corporate social programmes is akin to theft from shareholders unless motivated by profit maximization. Levitt (1972) has claimed that rather than being victims of advertising, consumers understand and enjoy the playfulness of persuasion. Finally, Gaski (1985) has argued that marketing managers have no role, nor even a right, to decide what is in the public's interest. Various refutations and counter-arguments for these claims have subsequently been presented in the marketing and business ethics literatures, by authors such as Abratt and Sacks (1988), Smith (1990) and Chryssides and Kaler (1996). As a result, the apologist position is only infrequently articulated in academic work now, particularly in comparison to the more obviously moral positions that I shall go on to discuss in a moment. This, however, is somewhat at odds with its importance to contemporary marketing thought, since the traditional justification of marketing represented by the apologist position remains very much at the core of the discipline. As Dixon (1992), Arnold and Fisher (1996) and Desmond (1998) note, conceptions of marketing more explicitly social or moral in purpose may have become to some extent accepted elements of contemporary marketing theory, but they still remain very much at the margin. Indeed, Arnold and Fisher conclude that:

> Although the Sixties had a powerful influence on the development of marketing thought, we are left wondering exactly what it is that we have learned. For all the expressions of idealism and hope embodied in the Sixties experience, marketing, some 25 years later, still seems to be firmly fixated on its place in business. For marketing academicians it appears to be business as usual.
>
> (Arnold and Fisher 1996: 132)

For all that, these 'new' marketings certainly represent an important response to the moral criticisms outlined above, and are more than worthy of further discussion.

Social marketing

Social marketing can be thought of as the extension of marketing knowledge, techniques and concepts into influencing the acceptability of social ideas and causes rather than just economic goods and services. Hence, we might consider typical social marketing contexts to be, for example, charity marketing, drug and AIDS awareness campaigns, church marketing and political campaigning. Whilst not formally defined in the academic literature until the publication of their seminal paper in the *Journal of Marketing*, Kotler and Zaltman (1971) recognized that social marketing had long been in use by marketers. It formed an important part of Kotler's project to expand the domain of marketing to ever more applications and contexts (see Kotler and Levy 1969). However, the social marketing project came to be represented by many of its protagonists as a promising response to criticisms of marketing's negative impacts on society. It was held up to illustrate that marketing could be, and indeed was, a useful and constructive force in society (see Lazer and Kelley 1973).

Social marketing has certainly by now become a firmly established subfield of marketing, and significant research has been applied in the case of political marketing (e.g. O'Shaughnessy 1990), charity marketing (e.g. Schlegelmilch 1988) and church marketing (e.g. Devlin *et al.* 1996) to name but a few. Indeed, whilst Kotler has consolidated his central role in the social marketing field with a number of further publications (e.g. Fox and Kotler 1980; Kotler and Roberto 1989), many mainstream textbooks now include sections on marketing in not-for-profit organizations (e.g. Dibb *et al.* 1994), and a number of specialist journals have emerged which include social marketing within their remit (e.g. *Journal of Public Policy and Marketing*; *Journal of Church Marketing*). Whilst fairly widely accepted then as a legitimate practice in itself, at least in principle, social marketing has, however, provoked further lines of enquiry into its moral dimensions (Laczniak and Murphy 1993). Laczniak *et al.* (1979) for example provide an important discussion of the ethical ramifications of social marketing, reporting evidence from a survey of various academics and marketing professionals. They found that social marketing was a double-edged sword, with significant unresolved accountability issues, and the potential for moral controversy. The possibility of marketing techniques being morally neutral was shown to be problematic in the case of social marketing since the social cause and the techniques could not easily be separated. Indeed, the persuasive aspects of marketing that I have already discussed might be particularly problematic from a moral point of view when one considers programmes explicitly focused on social issues. Notably, in Laczniak *et al.*'s (1979) survey these problems were perceived as less significant by marketing professionals than by academics. More recently O'Shaughnessy (1990) and Devlin *et al.* (1996) have explored the practice of social marketing in particular contexts, and in this way highlighted some of the moral ambiguities which might accompany the manipulation of social causes in order to appeal better to consumers. We only need to think about current concerns regarding political 'spindoctoring' and 'soundbite politics' to recognize that the continued expansion of the marketing domain brings with it its own moral debates.

Reconstructionists

If the development of social marketing represented an extension of existing marketing technologies into new social areas, the other strand of Kotler's attempt to conceptualize and legitimatize marketing's social role wrestled with a more fundamental reconstruction of marketing theory. The main thrust of the reconstructionist paradigm is the notion of societal marketing, and this was initially introduced specifically in response to the burgeoning 'consumerism' movement in the US of the mid–late 1960s (Kotler 1972; Arnold and Fischer 1996). Consumerism, defined by Kotler (1972: 49) as 'a social movement seeking to augment the rights and power of buyers in relation to sellers' was regarded by him as a positive force for establishing enhanced consumer sovereignty in the face of excessive seller power. Moreover, he claimed that if marketing recognized and embraced the 'opportunities' offered by the movement, then marketing could maintain its legitimacy and (by implication) avoid the increased regulation that had followed previous such movements. Kotler's response was in the form of a revised marketing concept that he labelled the *societal marketing concept* (SMC). This called for marketers to provide *in addition* to the basic elements of the marketing concept – customer satisfaction and profitability – a third element which he called 'long-run consumer welfare'. By doing so, Kotler was acknowledging the argument discussed previously that what was good for individual consumers might not be good for society (Levy and Zaltman 1975; Dixon 1992). Whilst Kotler proposed that one way to adopt the SMC was through a 'consumerist orientation' – as in a general culture of customer concern within the organization – his main emphasis was on setting out the types of product that might, or might not, be appropriate to a societal marketing orientation. By defining product benefits in terms of short-run consumer satisfaction and long-run consumer welfare, he claimed there were essentially four types of product. These were: *deficient products* which he said offered neither short- nor long-term benefits; *salutary products* which had low immediate appeal but high long-term consumer benefit; *pleasing products* which gave high immediate satisfaction but could cause harm in the long term; and *desirable products* which combined immediate satisfaction with long-run benefit. These are shown in Table 2.1.

Table 2.1 Kotler's (1972) classification of products according to the societal marketing concept

| | | *Immediate satisfaction* | |
		Low	*High*
Long-run consumer welfare	High	Salutary products	Desirable products
	Low	Deficient products	Pleasing products

Kotler suggested that for the implementation of the SMC, deficient products should be deleted from the product range altogether; salutary and pleasing products should undergo product modification in order to move them towards the top right-hand quadrant; and the development of desirable products should be the ultimate aim of marketing efforts. Kotler was therefore explicitly acknowledging that marketing should no longer be regarded as an amoral science, but that marketers should act as moral guardians against the unpalatable consequences of individual choice. Hence, it was accepted that the invisible hand of the market needed some degree of organizational integrity or social responsibility in order to ensure satisfactory social outcomes. In justifying and proselytizing the SMC then, Kotler (1972: 55) articulated a mixture of ethical and self-interest exhortations, with the emphasis falling slightly on the former:

The addition of long-run consumer welfare asks the businessman to include social and ecological considerations in his product and market planning. He is asked to do this not only to meet his social responsibilities but also because failure to do this may hurt his long-run interests as a producer.

Since this original formulation, the SMC has to some extent become an accepted part of the marketing lexicon, and makes an appearance in many contemporary textbooks. Usually, it is presented as an evolutionary step forward from the marketing concept.[6] However, as Dixon (1992) observes, the SMC is commonly noted in the introductory chapter of such texts, but then is essentially ignored during the main part of the text. This, he claims (p. 116), often distorts macromarketing issues by repeating and reinforcing 'the myth that the pursuit of profit by marketing managers maximises social welfare'. The SMC then has largely failed as yet to fulfil its potential in providing a significant moralization of marketing theory. Some further studies have however been conducted, including Gaski's (1985) criticism of the SMC (with a basic re-run of Friedman's argument that marketers should not be expected to determine what is in the public's interest) and Abratt and Sacks' (1989) rare empirical study. They trace the response made by companies in the South African tobacco and alcohol industries to social concerns, revealing reluctance and denial in the former and a relatively conciliatory, constructive approach in the latter. They conclude that the alcohol industry approach had indeed been of a societal marketing type response and that, as a result, appeared to be legitimating itself better in society than the tobacco industry. Finally, Prothero (1990) has set out the SMC in relation to social responsibility and green marketing, suggesting that in the context of increased consumer concern over environmental issues, firms would and should respond with the introduction of the SMC. As with Kotler, her argument is that the impetus for societal marketing strategies comes from a combination of self-interest (this time, the concerns or pressures of consumers rather than regulators and pressure groups) and social responsibility.

There are still, however, a number of important issues which remain problematic in terms of the SMC. First, existing conceptions tend to assume that what is good or bad for consumers in the long run is an objective, value-free fact. This disregards the possibility that competing positions may exist in a pluralist society and that these will have important implications for the identification of deficient, pleasing, salutary and desirable products. Indeed, Abratt and Sacks (1989) argue that many, if not most, products could be regarded as harmful or dangerous in *some* way, without them being demonized in the same way as alcohol and tobacco. For example, the marketing of motor vehicles has led to untold road casualties, unrestrained food promotion has resulted in increasing obesity and other health problems, and increased paper consumption has been accompanied by deforestation on a massive scale. By the same token, traditional 'bads' such as the manufacture of weapons might be defended by some on account of their contribution to peace and national defence, and 'goods' such as wind-powered electricity turbines might be criticized as 'inefficient' and a 'pollutant' of the aesthetics of the local environment.

A second problematic issue is that the SMC can be regarded as a somewhat blunt instrument of moralization. Although it accounts (albeit imperfectly) for long-term social welfare it takes no account of other moral issues involved in the marketing exchange, such as the rights of firms to market what they wish, and the rights of individuals to consume what they wish. Clearly then, whilst the SMC might be a important moral arena of marketing, particularly in the sense that it provides a perspective on marketing as a legitimizing practice, like social marketing it throws up its own complex moral issues and questions.

Ethical consumerism

Whilst the SMC has hardly succeeding in igniting a reconstruction of marketing theory, the 1990s have witnessed soaring interest in the potential for morality to provide a significant influence on consumer purchase decisions. Therefore, over the past decade or so, the marketing literature has paid increasing attention to consumers' ethical considerations, the effect of these concerns on purchase behaviour, and the role of marketing in understanding and responding to these concerns. However, the possibilities here have long been recognized by practitioners. For example, the UK Co-operative movement was established in the mid-nineteenth century partly in response to customer concerns over the questionable ethics of existing retailers (Bonner 1961; Birchall 1994), and 'enlightened' employee welfare policies on the part of large commercial enterprises during the early part of the twentieth century were at the time seen to have afforded products an ethical dimension. As Ashley (1912: xiii) commented nearly ninety years ago regarding the benefits of the British manufacturing firm, Cadbury's, progressive labour policies:

> [The labour policy] has been a splendid advertisement . . . I think this is a particularly encouraging fact, and highly creditable to human nature. It shows there is such a thing as a consumer's conscience. The whole essence of the Consumers' League work in America and of the white lists of the Christian Social Union in [Great Britain] is to make it 'good business' to be known to manufacture under satisfactory working conditions; and with increasing publicity and an increasing fellow-feeling among all classes, I expect that this is going to be the case more and more.

Academic researchers have only more recently focused attention on this issue, but early work in the 1970s on socially conscious consumption (Anderson and Cunningham 1972), responsible consumption (Fisk 1973) and ecologically concerned consumers (Kinnear *et al.* 1974) established a foundation for much of the work that now goes on under the labels of ethical and green consumption and purchasing (e.g. Drumwright 1994; Shrum *et al.* 1995; Schlegelmilch *et al.* 1996; Strong 1996). Broadly, what these studies have sought to achieve is the identification of such consumers, explanations for why they have emerged, delineation of their concerns and insight into how these concerns might impact upon purchase behaviour. However, whilst it has been shown that some consumers certainly do at times incorporate moral concerns into product evaluations, further investigation into the phenomenon has provided little additional insight. Indeed, attempts to segment consumers according to their moral evaluations, and ultimately to predict purchase behaviour, have yet to be suitably realized. The main problem here has been that many studies have been largely misconceived, either by failing to account for heterogeneity in any single consumer's moral concerns, or by viewing moral concerns in isolation from other 'conventional' (i.e. non-moral) product attributes.

Another stream of work has sought to establish whether there is indeed a benefit to firms for being ethical. Taking the 'enlightened self interest' position that good ethics is good for business (see Mintzberg 1983), various studies have investigated corporate ethics, social responsibility or social performance (or a reputation for these) in relation to financial performance (Aldag and Bartol 1978; Aupperle *et al.* 1985; McGuire *et al.* 1988; Dooley and Lerner 1994) or market share (Owen and Scherer 1993). As yet though, empirical evidence is somewhat equivocal regarding the ethics–performance relationship (Aldag and Bartol 1978; Owen and Scherer 1993; Burke and Logsdon 1996). Attention has also focused on identifying and analysing the use of social, moral and environmental themes in organizational communications (Lill *et al.* 1986; Phillips and Brown 1993; Iyer *et al.* 1994). Rising to a peak in the early 1990s, such themes are now perhaps less evident than they once were, but remain a significant part of the communications landscape. Moreover, it is quite clear that business leaders too, in their public pronouncements and corporate communications, have increasingly stressed the importance of ethical values in attracting and retaining customers. For example, following considerable time in the spotlight regarding its social and environmental policies, Shell UK in 1998 published its 'Report to Society'. In the introduction, Chris Fay the Chairman and CEO had this to say:

> Consumers have become more discriminating and more demanding. From ethical investments to rising demand for 'green' products, from concern over employment conditions in the developing world to consumer boycotts, the evidence of a more committed public is all around us. The public demands from us the highest standards of ethical and environmental responsibility.

Interest in morality from the point of view of consumer purchases has thus prevailed. Indeed, survey evidence throughout the 1990s has continued to show that consumers increasingly claim to include ethical criteria in their purchase decisions, and that boycotting of firms and products over ethical issues is a potential tactic for sizeable proportions of the populace (see CWS 1995; Strong 1996; Cooper 1998; Rogers 1998).

Although much of this work has been largely under-theorized, Smith (1990) has provided one of the first, and certainly one of the more scholarly, expositions of how ethics can be conceptualized as part of ethical purchase behaviour. Using Levitt's (1980) notion of the augmented product concept,[7] he shows that various aspects of morality can contribute to the overall meaning of the product in the consumer's eye, and can in turn affect the consumer's desire to purchase the product. Whilst Smith considers only the negative impact of undesirable moral choices on the part of sellers, there is clearly the potential for both positive and negative augmentation in this respect. The perceived ethics of any product offering can thus provide either an incentive or a disincentive to purchase. Moreover, this type of moral augmentation can pertain to any number of issues relating to the product. Hence, I am not just talking about moral concerns specific to the individual product, but also to the way in which it is marketed, the social behaviour of the supplying firm and even the country of origin of the product. Hence, the product might be regarded as composed of – in addition to other 'conventional' attributes – a bundle of positive and negative moral augmentations.[8] For example, Body Shop shampoo could (hypothetically) be *positively* augmented by *the product's* lack of animal testing, and *the company's* stand on recycling; by the same token it could be *negatively* augmented by *the company's* record of employee relations, and *the product's* use of non-renewable petrochemicals. The possibilities for such augmentation are in fact many and diverse – and as I said with respect to the SMC, it is dangerous to consider ethical augmentations as objective and value free. When reduced to product evaluations, morality is very much in the eye of the beholder.

The ethical consumer literature in its various guises appears to be becoming an established element of the marketing and morality literature. In terms of marketing theory, however, it offers little beyond the accepted sequence of consumer sovereignty upon which mainstream marketing is predicated. Marketers are generally portrayed as little more than the passive responders to the ethical whims of consumers. Morality is less a part of marketing, than it is of consumers. Smith (1990) writes of this in terms of ethical consumers providing a social control of business, at least when they are informed sufficiently to make 'rational' choices. At the same time though, he investigates only the case of consumer boycotts, where consumers are clearly more organized and powerful than they are as the solitary individuals conceived in traditional marketing theory. In this sense then, the pressure groups that form and direct boycotts might be thought of as a countervailing power in the marketing system. However, whether we think of consumers as individuals or as organized groups, we must still recognize the limitations of the ethical consumer model to achieve social good when there is insufficient demand or willingness to pay on the part of these consumers.

Taking a route rather more challenging to marketing theory, Prothero (1990) links green and ethical consumption with the SMC. She contends that a societal orientation should be adopted in the face of changed consumer demands. As with Smith then, Prothero sees the market as a social control of business, but in her work, one can also see a desire to moralize the marketing function. Crucial to Prothero's argument then (and indeed many other writers in this stream of literature[9]) is that consumer concerns with social and environmental issues are increasing, and will continue to do so, perhaps indefinitely – a relatively unsupported, untested and perhaps historically naïve claim. However, by combining this with similar assumptions regarding the growing interest of other stakeholders such as pressure groups and regulators, what is frequently suggested in the ethical and green marketing literature is that the development of products sophisticated enough to satisfy these demands necessitates a fundamental strategic reorientation. Hence, the need for more ethical vision, mission, values and leadership is seen by many within the literature as a critical element in the drive for ethical or green competitive advantage, and the development of an improved reputation. An 'ethical culture' thus becomes a prerequisite for satisfying increasingly demanding and cynical customers. Therefore, only by becoming a moral agent and adopting a positive social role can the firm construct a strategic response to indisputable and inescapable stakeholder pressures both current and anticipated. So, in a sense, the firm moves from being a market-led, externally controlled system characterized by a degree of passivity to one which is rather more strategic, moralistic, and internally driven.

These then are two quite distinct models: one where the firm simply responds to the ethical concerns of consumers, and one where the firm claims to be socially responsible itself and thus takes an active role in deciding what is in the public's best interest. Evidence from analysis of organizational communications suggests that corporate social responsibility of some kind is indeed a common claim for firms utilizing green themes (Iyer and Banerjee 1993; Iyer *et al.* 1994). However, debates within the accounting literature suggest that we might also question whether social and environmental communication has as much to do with maintaining organizational and institutional legitimacy as it does responding to consumer concerns (Puxty 1986; Patten 1992; Gray *et al.* 1995). As yet then, we have precious little evidence of how, or indeed whether, these models operate in practice, and what they require from the marketing function. For example, if the latter strategic mode is to be adopted, then what constitutes an 'ethical culture' and what values, beliefs and behaviours are likely to be manifest within one? The task of examining how marketing managers and other staff actually deal with moral issues in their work has in fact been dealt with most fully by our last stream of literature. The final response then to the moral criticisms of marketing that I want to deal with is the ethical decision making literature.

Ethical decision making

With marketing being so roundly criticized, and marketers widely seen as villains of unethical practice, the academic study of marketing and morality has almost inevitably examined the decision making processes leading to ostensibly 'ethical' and 'unethical' decisions. The core of this area of the literature has been the largely descriptive project concerned with modelling these processes and delineating the form and impact of various explanatory variables in determining their outcomes. The first significant model was devised by Bartels (1967), but it is Hunt and Vitell's (1986, 1993) rather more comprehensive version which has become more influential and widely cited. This model attempts to make more explicit the process by which moral decisions and resultant behaviours might be made, with

the avowed intention of constructing a base for empirical testing. The most recent
version of the model sets out a set of contextual variables, namely cultural,
professional, industry, organizational and personal characteristics. It is suggested
that these are the principal influences on the ethical decision making process.
The main part of the model then attempts to integrate the major ethics grand
narratives of deontology and teleology as different but complementary modes
of evaluation undertaken by the individual. It is this evaluation which is pre-
supposed as determining the consequent judgements, intentions and behaviour of
the individual. Whilst some aspects of this model have been tested, these have not
met with unqualified success, and various efforts are under way by Hunt and
colleagues to provide more persuasive empirical support (Hunt and Vitell 1993).

A number of other models of ethical decision making have also been
conceptualized within the marketing field (Ferrell *et al.* 1989) and more generally
within the business and organizational ethics fields (Treviño 1986; Jones 1991).
Central in much of this discussion is the relative impact of individual, contextual
and situational factors on decision making with moral content. Treviño (1986) for
example highlights the importance of individuals' moral development with situational factors such as the immediate job context, organizational culture and work
characteristics acting as moderating influences. Contextual factors have also been
examined and Corey (1993) has argued that certain conditions inherent to the
marketing function tend to create an environment for marketing managers which
is highly influential in prompting unethical behaviour. First, he says that marketing can be regarded as a boundary spanning relationship aimed at completing
transactions; hence the successful conclusion of deals may take precedence over
other (moral) considerations. Second, marketers act as agents for their organizations and are therefore in a position to receive benefits from conducting successful
transactions both as individuals (e.g. commission or bribes) and through the firm
they represent (e.g. increased sales). Third, Corey argues that marketers have
the capacity to wield significant economic power to influence, reward or punish
particular customer choices.

Of particular relevance, however, to the current study is the relatively recent
rise in interest in the role of organizational culture in affecting ethical judgements.
Aspects of organizational culture and climate have increasingly been the subjects
of academic scrutiny concerning morally relevant decision making in marketing
and in more general business applications (e.g. Robin and Reidenbach 1987;
Waters and Bird 1987; Sinclair 1993; Vitell *et al.* 1993; Dahler-Larsen 1994;
Treviño and Nelson 1995). Often this is centred on the notion of core values,
namely the central and fundamental guiding principles about which corporate
realities are said to be organized and corporate endeavours are ostensibly guided
(Deal and Kennedy 1982; Peters and Waterman 1982). Core organizational
values are proposed then to play a critical role in shaping decision making of all
kinds, but because they contain a strong normative element, are thought to play a
particularly prominent role in moral contexts (Starkey 1998).

Other cultural elements, such as norms and behavioural standards, have also
been argued to have a powerful influence on individual actions, and they can be

seen to support behaviour which may be considered ethical or unethical to non-group members (Turner 1971; Jackall 1988; Watson 1994a; Treviño and Nelson 1995). Individuals thus become socialized into certain accepted organizational behaviours which may prevail over (or replace) their personal (or previous) convictions or moralities (Van Maanen 1991). For example, Posner and Schmidt's (1984, 1992) widely cited surveys reveal the rising incidence of managers claiming to have been forced into compromising their personal principles in order to conform to their organizations' expectations.[10] Jackall's (1988: 6) influential study of US managers reveals that individuals 'bracket, while at work, the moralities that they might hold outside of the work place or that they might adhere to privately and to follow instead the prevailing morality of their particular organization situation'.

Culture is then in a sense an inherently moral terrain for it holds the key to the reciprocal relationships of obligation and responsibility – the moral rules and relationships – which define any particular community (Anthony 1994; Watson 1994a). For any social group, examination of its culture can reveal its values, ideologies and moral rules (Schein 1992). However, a recurring theme in much of this literature is the proposition that the 'right' culture, the 'right' values – i.e. an *ethical* culture, and *ethical* core values – can prompt improved ethical decision making from marketing and other staff (Robin and Reidenbach 1987; Freeman and Gilbert 1988; Treviño and Nelson 1995). These ideas have fed into a more prescriptive project within this literature aimed at suggesting how ethical decision making in marketing can be enhanced. If we return to Hunt and Vitell's (1993) model of ethical decision making, it is clear that the group of factors identified as contextual and personal factors are those that might be regarded as the potential root variables for improving ethical decision making in this respect. If we disregard the broad cultural environment as relatively fixed, we are left with personal characteristics, and the professional, industrial and organizational environments in which ethical decisions might arise. Prescriptions have therefore focused on such issues as ethics training, (e.g. Sharp Paine 1994; Treviño and Nelson 1995), industry programmes, (Simmons and Wynne 1993), corporate codes of ethics (Schlegelmilch and Houston 1989) and professional codes of conduct (Diacon and Ennew 1996).

Most commonly advanced though within the prescriptive literature, and indeed often cited as necessary for those possibilities above to succeed, has been the culture management approach. Much as with the arguments suggesting that movement towards a societal marketing orientation requires a fundamental moral transformation of the organizational culture, so too are improvements in ethical decision making argued to require a managed transformation of the organization's values (e.g. Robin and Reidenbach 1987; Stroup and Neubert 1987; Sharp Paine 1994; Treviño and Nelson 1995; Chen *et al.* 1997). Thus, Treviño and Nelson (1995: 195) suggest that 'organizations can proactively develop an ethical organizational culture, and that organizations with "ethics problems" should take a culture change approach to solving them'. Similar arguments are also present in relation to moral transformation in a wide range of subareas such as the environment (Elkington and Burke 1989; Bernstein 1992; Welford 1995), strategy (Freeman and Gilbert 1988) and governance (Diacon and Ennew 1996). Similarly in marketing, Robin and Reidenbach (1987: 48) argue that 'a major factor in developing successful socially responsible and ethical marketing programmes is management's ability to integrate ethical core values throughout the organization's culture', and hence, 'the approach we suggest might be defined as the development or re-formulation of a corporate culture'. Essentially, the argument here is that since the organization's culture has such a significant impact on how individuals perceive moral questions while at work, and how they subsequently reach decisions and behave, it is this which has to be manipulated in order to improve organizational ethics. Unfortunately, there has been rather limited attention focused on establishing how such a transformation might take place, why it might occur, or even if it is possible at all. As the organization studies literature has so effectively demonstrated, the deliberate management of culture is a difficult, lengthy process, which is rarely successful except at very superficial levels (see Martin 1985; Nord 1985; Ogbonna 1992; Ogbonna and Harris 1998). Indeed, the whole notion of a unitary, unambiguous and widely shared organizational culture has been widely questioned, and has been shown to be highly problematic (see Smircich 1983; Van Maanen and Barley 1985; Martin 1992). Again then, the study of marketing and morality leaves us with as many questions as it does answers.

Conclusion

In this chapter I began by discussing the moral criticisms of marketing, and followed this with an examination of the changing models of morality and marketing that have appeared in the literature. Whilst the former of these represents quite a complete body of research, the latter is less well developed. Notions such as social marketing, societal marketing, ethical consumerism and ethical marketing may have all entered the marketing lexicon, and even gone some way to enhancing the moral dimension of marketing, but they have yet to (and may never) really make much of an impression on mainstream marketing theory. Moreover, many of these concepts and theories remain as yet underdeveloped and under-theorized. This means that the various attempts that have been made in the literature to suggest how marketing should more properly be carried out seem somewhat premature. Moreover, it is my contention that a yet more deep-seated problem remains – and this calls into even more serious question these tenuous prescriptions. Almost without exception, models of marketing and morality begin with the assumption that any given decision or dilemma has moral content, and that it is treated as such by organizational members. Be it the development of products to satisfy ethical consumers, decisions to target potentially vulnerable consumers or the wording of green claims, the literature brings with the assumption that marketing personnel will treat these as decisions which are moral in nature and which require some degree of moral reflection and will *then* go on to engage in 'ethical' decision making. There is very little discussion of how these initial stages might happen, how they might be experienced, or indeed whether they happen at all. I want to argue in this book that knowledge of this kind of moral meaning is critical to how we understand marketing and morality. Without knowing how organization members think about, understand and communicate ostensibly social, moral and environmental issues within the organization, we cannot hope to develop appropriate and relevant theory.

In the next chapter I want to take up this theme, and develop it further. With moral meaning acting as the central organizing idea for the empirical work presented in this book, I want to show how a very considerable contribution can be made to the literature discussed in this chapter by developing a mode of research appropriate to exploring moral meaning. Also, I will discuss some of the implications of basing this investigation primarily on green marketing practices. Clearly these discussions will entail some debate of an epistemological and methodological nature, but essentially what I want to illustrate is how exploring moral meaning in green marketing can provide a valuable contribution to theory in marketing and morality.

3 Exploring moral meaning in green marketing

Introduction

I ended the previous chapter by arguing that in order to deal better with issues of morality, the marketing literature was in need of a more explicit treatment of moral meaning. Much can be learned from such an investigation, for it provides us with insight into what people actually think, feel and do in marketing situations. Without this kind of knowledge, I feel it is problematic to discuss issues of morality. After all, what can be gained in speaking of 'ethical' marketing if we don't know how those involved in the process understand and communicate notions of morality? How can we advocate a societal marketing orientation when we have little idea about the way that marketing shapes the moral consciousness of those involved in it? In that sense, what is needed in the marketing literature is a stronger bridge between micromarketing, i.e. the dynamics of the marketing process, and macromarketing, i.e. its relationship with wider society. To that end, I have focused this study principally on one particular area of marketing, namely that which relates to the natural environment – or as it is commonly known 'green marketing'.

My reasoning for focusing on green marketing is briefly outlined in Chapter 1. Basically I was concerned with narrowing my area of investigation, selecting an issue that was 'social' in nature, focusing on a social issue which would provide interesting and contemporary data, and contributing to a literature which would clearly benefit from some greater attention. Green marketing was highly appropriate on all four counts. Of course, by selecting green marketing, I was also opening up a whole new area of literature. However, I found that the green marketing literature, and indeed the more general green business literature, had rather little to say about morality, and almost nothing to say about moral meaning. None the less, there were certain aspects of this literature that I could bring to bear on my understanding of how (and how not) to investigate the area. Accordingly, this chapter is a discussion of the theoretical, epistemological and methodological implications of exploring moral meaning in green marketing.

The theoretical issues associated with moral meaning I have drawn largely from the organizational studies literature. As I shall explain shortly, the marketing literature has been dominated by very functionalist conceptions of morality that I feel are somewhat unconvincing, and which therefore provided only a limited theoretical basis for the study. There are important epistemological issues involved here, and as the chapter progresses, I want to draw these out. Having set out my epistemological position thus, the final aim of this chapter is to explain the methodology subsequently employed in the organizing, collecting and analysing of data during the study. Basically, the method adopted was an inductive, qualitative one, based around case studies in seven organizations. These organizations were selected to account for three organizational types – conventional, social mission and business–NGO collaboration. The rationale for this comparative case study approach will be explained later in this chapter. I begin though with a brief return to the ethical decision making literature discussed in the previous chapter. In this way I hope to be able to show what can be learnt from it in relation to understanding moral meaning in green marketing, but also, what it fails to contribute to this understanding.

Ethical decision making and moral meaning in marketing

When initially researching this area, I soon discovered that exploring morality in terms of what it might mean for and to practitioners was a rather novel approach in marketing. Most of the existing studies of morality in marketing begin with the assumption that the issue or decision is open for moral reasoning and debate. But in terms of the practical day-to-day business of marketing practice, this clearly ignores the very important dynamic that leads to the identification of this issue or question as moral in nature (or not) in the first place. Hunt and Vitell (1986) give passing reference to this in their model of ethical decision making, suggesting that some level of 'ethical sensitivity' on the part of the decision maker will determine whether an issue is subjected to moral reasoning. However, they do not explore this issue further. But how can they hope to model ethical decision making effectively without knowing with any certainty whether and how particular issues and decisions are granted moral status?

More recently, a handful of studies have actually begun to acknowledge the importance of this issue. Ferrell *et al.* (1989: 61), in their analysis of models of ethical decision making in marketing, have provided an important acknowledgement that, 'how managers recognize ethical dilemmas or know when ethical issues are present is a critical matter'. Moreover, two studies in the marketing literature have now reported empirical evidence relating to ethical sensitivity (Sparks and Hunt 1998) and moral reflection (Bone and Corey 1998) in marketing. Both of these concepts – which principally relate to cognitive aspects of individual awareness of ethical issues – add to our understanding of moral meaning for they help us to understand how issues and problems come to be recognized as moral in nature. Sparks and Hunt (1998) identify a key role for processes of organizational and professional socialization in 'learning' ethical sensitivity, whilst Bone and Corey (1998) emphasize the importance of positive organizational norms and non-bureaucratic structures in facilitating personal moral reflection by marketing professionals.

Despite their obvious contribution to the marketing ethics literature, studies such as these still very much typify the very functionalist conception of morality that is common to the marketing discipline. Morality is largely presented as an objective reality which individuals either identify in an issue or they do not. The possibility that these individuals and their organizations are actually involved in a process of *constructing* the whole idea and meaning of morality within their institutions is largely ignored. This, however, is the type of understanding that I am seeking to uncover in this book. Hence, the wealth of marketing ethics papers which adopt this positivist approach to morality – and I am thinking here of the work of Hunt, Vitell, Ferrell and others which habitually appears in the pages of the *Journal of Marketing*, *Journal of Macromarketing* and the *Journal of Business Ethics* – provides useful insights into morality, but generally fails to get to grips fully with the issues of moral meaning that I am concerned with here in this book. Given then, as I illustrated in the previous chapter, that morality is substantially influenced by situation, by context, and by culture, there is clearly a case for saying that organizational morality is in a very important sense socially constructed (Jackall 1988; Phillips 1991; Brigley 1995; Fineman 1995; Parker 1997). Jackall's (1988) study in the business ethics literature for example represents an important attempt to understand the working moralities of organization members (in this case, of US corporate managers). As he argues, organizational reality tends to induce a morality that is 'contextual, situational, highly specific, and, most often, unarticulated' (1988: 6). This view of morality as ambiguous and flexible is one which is in stark contrast to the one found in existing marketing literature, and one that is certainly in need of further exploration. The organization studies literature is extremely useful here then for we can trace a long history of concern with issues of moral meaning in this area. Accordingly, in the next section I shall draw quite heavily on this literature in order to explore what is already known about moral meaning, and thence to justify the approach taken in the empirical work presented in the following chapters. In this way I shall set out what insight might be dawn from the approach taken, and also how this might contribute to our understanding of marketing and morality.

Moral meaning in organizations

Morality as experienced, understood and communicated by organizational members has recently seen a renewed interest, but has long been dominated by Weber's (1947) contention that individual morality is subjugated to the functionally-specific rules and roles of the bureaucratic organization. In an important and influential study, Jackall (1988) took up Weber's theme of morality shaped by bureaucracy, and showed how the moral code of managers centred on rules for survival and success. He suggested that individuals would bracket their personal moralities whilst at work, and adopt the prevailing values of the organization. Further development of this argument has been enhanced in recent years by recourse to Bauman's (1989, 1993) influential critique of modernist rule-based ethical systems and the subsequent loss of individual moral impulse and feeling (e.g. ten Bos 1997; Desmond 1998; Letiche 1998). For Bauman (1993) bureau-cracy renders decisions 'adiophoric' – i.e. 'of a kind on which ethical authorities do not feel it necessary to make a stand' (p. 30). This is strongly related to the concepts of moralization and amoralization that I discuss later in this book. However Bauman (1993) presents adiophorization (that is, the process by which such moral neutrality is produced) as an inevitable and absolute process: the only logical consequence of bureaucracy is moral indifference to all organizational goals since it is the techno-rationalist process of the organizational system which is viewed as the arbiter of right and wrong. In contrast, by presenting some of my findings in terms of amoralization, my intention is not to suggest that morality is completely denied in the modern organization, but rather that it is frequently marginalized from green marketing in particular, or else enacted in a selective, contextual fashion. But more on this later.

The general picture presented by these authors then is an essentially gloomy one. Personal morality is seen as having little meaning within the organization, and behavioural norms and organizational values are coded into bureaucratic procedures and rules. Bauman's (1989) elegant rewriting of the holocaust in terms of modernist organizational bureaucracy, and its concomitant repression of moral autonomy and feeling, provides perhaps the most dramatic and certainly the most disturbing exemplar of this particular approach. However, this is not the only way that moral meaning has been understood within the organization studies literature. Watson's (1994a) ethnographic account of managerial work for example paints a highly moralized picture of managerial life, and this continues a long tradition of work which explores the morality implicit in everyday workplace behaviour (e.g. Turner 1971; Van Maanen 1973; Harvey *et al.* 1984). Watson's belief in the inherent morality of organizational life has led him more recently (1998: 253) to state that, 'the organization and the management of work involve moral matters and ethical dilemmas from top to bottom and from beginning to end'. Indeed, he provides rich and compelling evidence of moral engagement on the part of his managers, particularly in terms of trust, mutuality and co-operation (see Watson 1994a, 1998). Thus, his concern is mainly with the rela-tionships concluded within the work group, or the 'moral community' in which work is enacted. Watson acknowledges the parallels here with those enlisting the arguments of corporate culture to suggest that organizations can benefit from a more 'values-based' approach to management (e.g. Peters and Waterman 1982).

As we saw in the previous chapter, culture and morality are in many important respects inextricably entwined. Many writers have been moved to argue that the culture of the organization has a direct effect on the ethical decisions of its members (e.g. Robin and Reidenbach 1987; Vitell *et al.* 1993; Treviño and Nelson 1995), and at the beginning of this chapter we saw that cultural factors could also influence the degree of individual ethical awareness. But even if, as Watson claims, the culture of the firm is a tapestry of moral relationships and commit-ments, what does this mean for how the organization relates to the outside world, and for how it interacts with society and the natural environment? Marketing is after all a boundary-spanning function, and green marketing obviously has resonance beyond organizational walls. Our concern with morality in green marketing is therefore just as much about the impact of marketing on the external environment as it is about the moral community of the marketing function. Indeed, it could be said that the interconnection between these two realms – micromarketing and macromarketing if you prefer – is the principal terrain of my investigation.

When we consider morality from the perspective of organizational culture therefore, we tend to concentrate on the internal moral community at the expense of any external moral subject. For Dahler-Larsen (1994), this means that the whole notion of organizational culture is insufficient to deal with morality. For him, culture represents a substitution of a societal-based morality with an organizational one. This means that rather than being fixed on the notion of social good, moral attachment becomes internalized and rendered instrumental to organizational goals. Utilizing Durkheim's concept of the sacred realm, Dahler-Larsen (1994: 11) argues thus:

> [S]ociety is not only the source of morality . . . but it is also 'the only intrinsically desirable end of moral conduct' . . . In this sense corporate culture cannot qualify as 'morality'. It fails to have society as its ultimate aim.

According to Desmond (1998), marketing can accentuate this for it frequently works to introduce further distance between (a) organizational members and the moral 'other' outside the organization; and (b) corporate activities and their consequences. Organizational specialization in marketing practices such as advertising, public relations and consumer research often results in dispersal of marketing efforts across different companies. This can obfuscate aggregate moral consequences and diffuse moral responsibility. Desmond also suggests that marketing de-sensitizes marketers by codifying behaviour and removing moral autonomy; equally, individuals external to the organization are denied moral status by classifying them as consumers, as target markets, and as items of market research data. By the same token, though, we saw in the last chapter how some elements within the marketing discipline have sought to re-imagine a more moral marketing where marketers might be seen as morally committed, feeling individuals. Thus, both the societal marketing and ethical decision making literatures presuppose that marketing practitioners engage in moral reflection and have scope to consider the ethical implications of their decisions right through the organization's value chain.

Environmental considerations also introduce added complexities in terms of moral meaning. Theories of organizational greening frequently allude to the importance of organizational members establishing a sense of moral responsibility for the environment. Hence, writers such as Stead and Stead (1992), Shrivastava (1994, 1995a) and Welford (1995) have all emphasized that any attempt to develop sustainable business, i.e. that which aspires to have a zero 'adverse' affect on environmental quality, is possible only with a complete moral transformation within the corporation. This transformation is said to involve: the permeation of environmental considerations throughout the organization; the valuation of the environment for itself rather than instrumental to business; and the elevation of environmental goals alongside economic goals. The emphasis has therefore been laid less on formal environmental management systems, and more on the need to nurture new 'ethical' values, emotional connectivity and spiritual reawakening. Many green marketing writers have echoed such sentiments, with Prothero (1990), Peattie (1995) and Menon and Menon (1997) among others emphasizing that technical fixes for marketing cannot avoid long-term environmental degradation in the absence of a more profound cultural reorientation towards socially responsible and environmentally sensitive business. Taking a more radical position, Kilbourne *et al.* (1997) have even argued that environmentally sustainable marketing can only be possible following a paradigm shift in the economic, technological and political structures of society. Their argument is that these structures have privileged consumption as the principal means for achieving happiness, success and self-expression, whereas sustainable marketing and/or sustainable consumption require a completely new set of priorities and values.

To date however, these remain largely prescriptive positions, informed more by ideological conviction than empirical evidence. Indeed, there are few in-depth, academic studies to have examined the role of morality in corporate greening generally, or still less in green marketing specifically. Anecdotal and self-reported 'inspirational' accounts by 'new age' business leaders such as Anita Roddick of the Body Shop (see Roddick 1992), Tom Chappell of Tom's of Maine (see Chappell 1993), and Ben Cohen and Jerry Greenfield of Ben & Jerry's (see Lager 1994) have been largely predominant in the literature to date. Recently however, the work of Fineman (1996, 1997, 1998) has provided a valuable contribution to this debate. Taking, as I do, a social constructionist position on morality (Berger and Luckmann 1966; Phillips 1991; Parker 1997), Fineman presents moral status as fluid, subjective, and contestable. This means essentially that there are different moralities at work in the organization (Jackall 1988; Fineman 1995, 1997; Brigley 1995). Fineman (1995, 1997) provides an important categorization of these moralities, labelling them conventional, private and enacted. Conventional morality, he argues, is the ideal morality espoused by the organization to various publics through formal communication; private morality relates to the personal moral positions of individuals; and enacted morality is the accepted moral rules-in-use of the workplace. Not only are these moralities all coexistent but each can present a different lens with which to view the moral terrain of the organization.

It is clear to me that the marketing and the green literature has focused almost entirely on the former of Fineman's categories, i.e. the espoused, public, conventional morality of the organization, but has taken little account of the latter two. This, it would appear, gives only a very partial picture of marketing, morality and the natural environment. As yet then, we have little evidence of what morality actually means for those in the green marketing process. Fineman's work exploring green management more generally does however provide us with some clues. Crucially, despite uncovering wide variation in the quality of environmental management across organizations, he argues that even in the more progressive of firms, corporate environmentalism is largely bereft of moral substance (1998: 243):

> [C]orporate environmentalism is revealed to be morally hollow, while ethically pragmatic . . . We see shades of Bauman's (1989) views on the modern organization which encloses its members in a self-sustaining rationality, rendering morality invisible beyond a limited organizational boundary . . . [M]oral culpability ends with the 'customers' requirements'. The customer is the benchmark of goodness.

Thus, by refocusing on the personal and enacted moralities of the organization, Fineman returns us to the bureaucratic moral ethic described earlier. He offers little hope in terms of organizational culture change and moral transformation attending corporate greening. For a social, shared and very much external moral subject such as the environment then, Fineman (1998) suggests that we might expect to find an 'ethically pragmatic' morality, one which is internally focused and attuned to organizational interests and managerial advancement. However, in presenting corporate greening thus, Fineman's findings stand in clear contrast to the typical conventional morality professed by US and European corporations. In particular we might contrast them with the exudation of social responsibility found in many corporate mission statements (David 1989; Starkey 1998) and annual reports (Robertson and Nicholson 1996), as well the heavily moralized accounts related by the 'new-age' business managers. Even more confusingly, in the case of green marketing, US evidence from Drumwright's (1994) study of green purchasing describes a situation where enacted moral conviction and personal emotional attachment are very much crucial to the drives of marketing practitioners. In her study, greening is even presented in quasi-religious terms, such that it becomes 'the gospel' spread by green 'missionaries' and their 'converts'.

Overall then, we can identify little consensus regarding morality as experienced, understood and communicated by marketers, particularly when focused on environmental ends. My main objective therefore for the empirical work at the heart of this study was to sort out some of this confusion and develop a more coherent understanding of moral meaning in green marketing. In so doing, I was hoping, too, to develop some insight into the morality embedded in marketing more generally. Thus, my initial research aims were framed as follows:

1   To understand the green marketing process.
2   To articulate the role of moral meaning in that process.
3   To set out how and why morality is given (or denied) meaning in the green marketing process.

One area where the literature did however seem to present some degree of accord was in emphasizing the importance of cultural context in shaping the moral construction of greening (Drumwright 1994; Fineman 1996) and in influencing ethical and unethical behaviour (e.g. Nwachukwu and Vitell 1997; Treviño *et al.* 1998). Hence the empirical part of this study was specifically organized in order to explore moral meaning in green marketing in diverse organizational contexts. In this way, the differential impact of culture on these processes could be examined. In order to do this, three very distinct organizational types were identified, namely conventional companies, social mission companies and business–NGO collaborations.

A number of criteria could have been used in order to establish different categories of organization (e.g. industrial sector, organizational size or form of governance), but the main distinction I used was the espoused goals of the organization, namely whether social or economic goals were given prominence. I presumed that the moral meanings attached to green marketing might vary in some way according to the social orientation of the organization's mission. Hence, two polar types of organization were identified – *conventional companies* (i.e. those with economic goals prominent) and *social mission companies* (i.e. those with social goals prominent). Thus, whilst both might be regarded as being engaged in economic activity, the principal point of distinction was what those organizations said about *why* they were engaged in that activity. This did not mean that conventional companies could not have social goals, or that social mission companies could not have economic goals. Rather, it meant that the overall emphasis in corporate identity, branding, promotional texts and other company documentation, as well as independent published accounts, clearly indicated to me that one or the other was the more prominent.

As the fieldwork developed, I introduced a third category, *business–NGO collaboration*. What I mean by business–NGO collaboration is the temporary coalition between businesses and pressure groups to pursue mixed economic, social, ethical and/or environmental goal sets. Although relatively rare at the time that fieldwork was conducted, business–NGO collaboration was predicted to rise in incidence and significance (Elkington 1997), and had been touted by some as a new model of green business (see Hartman and Stafford 1997; Murphy and Bendell 1997). The mixed goal sets of business–NGO collaboration, plus their particular form of shared ownership, suggested that this was a rather novel organizational form, and one that might present a very different moral context in which to explore the green marketing process. In this, the emerging literature generally concurred, with authors such as Westley and Vredenburg (1991), Milne *et al.* (1996) and Hartman and Stafford (1997) all alluding to a very different set of cultural characteristics underpinning these kinds of alliance initiatives.

So this was the basic framework for the empirical work: comparative case studies from three organizational types, with a focus on understanding moral meaning in different green marketing contexts. However, I have alluded frequently in the preceding discussion to ideas of social constructionism and non-functionalist conceptions of morality underpinning this approach. Therefore, before proceeding to describe the mechanics of the research methods applied in the study, I feel it is necessary at this point to make clear, and perhaps to qualify, what exactly it is that I mean by these terms – and for that matter, to explain what implications these ontological and epistemological assumptions of mine have for the results and analysis subsequently laid out in the following chapters.

Ontological and epistemological issues

It is not my intention to delve too deeply into the philosophy of management research for I feel that this discussion has been extremely well rehearsed elsewhere.[1] However, I do feel it is essential to at least make explicit my thinking here – that is, my assumptions about how the social world is constructed and how it can be reflected and/or discovered through empirical research. This has important implications for the status that I am claiming for this research. Also, there are important implications in terms of how the 'truth' or 'validity' of this research should be assessed by you, the reader. As Morgan (1983: 13) states:

> [Researchers] engage a subject of study by interacting with it through means of a particular frame of reference, and what is observed and discovered in the object (i.e., its objectivity) is as much a product of this interaction and the protocol and technique through which it is operationalised as it is of the object itself.

This suggests that the discovered 'truth' about any given area of research is therefore inextricably bound up in the researcher's epistemological and method-ological perspective. For myself, it should be clear by now that I am predisposed to an interpretive mode of investigation, as premised on the notion of social constructionism. This, I feel, is the most appropriate way to explore moral meaning in green marketing. This does not necessarily mean that I feel there is no place for more positivist and quantitative approaches in management and marketing research (although I certainly have my reservations), but more that I do not feel they are at all appropriate here. They would constrain the potential boundaries and depth of knowledge that can be generated in this area. Let me set out then what the approach adopted here entails, and what it assumes in terms of the nature of reality.

The basic starting point for interpretism is that reality is socially constructed. This means that the social world is essentially a product of intersubjective experience and exists only through the meaning that social actors apply to it (Hassard 1993). According to these ontological assumptions, there cannot be an absolute concrete corporate morality, but rather one that exists through the subjective experience of various actors and groups of actors inside and outside the organization. It is the meanings that organizational actors apply to ethical principles and actions that become the research focus for studying morality in green marketing within the interpretive paradigm. Research of this kind is thus subjective yet reflexive. Furthermore, within the interpretive tradition, researchers have most commonly engaged their subjects phenomenologically, i.e. they are focused on meanings, and theory is induced from holistic data gathered in depth and over time in a small sample of organizations (Easterby-Smith *et al.* 1991). This data is frequently, indeed usually, qualitative in nature. There is a small but growing body of work associated with interpretive approaches to social responsibility, business ethics and green business. A number of researchers, such as Harvey *et al.* (1984) and Fineman (1996, 1997) in the UK and Jackall (1988) and Bird and Waters (Waters and Bird 1987; Bird and Waters 1989) in the USA provide important works in the field. More recent work has begun to focus more explicitly on the marketing function (Abratt and Sacks 1989; Drumwright 1994) although it is clear that the discipline has still not yet embraced interpretive approaches to nearly the same extent as it has the dominant positivist tradition.

What I mean by the positivist tradition is the mode of enquiry that is based upon the assumption that the method is objective and value-free. The focus is on facts, with measurable (principally quantitative) data being gathered from large samples in order to formulate and test hypotheses which can explain causality and fundamental laws (Easterby-Smith *et al.* 1991). Positivism thus rests upon the functionalist paradigm which contends that the ontological status of society is real, concrete, and systematic. To date, this has been by far the most prevalent mode of engagement in researching issues of morality (or at least ethics) and the environment in business and marketing. Indeed, in their review of the business ethics literature, Randall and Gibson (1990) revealed that 81 per cent of available empirical studies relied exclusively on survey data – a classic positivist research instrument.[2]

The implications for my adoption of an interpretive approach are quite significant. First, it means that I am not claiming that my role in collecting and analysing data and presenting these as results can be removed from the results themselves. My values are, by necessity, reflected in these results – at least to some extent. After all, it is I who have: chosen what to research; decided what is so interesting within this field that it demands attention; decided what is interesting and significant in my data; and determined which discoveries are worthy of being reported as results. Also, these findings are, by implication, to some extent subjective. The picture of organizational life set out in the following chapters is very much *my* interpretation of what my respondents were trying to suggest. Moreover, even the data provided by these respondents in the form of their interview responses were but *their* interpretations of the 'reality' *they* experienced. Subjectivity cannot be avoided. However, having made these points, I should emphasize that this does not mean that I feel my own account lacks value because of them. The view I have adopted is that management research might be best regarded as a craft (Watson 1994b). According to Watson (1994b), the crafting management researcher does not simply describe an objective reality that is observed as a scientist might, but then nor does he or she create a reality by seeing and knowing it as an artist might. In effect, crafting researchers *mediate* reality through informed selection, interpretation, colouring, emphasis, and shaping of their findings. Thus, 'we cannot see anything without a cultural and human mediation – but that is not to argue that there is nothing there other than that mediation,' (Watson 1994b: S79). Seen in this way, effective research requires that one acknowledge the subjectivity and the personal values that shape the research process. But it also means that effective research is reliant on the abilities of the researcher and the particular methods they apply. In the following section then, I shall set out the methodology applied in the study such that this can be assessed in a rather more informed way.

Methodology

This research study was firmly located within the interpretive tradition of 'inquiry from the inside' organizational research (Evered and Louis 1981). The principal purpose of this was to develop some level of empathy and understanding of the moral reference frames and conceptual schemes of those under examination (Geertz 1973; Martin and Turner 1986; Werhane 1998). I utilized an inductive research design whereby, as Eisenhardt (1989: 536) puts it, 'research [was] begun as close as possible to the ideal of no theory under consideration and no hypotheses to test'. This means that hypotheses, concepts, and theory constructs were not considered *a priori*, but were allowed to emerge from the field data as part of the research process (Glaser and Strauss 1967).

In truth, when I first entered the field, I had little idea of what I might discover. I had read around the subjects of marketing, business ethics and green marketing in some depth, but this had provided me with few insights into the particular issues of moral meaning that I was interested in. Of course, I brought with me my own values, moral frames of reference, and indeed a whole culturally shaped system of meaning and interpretation. Therefore, as Thompson (1995) has argued in relation to ethical reasoning, it would be impossible for me claim that in utilizing a descriptive approach to studying morality I could completely uncouple this from my normative assumptions. In attempting to describe moral meaning, I was making implicit assumptions about what moral meaning 'should' be; about the moral relevance of environmental issues in marketing; about why morality might be an important and valid area of research. Fineman and Mangham (1983) have claimed that this is intrinsic to *all* research, and have argued eloquently about the impossibility of value-free research:

> We, for our part, are not yet persuaded that researchers can suspend the filtering which affects us all; whatever the relationship [between researcher and subject], all parties to it are likely to 'see' events through a cloud of preconceptions, prejudices and theories. . . . The notion of an empty-headed qualitative researcher . . . is really rather a foolish one; the most collaborative of investigators is unlikely to deny himself or herself influence in the process of analysis.
>
> (Fineman and Mangham 1983: 298)

Despite this, the more grounded approach to theory development that I used in the study does require that one should attempt, to some extent, to bracket one's own point of view and seek to understand that of one's research subjects (Glaser and Strauss 1967). Certainly, I wanted to explore the moral meaning understood and communicated by organizational members, and in order to do so, I had to put aside for a time my own understandings of what was meant by morality, ethics, social responsibility, etc. It was important that I came to understand the culturally specific meanings as applied and utilized by my respondents, not by myself. Obviously, this involved some degree of reflexivity concerning my own values and what they represented. But in many ways, at the time that the fieldwork was conducted, my own beliefs regarding business ethics and corporate environmentalism were rather uncertain.

Within this overall inductive approach, a case study methodology was utilized in order to capture, organize and analyse data. The literature suggested that this was well suited to the research aims of generating and building theory in an area with relatively little existing theory or data (Bonoma 1985; Eisenhardt 1989; Yin 1989). Since they entail considerable quantities of data collection in particular organizations, cases can be an excellent way of delving deeply into organizational processes, and uncovering organizational meanings. Comparative cases were used in order to examine the process of green marketing in what I hoped were relatively extreme or polar cases (Eisenhardt 1989). This type of approach Glaser and Strauss (1967) would categorize as 'theoretical sampling' and Gummesson (1991), 'purposive sampling'. As I have said, these comparative cases consisted of organizations from three categories – conventional, social mission and business–NGO collaboration.

Whilst I do not believe that there is an optimum number of cases for any particular study – multiple and single cases both have their advantages[3] – seven cases were developed here in order to provide a reasonable degree of breadth across these different contexts without sacrificing too much in terms of within-case depth (Eisenhardt 1989). Since the main intention of the study was the generation of theory from data (as opposed to, say, the testing of existing theory), my principal concern was to generate reasonably consistent depth in data and understanding across the three types of organization, rather than to ensure similar numbers of cases (Glaser and Strauss 1967; Eisenhardt 1989). Accordingly, given certain restrictions on access, different numbers of organizations were sampled in each category: two conventional, four social mission, and one collaboration. These are shown in Table 3.1. More specifically, the organizations sampled in each category are described in the next three sections.

Table 3.1 Case study sample

Conventional companies	Social mission companies	Business–NGO collaboration
	ManufactureSoc	
RetailCo	RetailSoc	CollabOrg[1]
ManufactureCo	MarketingSoc	
	FinanceSoc	

Note
1 Data were collected from a sample of the participating organizations.

Conventional companies

Whilst it was acknowledged that significant variations could exist in this category (e.g. firms could have relatively strong social programmes or none at all; their economic motives could be espoused but not practised), in a sense this was intended to be a catch-all category for those firms not obviously operating an explicit social mission. Two companies were sampled in this category, a retailer (RetailCo) and a manufacturer (ManufactureCo), both of which were wholly owned subsidiaries of PLCs. RetailCo was a large firm with over 1,000 stores, around 50,000 employees, and stocking a large range of personal care products, gifts, cosmetics, household goods, health products, etc. In the business press it was generally portrayed as a firm with a good reputation and both RetailCo and its corporate parent were widely presented as good corporate citizens. The overall picture was not quite so rosy however. RetailCo had experienced considerable dissent from various pressure groups in respect of its position on a number of social and environmental issues and had even featured in *Ethical Consumer* magazine's survey of 'most boycotted firms'. By way of contrast, ManufactureCo was a far less visible organization. An SME with around 300 employees, ManufactureCo operated in the field of supply, installation and servicing of water-treatment technologies provided by its Scandinavian parent. Although both firms made some mention of social and environmental issues in at least some of their various internal and external communications, the prevailing impression was certainly one of two firms with conventional economic goals.

Social mission companies

Four organizations identified as social mission companies agreed to take part in the study, one a large co-operative retailer (RetailSoc) and three SMEs operating in cosmetic manufacture (ManufactureSoc), financial services (FinanceSoc) and marketing services (MarketingSoc). In many ways these four companies might be seen to constitute a fairly diverse group, particularly in terms of their differences in size, age and industrial sector. However, as I have already argued, the purpose of investigating social mission companies was to explore meaningfully different moral contexts for green marketing practices. In that sense I strongly felt that their similarities in terms of their founding missions far outweighed their differences in other more prosaic respects.

RetailSoc was a long-established consumer co-operative and its stated mission therefore focused on the principles of co-operation. Originally established in 1844 by the Rochdale Pioneers,[4] these have been set out by the International Co-operative Alliance as follows (cited in Butcher 1996): (i) education of the membership, staff and general public; (ii) co-operation among co-operatives; (iii) voluntary and open membership; (iv) democratically based control; (v) equitable use of profit/surplus; (vi) limits on the participation of capital. Although the continued relevance of the co-operative mission and its social ideals have come into question over the years, in many important ways the co-operative movement can be regarded as one of the most enduring examples of social responsibility in action (Churchill 1986; Thornhill 1992; Birchall 1994; Yeo 1995). Interestingly, as far back as 1857, one of the early central figures of the movement, George Holyoake (cited in Birchall 1994: 43), wrote of co-operative products in terms of their appeal to what must be one of the earliest conceptions of 'ethical' consumers: 'If there are to be moral sellers, there must be moral buyers . . . whether the price was high or low, the quality good or bad, they bought, because it was their duty to buy.' In more recent years, RetailSoc had attempted to revitalize and modernize its social ideals and mission. Following an ethical branding initiative by one of its subsidiaries, RetailSoc set out from the mid-1990s onwards to develop a more contemporary reaffirmation of its stance on social responsibility.

With around forty employees spread over three sites, and a turnover of approximately £1.5m p.a., ManufactureSoc was a fairly small organization. However, with more than thirty years experience as a social mission company, it was the second oldest and second largest of the sample in this category. It manufactured 'vegetarian' cosmetics, meaning that the firm did not permit any form of animal cruelty, including animal testing of products and ingredients nor the use of animal-derived ingredients such as musk and gelatine. Having initially been set up by an animal welfare charity, ManufactureSoc had since attained PLC status.

FinanceSoc was a smaller organization, with twelve staff and holding around £18m in assets. Founded in the early 1980s, FinanceSoc had remained part of the mutually-owned finance sector, despite the swathe of conversions that had occurred in the 1990s. Its avowed mission was to invest solely in environmental projects, often those overlooked or rejected by the more mainstream financial institutions.

Finally, MarketingSoc was a start-up organization, again developed out of a charitable institution that had remained as a majority shareholder. At the time the fieldwork took place, the firm was run on an informal and virtually voluntary basis by its two directors, both of whom continued to hold positions outside the company. Turnover was in the region of £40,000 p.a. The firm operated as a distribution and marketing agent for environmentally sensitive producers of timber-based products. Its mission was to develop a more localized and sustainable production base for national markets of its core products.

Business–NGO Collaboration

As mentioned, this third category was fairly rare at the time of fieldwork, and as such only one of these organizations, CollabOrg, was eventually sampled, albeit in some depth. The collaboration consisted of an environmental pressure group and over seventy-five firms. Its espoused aim was to provide a mechanism for securing and certifying a relatively advanced level of environmental management in member companies – but in respect to only a single environmental issue, timber-based product sourcing. The basic structure of CollabOrg was that members would sign up to certain commitments, and would nominate representatives to attend meetings and to set and implement policy; targets were set jointly by the corporate and NGO members.

Data collection and analysis

Initial research targets in the sampled organizations were environmental experts, protagonists, representatives and/or enthusiasts – usually identified by job title or by recommendation from company contacts. These were taken to be the principal environmental 'reality definers' in the case organizations (Fineman 1997), but other relevant informants and sources of data were also sought in order to gain a broader, more context-rich picture of green marketing processes. As far as possible, I also broached different organizational levels so that within-case variations in cultural context could be explored. Informants included board members, senior, middle and junior managers as well as shop floor workers. In all then, I conducted some sixty semi-structured interviews in the sampled organizations during a sixteen-month period over 1995 and 1996. These individuals came from a range of functional areas, including marketing, environmental management, quality, production, retailing and purchasing among others. The duration of interviews varied considerably, from as little as twenty minutes in a few cases to well over two hours in many others. On average though, interviews lasted approximately sixty minutes. A small number of focus groups were also conducted in order to make best use of the access provided, and to avoid intimidating inexperienced interviewees.

I used interview schedules, but in keeping with the exploratory nature of the research, I continually adjusted them in order to explore emergent themes. Crucially, I deliberately approached interviewees with an understanding that the focus of the study was green marketing; I made no mention of morality at the outset, and even as the interview progressed, this would only be introduced at the interviewee's instigation. The purpose of this was for me to investigate moral meaning in a more indirect way, such as to reduce levels of 'desirability bias' (see Crane 1999) and to try and gain more 'naturalistic' insights. I believe that this allowed respondents' everyday moral frames of reference to emerge from our discussions rather than those imposed by myself. Of course, I do not mean to deny that I had no influence over the responses of the people I talked to. Clearly, these people were talking to me, the academic and doctoral student (as I was then), and their words were undoubtedly coloured by this context. I attempted though to take this into account (as much as one can) when presenting my questions and later when analysing the data. This attempt at reflexivity involved me applying most of the prescribed interviewer techniques for dealing with such issues – ensuring confidentiality, putting respondents at ease, building up rapport, forming empathy, etc. But perhaps the main issue here is that if I anticipated some level of 'desirability bias' in discussions with corporate personnel over a sensitive subject such as the environment, then the picture presented in the following chapters is, if anything, a more upbeat, positive and moralized response than might have more 'naturally' emerged without my being present. Thus, given that the findings presented in the chapters that follow deal, at some length, with quite profound degrees of amorality in the way in which informants present green marketing issues, I do not feel that the results of the study contain within them unacceptable levels of 'presentational' data (see Van Maanen 1979). Indeed, I invite readers to draw their own conclusions regarding the more 'real' level of moral meaning present in the case organizations.

The interviews all took place at the respondents' places of work. Questions focused mainly on the motivations, processes and outcomes of green marketing programmes as well as other environmental initiatives introduced by the organizations or their competitors. Particular focus was placed on personal and group beliefs about the value, purpose and meaning of greening. Personal environmental convictions (of interviewees and other organizational members) were sought, as were respondents' impressions of broader shared attitudes, beliefs and behaviours within the organization. Where practicable, all interviews were recorded on audiotape and then transcribed; where this wasn't possible (for twelve interviews, at the respondents' request), and for all other data, comprehensive field notes were taken and then written up. Substantial quantities of additional data in the form of informal discussions, company documentation, communicative artefacts (e.g. products, adverts, press releases, etc.) and archival material were also collected and recorded.

Analysis was carried out inductively and relatively informally, with general descriptive interpretations of the data leading to pattern identification and hypothesizing regarding relationships. These were then tested back with other portions of data and used to direct further data collection and analysis (Glaser and Strauss 1967; Turner 1983; Martin and Turner 1986). Some degree of corroboration of analysis was sought by triangulation with content analyses of interview transcripts, and by referencing across cases, subcases, and with published data (Yin 1989). This parallel process of data collection, coding and analysis was conducted until interesting and plausible findings were developed. These were then gradually refined to ensure internal consistency and explicability.

Theory construction within the interpretive tradition has been variously described as 'semi-tacit craft skill' (Turner 1983: 334), 'disciplined imagination' (Weick 1989: 516), 'the telling of good stories' (Dyer and Wilkins 1991: 613) and 'a systematic set of procedures' (Strauss and Corbin 1990: 24). One of the key principles then of qualitative research is that theory building combines rational elements with creative, intuitive and imaginative elements. These can be regarded as different points on a continuum that runs between the rational and intuitive approaches to theory building. To a great extent, the position of a particular theory on this continuum owes more to the skills and specialities of the researcher than to any other factors. My intention has been to craft a powerful and evocative story depicting the moral experience of individuals who have been involved in the development of green marketing programmes. Hence, the relatively formal analytic procedures advocated by among others Glaser and Strauss (1967), Turner (1983), Eisenhardt (1989), Strauss and Corbin (1990) and Miles and Huberman (1994) have been used as a basis from which to develop a more informal 'emergent' analytical strategy that suited better the research field, the data collected and my own analytical skills (see Mintzberg 1979). The main elements of this approach were relatively 'rational' coding and memoing, combined with more 'intuitive' elements of 'thick description' (Geertz 1973), 'thought trials' (Weick 1989) and 'storytelling' (Dyer and Wilkins 1991).

I realize of course that my interpretations of the data, and the story that I try and weave around these interpretations, are not the only plausible ones that could have been derived from these data. To some extent though, the validity of my account must be assessed by you, the reader. Do my findings make intuitive sense? Are they logical? Does the story presented here 'feel' right? Of course, every attempt has been made here to ensure that the theoretical propositions put forward are internally consistent – that is, that they fit together without contradiction and are mutually reinforcing. Moreover, the exhaustive analytic process of constant comparison, and the extensive assessment and evaluation of rival explanations that I have gone through should contribute greatly to the credibility of the results and conclusions presented in the following chapters. But the findings are only as good as the impact they have on the reader. Dyer and Wilkins (1991) term this the 'aha experience'. If a description is sufficiently rich, vivid and theoretically strong to have revealed the dynamics of a situation in such a way that the reader can identify similar dynamics in his or her own experience – if the reader is compelled to register 'aha!' at the realization of the commonality of insight – then the account has clear validity. Again then, the quality of my theorizing is to be read not in my justifications, but in the eyes and minds of you, the reader.

Conclusion

In this chapter I have argued for a new way of approaching the study of marketing, morality and the natural environment. The existing literature was shown to be deficient in a number of important ways, and in particular in its positivistic, and overly objectivist approach to studying morality. Whilst being a crucial cornerstone in the conceptual basis of much of the extant literature, issues of moral meaning were shown, to date, to have been largely ignored. My own response to the problems encountered with the existing literature has been to focus specifically on moral meaning in green marketing, utilizing an interpretive, inductive approach. This approach has been centred on a comparative case study methodology and has used qualitative data and methods. In this chapter I have set out what kind of contribution can be made using such an approach, examined its epistemological and ontological assumptions and implications, and also detailed the mechanics of the methods actually applied.

This form of research methodology and method is unusual in the study of marketing and morality. Indeed, I would suggest that one of the principal contributions of my study is that it takes a new and original approach to empirical research in this area. However, the benefits of the approach utilized here are not simply that it is underdeveloped in this area. Rather, it can be seen to be extremely appropriate for many of the questions regarding moral meaning that are of relevance to this area of study, and more specifically, for the investigation of the broad research questions presented in this chapter.

In the next three chapters, the results and theoretical propositions which have emerged from analysis of the case study data are set out. The intention in Chapters 4, 5 and 6 is to present theory grounded in data for each of the three organizational forms for which case studies have been constructed; hence the chapters relate to conventional companies, social mission companies and business–NGO collaboration respectively. In this way it is hoped that the themes pertinent to individual cases can be developed and presented in some depth. In Chapters 7 and 8, however, more general theoretical propositions are set out and discussed, and these represent the outcome of systematic comparative analysis.

4 Conventional companies

Introduction

In this, the first of the chapters reporting results of the empirical research carried out for the study, findings relating to two case studies are presented: RetailCo and ManufactureCo. Taken together, they provide cases in both consumer marketing (RetailCo) and industrial marketing (ManufactureCo) and hence represent comparative cases 'nested' within the overall comparative case framework. As I have argued in the previous chapter, they are regarded here as 'conventional' companies in that they were firms espousing goals of growth and shareholder returns, and were neither committed to an explicit social mission nor directly positioned as 'green' or 'ethical' companies.

Despite being depicted as *conventional* companies, RetailCo and ManufactureCo should not necessarily be regarded as *typical* companies. I have no intention of claiming that the results presented here are representative of a wider sample of conventional business organizations. Indeed, as an exploratory study, the main intention was to elicit important themes and issues which might be subsequently utilized as building blocks for developing theory in this area. In particular, the study was designed in order that insights into moral meaning in green marketing could be developed in a number of different contexts. Nevertheless, having said that the results are not intended to be generalizeable, there is no reason to suggest that the picture presented here is particularly unique or unusual. Indeed, many of the people I talked to in the two conventional companies suggested that, in general, there was little substantial difference in the approach to greening in their firms compared to their immediate competitors – an interesting if empirically untested assertion.

So how is this chapter organized? Well, what follows is a broad description of both firms' approach to green marketing. Particular reference is made to how these approaches corresponded with notions of social responsibility and societal marketing. In the next section, the observed and reported cultural dynamics of green marketing in the case study companies are set out. Here, attention is focused in the main on RetailCo, mainly because this case offered far deeper and more useful data with which to build up a picture of moral meaning in a conventional firm. This was largely a product of access limitations at ManufactureCo, as well as the lack of any significant environmental programme at the company. The principal intention of this section is to draw out some emergent themes which help to explain how green marketing practices were enacted within the conventional companies, and to assess what implications this might have for understanding moral meaning in marketing. Finally, the main findings of the chapter are summarized and issues of concern for the following chapter are set out.

Green marketing in the conventional companies

In terms of their principal products and markets, the two companies were clearly in very different positions in relation to green marketing. RetailCo, as a retailer of branded and own-label personal care products, gifts, food products, etc. certainly could not be regarded as operating in a 'dirty' industry, but many areas within its scope of operations could be environmentally controversial. It had, for example, been the subject of demonstrations and boycotts regarding animal testing. Also, the own-label products and retailing services provided by RetailCo could, at best, only conceivably be regarded as what Peattie (1995: 181) calls 'relative green products', i.e. their claim to greenness would lie in the reduction of actual or potential harm they might cause to the environment. Simply by being a retailer though, and a fairly prominent one at that, it had been involved in the publicity (both positive and negative) surrounding the green business movement in the UK. ManufactureCo, on the other hand, as a supplier of water treatment products widely used in the environmental industry, could be regarded as a provider of what Peattie (1995: 181) calls 'absolute green products', i.e. those which contribute positively to the improvement of the environment. However, its small size, foreign ownership and lack of involvement in consumer markets limited its public profile on environmental issues. Let us look at the two firms' green marketing approaches in more detail.

RetailCo

RetailCo could be seen to have a fairly well advanced environmental agenda, albeit within a relatively 'clean' area of business. Although several respondents indicated to me that the firm had introduced a few environmentally friendly practices quite some time ago (such as the re-use of transport packing materials) it was clear that at the time this had been done on grounds of cost effectiveness rather than environmental concern. An allegedly 'coherent' and 'structured' approach to the environment had, however, been attempted from around 1990 when a dedicated Environmental Co-ordinator position was established within the Product Quality section of the company. The first environmental policy statement was subsequently issued in 1991, and internal environmental reporting was begun in 1993, with the intention, according to the environmental co-ordinator, of setting up an external reporting procedure across the parent group, 'hopefully in a couple of years'. At the time of fieldwork in 1995/6 there were three dedicated environment positions in the company, as well as a number of 'green teams' comprising volunteers throughout the company. The role of these green teams had been defined by the firm in its documentation as: 'to investigate opportunities for further environmental improvement and to ensure the implementation of our existing policies at a "grass roots" level'.

Organizational greening in RetailCo could therefore be seen to have been broadly consistent with developments in other large established retail firms (see Simms 1992; Taylor and Welford 1994; Fineman 1996). Green marketing activities in the company had spanned the four P's marketing mix framework, extending into Peattie's (1992) expanded green mix of processes, policies, people and providing information. Indeed, greening at RetailCo could be said to have impacted to some extent throughout the company, and certainly beyond marketing activities alone. However, it is those aspects of greening which principally centred on marketing concerns – most notably new product development, corporate communications, promotions, labelling and pricing – which were particularly of interest to me, and which are primarily the ones reported here. Interestingly though, respondents themselves did not refer to their company as employing 'green marketing' in their discussions with me. Indeed, the term appeared to carry a pejorative meaning in RetailCo akin to Peattie and Ratnayaka's (1992) 'green selling', i.e. using the environment as a selling point without any appreciable alteration to the product. Hence, it should be noted that these are *my* constructions of 'green marketing' activity at RetailCo and not the respondents' own.

It is also notable that RetailCo managers couched our discussions of environmental product concerns in the company in terms of their own-label goods, and generally excluded proprietary brands. Among these own-label products, the principal environmental developments had been: the incorporation of recycled materials into product formulations (e.g. for video tapes, dustbin liners and kitchen knives); the introduction of so-called 'natural' cosmetics ranges; organic or sustainable product ranges; energy-saving products; and various products using recyclable and re-usable components. Along with changes in product formulations, RetailCo had also attempted to 'audit' and subsequently reduce packaging. Moreover, it had introduced communications initiatives such as an in-house eco-label, collaboration with NGOs on establishing national eco-labelling schemes, provision of on-pack environmental information and the publishing of environment brochures and leaflets.

Environmental concerns, however, clearly made little impact on pricing decisions, and executives regularly claimed to me that before green developments could be introduced, they had to be shown to be cost effective:

> Everything doesn't have to make a profit. But at the end of the day, most – well I'd say all – of the successful environmental issues [in RetailCo] are cost effective. We're doing it because it's sound business sense.

The avowed intention of the company then, was to maintain prices whilst attempting to introduce incremental environmental improvements in product formulations. Hence, both premium and penetration pricing had been avoided, reinforcing executives' claims that at RetailCo, the intention had not been to highlight the environment as a prominent marketing issue, but to render it as 'just another part of doing business'.

This attitude was also reflected in the company's overall green marketing strategy. Despite a range of greening activities, few, if any, of RetailCo's products were marketed on an explicit green platform, or positioned to appeal directly to 'green' or 'ethical' consumers. My interpretation of this was that it should be regarded as a strategy of *muted greening*, that is, a strategy for green marketing whereby environmental considerations are incorporated into business practice, but where external environmental promotions are low key and predominantly public relations based. Hence in RetailCo, environmental 'auditing' or assessment procedures had been introduced (e.g. store environmental reviews, supplier questionnaires and a packaging audit) whereas little emphasis had been afforded to corresponding green claims on product packs or in advertising. However, environmental responsibility was emphasized relatively strongly in press releases, information packs, and through local community and philanthropic gestures. Equally, it was obvious that internal communications were fairly well developed, with managers and staff able to show me an annual environmental report, a regular environmental section in the in-house magazine, environmental news-letters, as well as evidence of informal communication through the green team network.

According to respondents, this muted strategy was principally driven by changes in the marketing environment. It was generally suggested that it had become increasingly important for RetailCo to remain credible and responsible in the eyes of a sceptical public, but at the same time, as one respondent put it, to avoid risking 'putting our heads above the parapet'. This kind of grab for positive environmentally based publicity was widely disparaged due its potential to incite unwanted or inappropriate attention from outside bodies. Hence, senior executives suggested that they had not wanted the firm to be seen to be doing too little, as this may have led to reputation problems; but equally, it was potentially dangerous to, as they put it, 'go around shouting about it like other companies have', since this could have drawn attention from latent critics in pressure groups and the media. Such a balancing act was regarded as a pragmatic response by the company to the perceived (and often conflicting) pressures of increased external scrutiny, market pressure, consumer confusion and scepticism towards green claims, and increasingly onerous regulation.

Interestingly, within this perceived mixture of forces and pressures, the consumer was depicted by different respondents (and sometimes by the same respondent) as both 'the key driver' of organizational greening, and also a significant barrier to more explicit green marketing. As a driver for greening, the customer was held up as a strong influence on the motivation to develop and enhance the firm's image for environmental responsibility. The cause of a cus-tomer barrier to greening was a widely alluded to (but largely undocumented) perception of consumer antipathy towards green products.[1] Green branding was seen as sure to 'cause sales to bomb', implying that consumers were negatively motivated towards purchasing green products. In the main this was seen as a result of: (a) consumer doubts over the quality of green products; and (b) a lack of trust in green claims. Specific citations of these problems tended to rely on examples from the cleaning products and detergents sector, and in particular on green washing powders and liquids which were depicted as having seriously under-performed in the market. None of these products were sold by RetailCo in any significant quantity. The main example cited of this phenomenon actually relating to RetailCo products however was the case of a range of dustbin liners which, having apparently failed under green branding, were successfully re-launched later as a non-green product. Essentially, despite maintaining an identical product formulation, the recycled nature of the product was abandoned as a key element in the product's communication strategy in order to address customer perceptions of product weakness. For RetailCo managers, the customer was seen as equating 'recycled' with 'flawed' and 'feeble'.

Overall then, managers at RetailCo tended to emphasize that rather than attempting to use the environment to present an overtly positive corporate image, 'we had to manage the environment such that it didn't *damage* our reputation' – a more cautious and conservative reputation management approach.[2] These findings provide strong supporting evidence for Wong *et al.*'s (1996) conclusions that UK consumer marketing firms were playing down their environmental credentials in response to an emergent consumer backlash in the early–mid 1990s. According to Wong *et al.* (1996), this backlash had largely arisen from a mismatch between consumers' expectations and the reality of firms' product offerings, much of it due to ineffective communications and promotional policies. This in many ways was a key aspect of the business context in which the case organizations were developing green marketing policies and programmes at the time that fieldwork was conducted. I shall return to this issue in the following chapters and elaborate on it more fully in Chapter 7.

In a sense then, the strategy for greening adopted by RetailCo cut across Peattie and Ratnayaka's (1992) off-the-peg potential strategies. Changes were issue-based and cautiously attuned to the exigencies of specific markets and market environments rather than being simply 'piecemeal'. Hence, on issues such as responsibility for packaging the company might be regarded as having adopted a 'defensive' strategy; on animal testing a 'knee-jerk reaction' strategy; on natural ingredients a 'follow the herd' strategy; on wood sourcing a broader 'greening the company' strategy; and so on (see Peattie and Ratnayaka 1992).

ManufactureCo

ManufactureCo's approach to incorporating environmental considerations into its marketing activities revealed an equally interesting picture. The firm's Scandinavian parent company could be seen to have publicly presented itself as an intrinsically green company, due in the main to its marketing of environmental technologies for water treatment. For example, of the ten major stories featured in the parent company's 1995 Annual Report, no less than seven were concerned with the environment. In addition, the marketing report in the same publication claimed:

> We are also a leader in environmentally-related technology. Environmental considerations play an important part in both product development, and generally at work, where the company has a comprehensive Environment, Safety and Health program in place.

This emphasis on the environment was repeated in company magazines and other publications for customers and various stakeholders that were published by the parent company.

In stark contrast to this polished green image of the parent company, I could find little evidence that staff at the UK subsidiary believed their own firm echoed similar sentiments, either publicly or privately. Indeed, respondents generally expressed little conviction to me that their business had developed any kind of coherent environmental programme outside an apparent 'general awareness' of the issues. Hence, illustrative staff responses were: 'to be honest with you, I'm not sure we do have an environmental agenda' . . . 'we don't get involved in the environment all that much' . . . 'the environment is only marginal to our business'. Indeed, whilst the use of the company's products was clearly environmental in nature (e.g. in the treatment of effluent) this was afforded scant significance by ManufactureCo executives in my discussions with them. Rather, they suggested that the equivalence of environmental credentials for all competing firms in this particular industry made such concerns fairly redundant. In addition, they presented their customers as having only very limited interest in environmental issues. As a result, it appeared to be widely believed that little adaptation to environmental concerns had been necessary in marketing terms. There was, though, some suggestion that environmental considerations were beginning to feature in customers' demands, although respondents were quick to emphasize that this was almost certainly due to increasing regulatory pressure rather than any kind of moral impetus in the customer firms. Indeed, it seemed to be inconceivable to ManufactureCo staff that the environment would feature in industrial marketing exchanges unless driven to by external pressure. Thus, one manager claimed to me: 'the customers will often be forced into doing it. No one does it unless he has to.'

This is not to say that respondents made no claims at all for the inclusion of environmental concerns into marketing activity. The environmental performance of product features such as noise, oil and coatings were all clearly of consequence to the overall product offering. Some opportunistic public relations activity had also been initiated and this had seen the company involved in public programmes with varying environmental consequences. Moreover, some communications and promotional texts made at least limited reference to the environmental qualities of the firm's products. This was principally by specifying the components' accordance with regulations of various kinds, and by some reporting of the practical role of their products in environmental management systems or in meeting customers' environmental objectives. The 'caring' or custodial type themes typified by the communications programmes of RetailCo were not however in evidence, possibly as a result of perceived differences in market needs.

Overall, the green marketing strategy adopted by ManufactureCo was probably closest to what Peattie and Ratnayaka (1992) describe as a 'knee-jerk' strategy: compliance with regulation and response to strong external pressures. Hence, green marketing at the company appeared to be fragmented, unmanaged and opportunistic in the context of potential changes in the marketing environment. Moreover, in their conversations with me, respondents from ManufactureCo made no attempt to hide greening initiatives behind protestations of ethical motives, as the following manager illustrates:

> The [customers] are trying to change their image so that they are seen as green . . . and we can be part of the bandwagon to sell some product and develop new markets.

Green marketing and corporate social responsibility

In many ways then, it is difficult to ascribe an overall social responsibility strategy to the practice of green marketing at these two companies. However, at RetailCo, where the environmental agenda was considerably more developed, a clear discourse had begun to be developed around the greening programme, as examined in more detail later. The recurrent theme pervading the organization, evident both in formal documentation (reports, etc.), informal documentation (newsletters, training videos, etc.) and routinely incanted by executives in the company was this:

> 'Sound environmental sense makes good business sense.'

This theme could be seen to be firmly located in the discourse of enlightened self-interest, i.e. where ostensibly 'ethical' actions are viewed in the context of their long-term performance benefits. Correspondingly, at RetailCo this theme had tended to be articulated to me with particular reference to the cost savings that could, or had, been made from introducing certain environmental policies. This might have been through various policies such as packaging reductions and energy efficiencies. There were also significant incidences in my discussions with RetailCo managers when respondents would rationalize *all* organizational greening practices in terms of economic performance criteria, or as they tended to put it, 'good business sense'.

Whilst this notion of enlightened self-interest was clearly central to the framing of green marketing in RetailCo, it had also begun, to some extent, to emerge in relation to ManufactureCo's incipient greening policy. Although at the time of fieldwork, this could not be said to constitute a clear moral discourse at the firm, there were certainly signals from the parent company that such an instrumental, self-interest conception of the environment was likely to be promoted. Hence, in this quote from the parent's annual report, environmental policies were presented in much the same way as at RetailCo:

> Good environmental management can pinpoint opportunities for cost savings. It encourages energy efficiencies and reduces waste. It gives you a nice, clean corporate image. In short, it's good for your bottom line . . . and rather than being a constraint, it just makes good business sense.

Clearly then, green marketing at the conventional organizations was constructed very much in terms of notions of self-interest. How these notions actually came to be established, legitimatized and subsequently integrated into the fabric of the company, however, is not evident at this current level of analysis; nor indeed does it provide clear insight into what implications such meanings might have for the marketing strategies and tactics adopted by the companies as revealed above. The following section then seeks to explain in more detail the processes underlying the introduction of green marketing programmes at RetailCo and ManufactureCo. In so doing, the aim is to explore how attendant notions of morality were given or denied expression within this process, how the self-interest discourse came to be accepted, and how this can be related to manifest marketing phenomena.

Cultural dynamics and moral meanings in green marketing

Overall, the prevailing ethos of both of the conventional organizations was characterized by informants as conservative and business-like. They were seen as typified by well-established and fairly rigid attitudinal and behavioural norms that were reflected in sizeable populations of long-term, and to some extent homogeneous, employees. In the context of such orthodoxy, the environment might be considered to be a potentially radical introduction into the cultural knowledge of the firm and its members (Fineman 1996). Indeed, respondents from both companies tended to present the extant corporate culture as potentially resistant to greening, unless it could be shown to be consistent with existing commercial priorities and norms. However, it is important to note that at the time of introduction for the companies' nascent environmental agendas (for RetailCo in the early 1990s; for ManufactureCo in the mid-1990s) green and/or ethical marketing issues were still considered 'new' to the organizations. Hence moral meanings for the environment were open to interpretation and were, to a large extent, negotiable.

At a micro level, it was evident that the process of institutionalizing such green meanings centred around the presence or otherwise of certain 'environment champions' who would facilitate and expedite the introduction of environmental considerations into marketing activity (Chakrabarti 1974; Drumwright 1994). Indeed, in the green marketing context Drumwright (1994) refers to such individuals as environmental 'policy entrepreneurs' and I shall similarly adopt this terminology. Such policy entrepreneurs were found to be present in both

RetailCo and ManufactureCo, but in the latter were only very marginally focused on environmental issues. Therefore, significantly different dynamics were revealed in the two companies, most notably in the sense that only in RetailCo could the process of institutionalizing the green agenda be regarded as managed in any way. The following section looks at this role of the policy entrepreneurs in the two conventional companies. Then I go on to analyse in some detail the processes associated with these actors specifically in RetailCo and draw out insights pertaining to attendant moral meanings.

Policy entrepreneurs and processes of institutionalization

Whilst the existence and importance of environmental managers, advocates, leaders and/or champions has been fairly widely recognized in the organizational greening literature (see for example, Elkington and Burke 1989; Dillon and Fischer 1992), little examination has emerged concerning their personal and professional roles in the process of greening (Fineman 1997). However, Drumwright (1994), in her study of socially responsible organizational buying, provides an important and illuminating description of such 'policy entrepreneurs'. In many ways Drumwright's (1994: 4) descriptions bear a striking similarity to the key environmental protagonists I came across in RetailCo:

> Policy entrepreneurs . . . usually were facile at both motivating people and making the system work for them . . . had tenacious persistence and a high energy level . . . were undaunted by resisters and operational problems.

At RetailCo, I saw policy entrepreneurs or environmental champions who had fulfilled similar roles in fuelling and driving the internal green agenda. Indeed, without strenuous campaigning on their part, it was clear that far less positive green marketing activity would have been contemplated by the company. Such campaigning was mainly achieved through energetic attempts to maximize personal interaction between themselves and their less environmentally motivated colleagues, and through constantly reiterating and revitalizing environmental themes, as this particular RetailCo policy entrepreneur explains:

> I get round all of what we call our group product managers . . . as frequently as possible. And what we have to do is . . . get those meetings in the diary and get out to the business centres. And that's the only way to do it. You get yourself about. It's hard work but it's got to be done.

Executives also attested to the importance of environmental protagonists being highly motivated and, in particular, being persistent in seeing environmental initiatives through. Hence, as one informant suggested: 'everything's possible – it just depends if someone is willing to put the effort in'. In addition, respondents also highlighted the importance of their exercising subtlety and guile in the 'highly political' process of securing support and acceptance for environmental initiatives at RetailCo.

Interestingly, environmental protagonists at RetailCo did not particularly exhibit an evangelistic sense of mission towards the greening of their organization. Executives with direct green marketing responsibility appeared to harbour a range of environmental standards and ideals. Whilst some exhibited a clear concern for the environment, others were obviously less personally committed. Environmental responsibilities were generally taken on more for career advancement than they were for moral or environmental commitment, evidenced by statements such as, 'I certainly never had any personal desire to get involved in the environment', and 'I wanted to get the environment on my CV'. The personal moralities of RetailCo environmental executives then were on the whole less instrumental in the adoption of their policy entrepreneurship role than were traditional drives for organization success; the role was simply regarded as a necessary one to do a good job in a new and problematic organizational function. This corresponds with extant UK evidence (Fineman 1996, 1997), but stands in contrast to that from the US (Drumwright 1994),[3] suggesting the possibility of a country effect. That is, US managers might be more likely to present themselves as emotionally committed to greening than their British counterparts. I shall return to this later in the book, in Chapter 9.

In contrast to this situation in RetailCo, no such environmental policy entrepreneur role appeared to be filled at ManufactureCo. In general, direction and meaning seemed to be derived from intermittent and irregular signals from the parent company rather than from an internal source. These external messages, however, appeared to have had little impact on the cultural knowledge of the firm or its employees, reflected in turn by the general lack of environmental awareness in the firm. As one manager put it:

> I don't think that making environmental products will make you more environmentally conscious. You may become more aware of some of the problems, but you do tend to get blasé about it.

Conversely, the issue of health and safety (H&S) appeared to be prominent in respondents' consciousness. Not only was it widely attested to be central to the firm's operations, but respondents suggested that it was one of the key issues which set ManufactureCo apart from its competitors. Hence, informants would say things to me like, 'our health and safety is second to none' . . . 'the company has used safety as a selling point' . . . 'because of the health and safety rules on site, we make quite a show of it'. Equally, in much the same way that the progression of the environmental agenda at RetailCo apparently relied on environmental policy entrepreneurs, respondents from ManufactureCo suggested that the H&S issue had been propelled to such prominence by the commitment of particular individuals. As one informant suggested, 'the Health and Safety Manager is very hot on safety . . . she's been here about five years I think, and she's made a big difference.'

Therefore, the presence of H&S advocates and absence of environmental advocates had clearly had a significant effect on the cultural knowledge of the firm and its members. Without such championing, the environment had received little attention in ManufactureCo compared to H&S issues. As a result, it appeared that environmental meaning on the part of respondents largely mirrored the firm's mode of environmental management, i.e. unfocused, scattered and idiosyncratic. In search of some kind of frame of reference for environmental activities in the company, when discussing such issues with me, respondents tended if anything to link the environment to this highly prominent H&S function. However, as one respondent from the H&S function itself lamented, this assumption was decidedly misplaced:

> Environment is becoming more high profile. The parent company has just done their ISO 14000 . . . and so everyone is phoning us up [H&S] and asking us about it . . . but we don't know any more than they do!

Policy entrepreneurs were clearly integral to the development or otherwise of an explicit environment agenda in the sampled conventional companies. Evidence suggests however that such internal marketing of green initiatives is likely to be a difficult task, particularly in the context of confusing or unsupportive market signals (Wong *et al.* 1996; Fineman 1997) and/or a lack of attendant cultural endorsement (Drumwright 1994; Fineman 1996). The following sub-sections therefore seek to reveal in more detail the processes by which such individuals appeared to attempt to incorporate environmental understandings into their organization, and in particular how this may have affected the notions of morality attached to the company's green marketing programmes. Accordingly, in the remaineder of this section attention is focused on RetailCo rather than ManufactureCo since it was only in the former that such individuals were readily discovered, and where appropriate data could be collected. Analysis of this data revealed that policy entrepreneurs appeared to have developed a set of articulated and unarticulated micropolitical manoeuvres which were generally believed to constitute a recipe for success for the selling of green initiatives within the organization. Broadly speaking, these can be categorized as image making, moral framing, narrative surfing and value dissemination.

Image making

It was recognized by the policy entrepreneurs I spoke to in RetailCo that, in what they perceived to be a relatively conventional corporate milieu, and one not particularly open to radical ideas, the environment as a concept could be viewed in some way as inappropriate or challenging to the status quo if associated with the wrong images. Accordingly, the position and status of environmental executives compared to more traditional roles in the firm was an issue of some consternation to the post holders. In particular, they related how in the early stages of RetailCo's environmental policy implementation, they were regarded by most of their colleagues as 'out on a limb', and considered peripheral to the main business of manufacturing and marketing products. One respondent for example described their colleagues' reaction thus:

I think we were tolerated . . . just leave them alone . . . they are doing a good job elsewhere . . . just let them get on with it.

In response to this possibility of being marginalized and subsequently manoeuvred away from having any real organizational respect and power, environmental executives consciously, and at times unconsciously, appeared to practice a subtle form of personal and group image making. Most obviously, they sought to distance themselves from what they regarded as the corporately unacceptable image of the environmentalist – 'the beads and braids brigade' . . . 'the beard and sandals lot' . . . 'the cranks'. A deliberate adoption of what was termed a sober and 'professional', 'businesslike' appearance and manner was supplemented by an avoidance of 'emotive' or ethical arguments in favour of 'rational', technical ones. Since the term was used fairly frequently by RetailCo policy entrepreneurs, this can be usefully categorized as the 'responsible management' image:

> [The first RetailCo environmental executive] was meticulously carefully to make sure that he was always taking a very responsible management approach, and so he built up a reputation that this isn't just some sort of open-toed sandal, you know, thongs and braids brigade going in . . . It's that perception thing again. I think it's grown up that we do take a professional approach and I make sure that, you know, that sticks.

The need to be seen as professional managers in the same way as their colleagues was felt acutely by the environmental executives I spoke to in RetailCo. It was important to them that they fitted into a corporate culture which they routinely depicted as 'professional' and 'businesslike'. This cultural integration could be argued to have served two purposes. First, it provided managers with the correct and unchallenging image with which to pursue initiatives that may otherwise have been regarded as suspicious, inappropriate, or controversial. As a result, they were able to progress relatively unhindered by their non-traditional role towards the customary rewards of organizational success, namely job security and career advancement. Second, it could also have enabled these individuals to engage their organization more intimately, to express loyalty to their company and pride in their job. Consequently, it may have contributed to the satisfaction of their needs for respect and belongingness (Fineman 1996).

A possible side-effect of these acts of image making appeared to be some form of minor 'moral stress' (Bird and Waters 1989), brought on by the relinquishing of personal moralities to the 'enacted' morality of the organization (Fineman 1995, 1997). In some situations, clear differences could at times be discerned between: (a) the moral certainties articulated in response to my questions regarding *the company's* policies and practices and (b) admissions of moral ambiguity and outcome uncertainty when questioned on respondents' own *personal* opinions. In the most compelling example of this private–public tension, one respondent had claimed *not* to be an environmentalist while our discussion was focused on company policies. However, later in the interview, when the respondent's personal moral position was sought, this claim was retracted – even to the extent of emphasizing membership of environmental organizations *and* resignation from a previous company on the grounds of maintaining a clear environmental conscience!

Moral framing

This carefully constructed image of the professional manager was bolstered in a number of ways by environmental executives in RetailCo, but it was most apparent in the arguments which they presented in order to describe and justify the adoption of environmental initiatives. In the main, informants were at ease when discussing environmental marketing projects that could be readily subsumed within a context of cost savings and other commercial justifications. These had generally been the issues which RetailCo had tackled earliest in its environmental programme, the 'low hanging fruits' of win–win solutions which offered bottom-line benefits along with reductions in environmental impacts. However, even those activities which may have been broader in scope and which may not have so obviously generated immediate quantifiable benefits for the company (such as environmental 'auditing' and efforts to improve environmental labelling) were also assimilated within a highly instrumental conception of the environment. Indeed, managers routinely emphasized to me the lack of conflict between 'environment' and 'economics', and they frequently related back to the enlightened self-interest theme of 'sound environmental sense makes good business sense'.

Interestingly, at times this logic was even inverted such that environmental benefits were argued to *only* occur in the context of economic benefits. For example, typical comments were, 'the cost is often a good guide [to the best environmental solution]' and 'if it's not making sense economically, then it is probably not making sense environmentally, and so we haven't found really that that causes us a conflict.' This finding is crucial. These managers were claiming that the *environmental* impacts of competing solutions could be best assessed according to their relative *cost*. Hence, if a particular proposal demanded a greater commitment of resources than its forecasted returns, then it was not deemed to be environmentally appropriate. This was a curious, perhaps disturbing, rationale that can perhaps only be adequately explained by the total immersion of these managers in the cost and enterprise culture of their departments.

In general then, managers' rationalizations for environmental activities (both to me and, they suggested, to their colleagues) almost exclusively emphasized commercial considerations rather than ideological, ethical, cultural or personal motivations, even though there was the very real possibility that organizational resources may have secured a better economic return elsewhere. The invocation of consumer need was much in evidence, and the careful interpretation of, as yet inconclusive market research, appeared to be a powerful legitimating device in support of executives' green projects (see for example, Brown and Ennew 1995). Such 'rational' and 'commercial' arguments were seen as central to the responsible management approach and other 'emotive' arguments were condemned in comparison:

> I don't react emotively. I react based on scientific evidence that is put in front of me. So that if you take that approach, it is often a lot easier to combine the sort of professional, commercial approach to environmental management as opposed to the emotive, reactive sort of approach.

The perceived need for executives to negotiate the embedded culture of the organization in securing support and commitment for environmental marketing initiatives can be seen to have had the effect of them enacting a moral frame that effectively castrated moral meanings from the environment. Clearly, from an ethical point of view, this would correspond more with teleological conceptions of morality than deontological ones. In other words, managers did not emphasize any intrinsic *duty* to protect the environment, but rather would suggest that environmental protection had beneficial *outcomes*, namely cost reductions (which could then be used to reduce prices), improved company reputation or enhanced public legitimacy.

Moreover, it is also significant that any notions of societal marketing in this scenario (i.e. marketing activities conducted with the long-term interests of consumers in mind) appeared to be very much divorced from moral reflection and consideration. The commodification of social and environmental concerns in the form of green products appeared to shape the nature of those concerns for the individuals and companies involved. Hence, in RetailCo it was apparent that the marketing process itself acted to neutralize concepts of morality or ethics, or rather *amoralized* green marketing. The invocation of commercial arguments for specific projects can be seen to be the most obvious manifestation of this process of amoralization. However, I also detected more subtle elements, such as the setting out of moral boundaries and the avoidance of moral vocabularies, which appeared to underpin and interplay with this approach.

Setting moral boundaries

As the main environmental reality definers in RetailCo, policy entrepreneurs had attempted to set the boundaries within which the environment was considered to be a social or ethical responsibility of the firm. It is revealing then that many of these individuals made a distinction between issues that were to be perceived as 'ethical' and those which were to be perceived as 'environmental'. This reluctance to categorize environmental products within the rubric of ethical business was manifested in comments such as those relating how the prominence and 'fashion' for environmentalism was beginning to be overshadowed by that of ethical issues, e.g. 'it's difficult keeping the spotlight on core [environmental] issues. Now we're having to move into the ethical thing'. This position was reiterated even more explicitly when respondents were asked to clarify the scope of the company's environmental policy, and how this translated into defining their own functional responsibilities:

> We . . . are careful about the language we use – ethical and environmental . . . but there are some ethical issues which are fairly close. . . . They are actually reporting to different boards of directors, so as a company we do actually separate out the two.

It is clear then that quite specific moral boundaries had been set out among managers at RetailCo. As much as possible, 'ethical' issues were marginalized and frequently excluded from the mindsets of executives who had to deal with 'environmental' products and problems on a daily basis. Those environmental products that they had to contend with were therefore not consciously framed in terms of explicit moral responsibilities or dilemmas, but rather as technical problems which demanded technical solutions. Moral reflection, as much as possible, was apparently avoided. These findings are broadly in keeping with those of other qualitative studies in the business ethics field where managers have been found to avoid moral discourse (Bird and Waters 1989) and become de-sensitized to the moral dimension of their activities through bureaucracy, formalization and task repetition (Jackall 1988).

Semantic suspects

Content analysis of research interviews and various forms of company documen-tation collected at RetailCo revealed that at, its most extreme, this avoidance of 'ethical' themes in 'environmental' discourse at RetailCo could take the form of a wholesale avoidance of certain words and concepts. These can be subsumed within a category of *semantic suspects*, i.e. symbols which may have translated meanings that environmental executives felt would damage both their personal image and the status of environmental business in RetailCo generally. In particular, organizational conceptions of the environment were channelled away from morally contestable notions such as 'deep ecology' concepts of sustainability, biodiversity and ecocentrism. For example, although arguments for sustain-ability have been held to be less confrontational towards business than many other environmental positions (Peattie 1995), they were still assiduously avoided by environmental executives at RetailCo. The term itself was almost never used by respondents in my interviews with them, nor did it appear in external communications. Indeed, in the RetailCo environmental policy statement, sustainability was not directly mentioned despite the use of a phrase – 'our aim is to meet current needs, without compromising the ability of future generations to meet their own needs' – which was almost identical to the much-quoted World Commission on Environment and Development definition of the term.[4] The avoidance of sustainability here was all the more striking for the inclusion in its place of its principal tenet; it might thus be reasonably argued to be the result of a deliberate and calculated semantic choice.

At one level, this reflects RetailCo's muted greening strategy, and respondents were quick to emphasize the potential pitfalls of using terms in the public realm where definitions might be open to differing interpretations. Also, at a deeper level, it probably reflected attempts by environment executives in RetailCo to reframe the environment in order to present it as a 'normal' and 'rational' business function rather than a soft 'emotive' issue:

> As soon as you mention it [sustainability], people's eyes glaze over. If you are talking to senior managers, they think you are going back to the hippie days, you know. Sustainability? We are running a business to make profits. It's not about furry things.

Whist interview protocol was designed so as to focus our discussions directly on environmental issues, it was somewhat surprising that executives made little or no attempt to incorporate the environment within a discussion of social responsibility or corporate morality. Morality terms such as 'ethical', 'moral', 'responsibility', 'duty', 'right' and 'wrong' were rarely if ever used by my informants. The company's twenty-page environment information pack also avoided direct morality terms, preferring instead to emphasize the size and importance of the company and its policy of 'caring' for customers. In general then, executives at RetailCo involved in the processes of environmental marketing acted to neutralize morality or to *amoralize* the environment in order to secure organizational endorsement for their activities. This can be seen to have been a deliberate strategy adopted by the firm's first environment manager, as he relates here:

> You have to be realistic. Things like sustainability – unless you dress them up in more business language, they are going to be resisted. You have to accept that there are certain words and phrases and approaches that turn the locks in a business. And if you can't get the right managers to buy into what you are doing, because you are using the wrong language or the wrong keys, then it doesn't matter how sensible you are, or what you are trying to push, you've had it.

Hence the muted greening strategy revealed earlier can be seen to have been a product of the way in which environmental protagonists within the company had sought to balance internal and external pressures for and against greening. Their tactics clearly focused on finding a vocabulary for greening that was appropriate for the conservative and cost-focused corporate milieu of RetailCo, but also one which reflected their embedded notions of professional retailing. The discourse subsequently established appeared almost entirely amoralized.

Narrative surfing

Managers had also sought to integrate the environment into the fabric of the company by aligning green marketing activities with existing prominent corporate narratives. This process is referred to here as narrative surfing since the choice of narrative appeared to reflect the particular demands of the situation, and executives seemed adept at invoking different narratives as needs arose. For instance, the introduction of the environment into everyday operations of the company was compared by almost all respondents to the integration of (total) quality concerns during the 1980s:

> Environment is very often linked to quality . . . many people find that it mimics quality maybe ten, fifteen-years lagged behind where quality is now . . . so it's really from a quality background.

This association of the environment with the quality narrative can be argued to represent an attempt to de-mystify the greening process by comparing it to a process that was already known and considered to have been a successful and relatively unproblematic transition for the company. Further credibility was garnered by the fact that the source of most early environmental developments in the company was also associated with the quality division – and several key individuals had been involved in both schemes.

It is evident, however, that environmental policy entrepreneurs did not limit themselves only to attaching the environmental marketing activities to the quality narrative, but rather 'surfed' various narratives as appropriate given the particular contextual and political exigencies of the situation. For example, the quality narrative appeared to be principally invoked with reference to new product development, production, and process decisions. However, when contesting promotion decisions with other managers, the preferred narrative appeared to be that of 'concern'.

'Concern' refers to RetailCo's umbrella corporate marketing campaign at the time that fieldwork was conducted.[5] The phrases 'Who's concerned? . . .', 'Someone is concerned . . .' and 'RetailCo is concerned' formed the context for all RetailCo marketing communications at this time. As such, the campaign had been adeptly invoked by senior environmental executives in order to contrive an effective bargaining position with senior marketing executives:

> The Director of Marketing . . . accepted as a principle that . . . if [RetailCo] was not seen to be environmentally sound then the whole Concern campaign had a major flaw in it. Because if you can't be concerned about the environment, something as fundamental as that, how can you be concerned about the rest of it?

However, the integration of the environment within the concern narrative had not been restricted merely to internal political uses, but can be seen to have also manifested itself explicitly in formal policy documents and marketing texts, with comments of the type, 'concern for the environment and the people in it goes hand in hand with RetailCo's policy of being concerned for its customers'. Crucially, the use of the concern narrative can be seen to have been used in preference to a competing narrative of social responsibility which may arguably be regarded as having been equally, if not more, applicable in these contexts. Again, however, the use of an explicit moral term such as social responsibility may have been adjudged to be overly challenging to the existing corporate ethos. But 'concern' may have been perceived to be both less suspect and more in line with other marketing texts. The use of this narrative thus normalized the greening process.

One final narrative with which respondents can be seen to have fused environmental considerations was that of RetailCo's cultural traditions. RetailCo's philanthropic founder acted as a useful narrative for contemporary employees in terms of establishing a meaningful frame of reference for interpretations of, and justifications for, recent environmental activities in the company:

> When we issued the environmental policy and we started looking at it in a structured sort of way . . . we even related it back to [the founder's] days, when he founded the company, and was founding it on a social and ethically responsible premise.

This manifested itself to a greater degree, however, in various marketing communication texts. Key environmental documents, directed at internal as well as external audiences, habitually began by integrating environmental activities within a wider historical narrative (and also invoking the concern theme), using statements of the kind: 'Since the Company was founded RetailCo's philosophy has been to be concerned for its customers, staff and the local community.'

In marketing communications then, the philanthropy of the founder was mobilized in order to give credence to claims for a long unbroken tradition of 'concern' at the company. In contrast, the living history of the firm, the stories recounted by present employees, provided little insight into this legacy of social and environmental responsibility. Rowlinson and Hassard (1993) refer to this as the 'invention' of corporate culture: the process of giving meaning to events through the implication of a largely factitious continuity with the past. Certainly respondents' use of the historical narrative in this study was indeed limited to specific references to the company's founder, and to claims of a well-established reputation for concern amongst consumers which had to be fulfilled. In general then, the cultural tradition narrative served as a useful symbolic device for green marketing communications, particularly in terms of creating an historical embeddedness for environmental activities. Moreover, internally it had more currency when translated into a consumer demand, i.e. a reputation for social and environmental responsibility that had to be maintained. Once more this had the effect of suppressing the distinctly moral component (an internal, cultural drive to 'care') in order to stress the instrumental (an external demand to 'live up to' the existing reputation) – again adding to the reframing of the environment as an amoral and 'normal' business activity.

In short then, the surfing of appropriate existing company narratives allowed the environment to be presented as something which was neither strange (through the quality narrative), nor different (through the concern narrative), nor new (through the tradition narrative). When considered in association with the other emergent themes of image making and moral framing, the practice by which policy entrepreneurs in RetailCo had sought to secure commitment and support for green marketing is fairly evident. Most notably, it had involved the neutralization of morality in relation to the environment. The intention in the company had been to render the environment as just another business problem with no more and no less relevance to notions of ethics or morality than for any other issue. In the final section focusing on RetailCo, the analysis moves on to an exploration of the processes by which these relatively well established and legitimatized environmental values had been disseminated through to areas of the organization outside the direct contact of the main environmental protagonists.

Value dissemination

Whilst the environment as an issue was clearly not central enough to be at all consequential in recruitment and selection decisions in RetailCo (other than for dedicated environmental positions), once employees had joined the company several mechanisms were in place by which they could garner environmental knowledge, awareness and meaning. Environmental newsletters, bulletins and leaflets of various kinds acted as useful vehicles for communication of issues and for raising the profile of the environment within the company. Whilst these may have included fairly general environmental information and tips, little opportunity was lost to reinforce in these publications the prevailing theme of 'sound environmental sense makes good business sense'. Hence, this message was reiterated in various texts such as the environmental policy statement, a staff information video, customer environment leaflets, and so on.

The informal green team network was generally seen by green policy entrepreneurs as the most important vehicle for raising environmental awareness in the company, particularly in the formative period of greening. As groups of interested volunteers, working outside company time, these tended to comprise individuals with some level of explicit moral motivation. Hence informants (both members and non-members) would say things like: 'it's mainly people who are interested in green issues personally' . . . 'on a personal view, it is something that I am interested in, something that I want to be involved in. I feel quite strongly about it.' Green teams consequently concentrated on issues of immediate concern to their members, particularly the establishment of local recycling and re-use systems within individual departments. And whilst they had limited, if any, impact on company policies, even at the most basic tactical level, these teams could be seen to occupy an important role in informing and motivating people about environmental issues generally, and also in relation to their particular sections and roles. Policy entrepreneurs then had utilized the enthusiasm of their colleagues to generate a more conducive context for greening activities. Hence they saw the environment as an 'empowering tool' with which they had 'persuaded a lot of people to do things different ways'. None the less, since green team members tended to be involved for personal rather than for professional reasons, the teams could be, as one senior executive put it, 'a double-edged sword' that may have impeded the crucial support and attention of line managers. So although the team meetings clearly allowed members to speculate fairly openly about environmental issues and problems at the company, there was also a general recognition that proposals had to be local, practical, quantifiable and cost effective. This had called for careful management in order to focus the teams' attention on parochial concerns and to ensure credibility of the overall greening project.

Some evidence of the environmental agenda having successfully permeated at store level could also be detected, although in a substantially diluted form. The muted greening strategy and the attachment of the environment to existing narratives and discourses within the company meant that, at the front line, what little environmental meaning that had been present back at the head office tended to be lost. Hence, my conversations at RetailCo stores suggested that store staff saw issues in terms of 'costs' and 'customers' rather than 'nature' or 'morality'. In this sense, energy efficiencies were seen to be primarily cost-motivated, and green products were regarded as being stocked to offer choice rather than because they were of environmental benefit. Despite at least some environmental training having then been activated at store level, knowledge of RetailCo's environmental policies and programmes appeared limited, and store staff's comments were typically of the type: 'I *think* they are recycled' . . . 'I *assume* it's used in some environmentally friendly way' . . . 'I *think* there was a document or something that we were given in training' (emphases added). This lack of certainty and involvement seemed to be exacerbated by a perceived lack of concern amongst the majority of consumers, and therefore greater personal involvement in the environment was considered to be valid only 'where it meant you could give a better service or do a better job'.

In general, policy entrepreneurs did not appear to regard the dissemination of environmental *values* throughout the company as importantly as the diffusion of environmental *responsibility*. Specifically, the intention had been 'to get the environment integrated into everybody's day to day's business'. This had taken the form of working towards integrating environmental responsibilities into staff job descriptions and responsibilities, whilst at the same time preventing the growth of a dedicated environment section. Respondents presented this as akin to integrating total environmental quality through broad cultural change rather then through the appointment of a quality officer. Equally, in this way it was possible to prevent environmental management from becoming an environmental 'dustbin', i.e. a marginal repository for all of RetailCo's environmental problems. Accordingly, the environment could be further uncoupled from any notions of a personal moral crusade, and legitimately established as 'just another part of doing business'.

Conclusion

The analysis presented above provides some important insights into green marketing in conventional business organizations, and in particular into the tactics adopted by individuals within one such organization to secure support and commitment for these activities. First, the extent of the greening programmes in these companies appeared to be directly related to their susceptibility to such external threats as regulatory attention, media exposure and adverse publicity. The high visibility of a retailing organization such as RetailCo was clearly felt to project it into a more vulnerable position than that of an industrial marketing company such as ManufactureCo, despite the latter's involvement in environmental technologies. Indeed, respondents at ManufactureCo presented a picture of only limited environmental awareness and concern compared to that at RetailCo. Hence, potential threats to corporate legitimacy appear to have more bearing on the attention afforded to environmental issues than do the intrinsic environmental qualities of a firm's products. More on this in Chapter 7.

Second, in the absence of any clear evidence of the environment having impacted significantly upon consumers' purchasing behaviour, except where required by law, the firms had attempted only limited incorporation of the environment into pricing, communications and promotion policies. The environmental performance of products was, however, an issue, at least in specific markets. Hence, the firms' adopted marketing strategies might be referred to as 'muted' greening, i.e. claims for green product benefits were low key and predominantly public relations based in order to deflect potential criticisms rather than to attract customers. In RetailCo at least, protestations that environmental initiatives were consumer driven appeared to owe more to managers having been socialized into the rhetoric of customer focus than it did to manifest policy.

Third, it was found that green marketing in these companies tended to be introduced under a banner of enlightened self-interest. This was typified by the recurrent theme of 'sound environmental sense makes good business sense' in RetailCo. A remarkably similar situation appeared to be arising also at ManufactureCo's parent company, suggesting that the firm's as yet underdeveloped environmental agenda might emerge within a broadly similar (a)moral discourse.

Fourth, this instrumental conception of the environment was further underlined by the efforts of policy entrepreneurs to establish support and commitment for greening, at least in RetailCo. This arose from the focusing of these attempts on presenting the environment as 'just another part of doing business'. Four emergent themes, image making, moral framing, narrative surfing and value dissemination, have been set out during this chapter in order to conceptualize this process of constructing the environment and to illustrate how moral meaning within the organization was directed. These themes are considered to be important explanatory variables in understanding the cultural dynamics of green marketing in conventional organizations. However, since similar advocacy roles were not fulfilled in ManufactureCo, little insight could be developed in relation to these themes from this case. Indeed, (at least partly) as a consequence of the absence of environmental policy entrepreneurs, far less environmental awareness and understanding, and fewer practices, were evident among respondents in ManufactureCo, rendering further data collection on these issues problematic.

Finally, and perhaps most importantly, the process of institutionalizing environmental concerns into marketing activity at RetailCo had the effect of moral meaning being stripped from the environment, and as a consequence *amoralizing* green marketing. This appeared to be seen as a necessary condition for negotiating the embedded culture of the organization and realizing the policy entrepreneurs' principal goal of establishing the environment as a 'normal' element in the firm's day-to-day business activities. In the following two chapters, two rather different organizational contexts will be explored in order to provide some comparison with the findings presented here. These are the cases of social mission companies (Chapter 5) and business–NGO collaboration (Chapter 6).

5 Social mission companies

Introduction

Whilst the previous chapter concentrated on conventional business organizations, this chapter focuses attention on a very different type of organization – what I have called social mission companies. The notion of a social mission company was broadly defined in Chapter 3. I suggested that the main criterion for inclusion into this category was an explicit pursuit of particular social goals through economic activity. This chapter reports results relating to case studies of four such organizations: a retail consumer co-operative (RetailSoc) a mutually owned, environmentally branded financial services provider (FinanceSoc), a manufacturer of 'vegetarian' cosmetics (ManufactureSoc) and a broker and marketer of 'sustainable' wood products (MarketingSoc). In many ways these four companies were a fairly diverse group. However, as argued in Chapter 3, the purpose of investigating social mission companies was to provide a comparative case study methodology with which to explore significantly different organizational contexts for the enactment of morally relevant green marketing practices. The explicit integration of social goals into the founding mission of these companies was thought to provide such a distinction. This is not to say though that we should consider the social mission companies to be a wholly homogeneous group. In particular, one of the case organizations, RetailSoc, was clearly much larger and much longer established than the other three. Not only did this mean that a far greater volume of useful data could be collected for RetailSoc, but also its age and size were seen to distinguish it from the rest of the group in certain important aspects. Accordingly, over the course of this chapter, certain commonalties and contrarieties between the case organizations as a result of size and age differences will be indicated and discussed.

There is also a second sampling issue to take into account. Although it was not a deliberate decision, it is significant to note that the social mission companies I concerned myself with also differed markedly from the conventional companies in terms of their ownership and governance. Where RetailCo and ManufactureCo were wholly owned subsidiaries of joint stock companies, two of the social mission companies, RetailSoc and FinanceSoc, were from the mutuality sector; one, MarketingSoc, was a private limited company; and one, ManufactureSoc, had PLC status. In addition, the latter pair were also both founded out of charitable institutions – and indeed these institutions had remained as part of the firms' governance structure. Overall then, the ownership and governance of the social mission companies discussed here might be regarded as providing a more favourable context in which to set their specific social goals alongside (even above) economic goals. Whilst such differences in governance structure should not be over-emphasized, they could well be important in terms of influencing the moral tone of the organization (Diacon and Ennew 1996). Hence, the potential role of governance in this respect is highlighted and discussed throughout this chapter where relevant. It is also returned to in more detail in Chapter 8.

As was the case with the last chapter, the intention of this one is to explore the practice of green marketing at these companies with a view to drawing out in particular those issues considered to impinge upon notions of morality and moral meaning in some way. Clearly, however, I could not even attempt to do this without locating morality and organizational greening within the context of the companies' overall missions and espoused social goals. Indeed, given that I found a severe lack of scholarly empirical research in relation to companies of this type, I consider this study of social mission companies – their marketing, their strategy and their management – to be an important addition to the literature. These issues have consequently been accorded considerable attention in this chapter *in addition* to the kinds of issues that were covered in Chapter 4. The format for this chapter therefore is as follows. In the section following, some additional analysis of the missions of the four firms is presented. Following this, I look at how the companies operationalized their missions, particularly in terms of green marketing practices. Then, the cultural dynamics of green marketing in the companies are explored in some detail, seeking, as with the previous chapter, to focus on their moral substance and countenance. Finally, once this has been accomplished, the findings of the chapter are summarized, and some brief implications are considered.

Social missions and the social mission companies

In recent years, increasing numbers of firms have claimed to operate with 'dual bottom lines', i.e. a mixture of social and economic goals. Although in the past, this has tended to be seen as appropriate only for boutique firms targeting an 'ethical' or 'green' niche, there is evidence that at least the principle of establishing social goals alongside conventional economic goals has begun to cross over into the mainstream. As a result, even large multinationals such as McDonald's, Shell, Levi Strauss and others have of late espoused an ostensibly 'genuine' pursuit of social missions (albeit alongside and probably subordinate to, their economic missions).

My particular focus, however, was on companies that had adopted a very clear and explicit social stance, rather than those that might be more open to dispute. To that end, in this book I use the term social mission company to refer to firms which: (a) have been predicated *right from their founding* on pursuing a social mission through economic activity; and (b) which have subsequently presented this mission as equally, if not more, important than their more general economic goals. Although in practice there have been relatively few in number, commonly cited examples of such social mission companies operating today include US businesses Tom's of Maine and Ben & Jerry's, and European-based enterprises the Body Shop and the Co-operative Bank.[1] These particular businesses, however, are not the focus of this chapter but rather I am concerned with the four anonymous social mission companies outlined previously – all of which, it is probably fair to say, have enjoyed a substantially lower public profile than these examples in the UK (and certainly overseas) over recent years.

Despite receiving fairly prominent media attention throughout the past decade, attempts to affect some form of avowedly social posture have been subjected to little of what might be regarded as rigorous or scholarly enquiry. Most accounts have been either self-reported (see Roddick 1992; Chappell 1993; Lager 1994) or of the anecdotal or vignette style (see Bernstein 1992; Clutterbuck *et al.* 1992; Smart 1992). They have also been used in a generally uncritical way to present the potential benefits of socially responsible business with little regard for the possible problems, pitfalls and drawbacks. Newton and Harte (1997) refer to this type of approach as 'sentimental' and 'kitsch', arguing that it relies too much on the well-meaning evangelism of the authors, and too little on insights derived from the practical experience of those actually involved in such businesses. Ultimately, as Newton and Harte (1997) suggest, such an approach is likely to be self-deluding and self-defeating. It is my contention therefore that there is a pressing need for a more critical and empirically driven approach to understanding these types of organization. True, there is no shortage of literature on issues of social responsibility, but this has tended to concentrate mainly on the issue of whether and why firms should be responsible for social goals (e.g. Carroll 1979; Mintzberg 1984; Bowie 1991), and which goals they should focus on (e.g. Freeman 1984; Burke and Logsdon 1996). Such concerns have also been largely mirrored in the societal marketing literature, albeit with some discussion of how and why the marketing of particular products might be regarded as socially responsible or irresponsible (see Kotler 1972; Abratt and Sacks 1988, 1989; Prothero 1990). However, whilst these are clearly crucial and quite fundamental issues, it leaves us asking the question of how exactly it is that social mission firms *in particular* can and do develop ostensibly responsible strategic positions, processes and perspectives.

This general paucity of literature therefore led me to examine my four social mission companies in some depth. Rather than looking only at green marketing and morality, I also sought to explore how they defined and operationalized their missions in terms of marketing and strategy. This, in turn, I reflected back to see how it helped me to understand my insights regarding issues of environmental responsibility and moral meaning. Overall, as will become evident as the chapter progresses, the picture that emerged was a complex one, with a number of surprising findings being revealed. Crucially, much of the extant literature on social responsibility, organizational mission, societal marketing, social marketing and the like, seemed to be of little use in understanding the behaviours of these companies as experienced and filtered through the perceptions of my respondents. It seemed that their very nature as social mission companies meant that the usual ways of understanding organizational purpose, strategy and marketing could not be retrospectively fitted around their actions in any comprehensive and conclusive way.

So what was it about the missions of these firms that was so distinctive? Well, as I have said, they all emphasized that certain social goals were at least equally as important as economic goals. They also had all been in place since the founding of the organizations. However, the precise social goals articulated by the firms differed quite substantially. For RetailSoc, the social purpose of the wider Co-operative Movement had long been an issue of concern, both for observers and members of the Movement (see for example Carr-Saunders *et al.* 1938; Ostergaard and Halsey 1965). In particular, the devastating postwar incursions into the market share of retail co-operatives at the hands of the grocery multiples had repeatedly brought into question the problems of balancing commercial needs with co-operative principles (see Bailey 1955; Stephenson 1963; Birchall 1994). In its latest attempts to revitalize and modernize its mission RetailSoc had tended to emphasize issues of consumer protection and fairness, including freedom of information, access for all, and health and labelling issues. This had been packaged within an 'ethical retailing' initiative by the firm, launched in 1995 following an extensive survey of customers and members. Environmental issues were included within this initiative, but as one of a number of more general promises rather than a primary theme.

The social mission of ManufactureSoc was primarily concerned with animal welfare. Company literature stated this mission thus:

1   To set an example to the cosmetics industry by not testing on animals and, more importantly in the current context, to discourage the use of new ingredients through our strong Fixed Cut-Off Date criterion of 1976.
2   To leave a fund to help animals through the eventual disposal of its shares.
3   To provide cosmetics of the finest possible quality at very reasonable prices for people who care about animal welfare.

Having described itself variously as a 'vegetarian' company or one 'dedicated to animal welfare', ManufactureSoc had also claimed in its literature that all of its directors and shareholders were animal welfarists and vegetarians. Therefore despite its PLC status, ManufactureSoc's ownership structure was similarly supportive of its social mission as with the other social mission companies. Equally, it had stated publicly that its espoused 'ethical' mission was primary and that products which could not be produced within its ethical parameters would not be manufactured. Again its mission mentioned environmental issues, but aside from animal welfare issues, only marginally. Indeed, the chief executive set out the company's priorities to me thus: 'we care about the environment but we put animal welfare foremost'.

In contrast, FinanceSoc *did* concern itself principally with protection of the environment. Internal documentation set out the firm's lending policy as follows:

Advances shall be made to persons or on property which, in the opinion of the Board, are most likely to lead to the saving of non-renewable resources, the promotion of self-sufficiency in individuals or communities, or the most ecologically efficient use of land.

Accordingly, company literature claimed that it was the only financial institution whose 'sole purpose [was] to seek ecological and environmental gain through its lending policies'.

Finally, MarketingSoc focused on local social and environmental issues under the banner of *bioregionalism*, i.e. local production for local needs. With its origins in an environmental charity, there was little doubt that the founding of the company was instituted on social grounds. One of the firm's directors explained the evolution of the company thus:

> [An environmental NGO] funded us [the charity] to look at this whole issue as a sustainable development issue about integrating employment and environment in the UK, putting money back into our own woodland, and their management. And offering a local alternative to imports from tropical forests – which also means cutting down on road miles, and the issue of transporting goods.
>
> So it was initially funded by the [environmental NGO]. And two years ago we started some trials with [the product] to [company A], which went very well. So then they said, well why not put a proposal together to look at supplying thirty stores? Which was last year. And at that point, we had to set up a company, because you can't trade through the charity. The research and educational work was all done through the charity and when it came to trading the products, we set up the company.

Clearly then, environmental protection was central to the social mission of MarketingSoc, and had been instrumental in its initial founding. Hence, altogether we have three different social issues which the social mission firms had committed themselves to addressing: protection of consumers, animals and the environment (both generally and locally). However, as I was talking to the managers and directors of these companies, it became clear to me that in order to understand how the mission of the firm shaped the moral meaning applied to green marketing, I had to first uncover how the mission was translated into the overall marketing strategy of the firm. And as I discussed this with my informants, it became clear that a number of different approaches could be divined. It is these that I shall turn to now.

Marketing strategies

Understanding the marketing strategies of the social mission companies was in many ways an exercise in determining how organizational purposes could be operationalized. In particular, important questions arose as to how strategies could be developed which balanced in some way the dual demands of profits and principles. However, the managers I spoke to used little of the vocabulary and terminology of the concepts typically employed in the literature to model these phenomena, such as social or societal marketing (see Chapter 2). They did, however, freely, and apparently unconsciously, explain their strategies in terms of several of the core principles of these concepts (see also Abratt and Sacks 1989). In fact, data analysis of the responses of senior marketing and general managers to my questions regarding their firms' overall external orientations and marketing strategies revealed two key constructs – what I call here 'campaigning priorities' and 'mission positioning'. Whilst these constructs were found to draw substantially from the concepts typically found in the literature, they did so without directly mirroring them. In this section then I shall describe the social mission companies' marketing strategies in terms of these two themes, whilst at the same time enriching the analysis with reference to some of the more familiar concepts from the literature. Finally, I shall tie the analysis together by using the two constructs of mission positioning and campaigning priorities to conceptualize the different potential marketing strategies of the social mission companies.

Campaigning priorities

The first key feature of the social mission companies' strategies that for me distinguished them from those of the conventional companies was the importance attached by the firms' leaders to campaigning for social and environmental change of some kind. Senior executives articulated to me a common goal of converting external publics to their world-view; and whilst this was also true to some (lesser) extent of the companies considered in Chapter 4 (e.g. through political lobbying and school information packs), in the social mission companies this was portrayed as more than simply a benefit for the company, *but as an end in itself.* Hence, rather than it being merely a means of ensuring a favourable business environment (as was the case with RetailCo), promoting the cause was seen as an important organizational goal for the social mission companies. Clearly, the system of governance in the company was important here, and the collusion of members/owners was essential in allowing the company to be used as a vehicle for social change in this way. A useful approach to understanding this construct is thus provided by Kotler and Zaltman's (1971) notion of social marketing. Although originally formulated in relation to non-business organizations, Kotler and Zaltman's definition (p. 5) reflects very much the practice of the social mission companies:

> The design, implementation and control of programs calculated to influence the acceptability of social ideas and involving considerations of product planning, pricing, communication, distribution, and marketing research.

According to Kotler and Zaltman, the core product offering within social marketing is the cause itself. This is made tangible by the supply of products and services which advance the social cause. In the four sampled companies, such linkages between cause and product were certainly evident, although not always to the same degree. Hence, MarketingSoc's mission to promote bioregionalism was made tangible by woodland products; RetailSoc's mission to promote fairness, equality and democracy was made tangible through the provision of retail services; and so on. However, senior executives from the social mission companies clearly differed in the relative marketing emphasis that they applied to promoting (intangible) cause and (relatively tangible) product.

In general, most informants saw the basic role of their companies in promoting their cause as simply information providers, e.g. through customer leaflets, newsletters, reports, publicity, etc. Moreover, the material existence of the firms in the market was also presented to me by executives as an important indirect influence on society: first, because it provided an example to government and industry that social and environmental goals could be achieved in a commercial context; and second, because it enabled the provision of social or environmental products that would not otherwise be available to consumers. The companies could also be seen to adopt more direct campaigning tactics such as political lobbying, educational visits and materials for schools and colleges, public relations activity, supplier seminars, etc. However, these were not uniformly applied, and there were clear differences in the priority accorded to campaigning as a company activity in the social mission firms. It was not so much that the firms' leaders were necessarily confronted with the option of pursuing profit or principle, but more a question of resolving why the firm was in existence in the first place, and how this could translate into an appropriate balance between social and economic goals. For example, we might ask whether the foremost goal of a social mission company was to promote social change, as indeed Kotler and Zaltman (1971) suggest in the case of social marketing. Or conversely, was their major priority to provide a socially beneficial product, and in so doing promote social change indirectly, as might more befit a societal marketing orientation? Finally, there is the possibility of seeking to maximize profitability through the marketing of a socially acceptable product in order that funds be made available to support the promotion of the particular social cause. This can be regarded as a question of organizational purpose (see Freeman and Gilbert 1988).

Broadly speaking, the companies could be classified into two categories: those that claimed that campaigning was a (even the) primary corporate activity (ManufactureSoc and MarketingSoc) and those that claimed it was a secondary activity (RetailSoc and FinanceSoc). The principal difference here was how the managers suggested the resources of the firm were balanced between, on the one hand, promoting social and environmental change, and on the other, furthering the firm's economic success. The 'primary' group clearly laid more importance on the former than did the 'secondary' group. Indeed, for the 'primary' group, campaigning on the part of company leaders was shown to take up a substantial amount of their time, and it was acknowledged that economic success had to take a subordinate role to the firm's social mission. The chief executive of ManufactureSoc for example argued:

> The goals of being ethical and maximizing profit and growth are incompatible . . . for us the balance is always towards animal welfare.

In the case of MarketingSoc, this had even had the unfortunate consequence of its directors at times forgoing remuneration in order to ensure the survival of the firm with its principles intact. However, for the 'secondary' group companies, campaigning that was not directly related to firm performance was principally seen as something that should only be undertaken once sufficient resources had been accumulated, as this manager from FinanceSoc suggested:

> It hasn't really been appropriate for us . . . perhaps we'll attempt more of a campaigning role now that we have the resources . . . but at the end of the day it's not what we are here for.

Equally, campaigning would be resourced *after* a certain degree of profitability had been attained, or as one executive from RetailSoc put it, 'between what I call the gross, net profit and the net, net profit'. Hence, it was not so much that managers from these firms claimed that principles would have to be sacrificed in the pursuit of profit, but rather that they were likely to spend less time and resources on actually pushing forward certain social and environmental issues, should profitability be threatened in any way. In these firms social marketing was therefore principally centred around indirect campaigning tactics and PR activity.

Whilst clearly representing important differences between the group of social mission companies, these categorizations of campaigning priorities should not be regarded as static. In fact, the firms' campaigning priorities appeared to be a direct consequence of the personal inclination of its leadership. In FinanceSoc for example, it was related how one of the original founders of the company had departed acrimoniously due to a refusal by the rest of the board to adopt a more substantial campaigning profile. A more agreeable reaction may have precipitated an entirely different social marketing strategy. However, the entrenched antipathy towards such an approach was made evident by the current chief executive, who warned, 'if we'd gone down the campaigning route, we wouldn't be here now'. Also, it appeared that priorities altered over time. Several respondents in the social mission companies described actual or potential developments in their firm's social marketing strategy. None the less, whilst there was some recognition that growth and economic success provided opportunities for increased attention to campaigning, there was also evidence of concern over the potential trans-formation in priorities that such a commitment to growth might bring. Hence, the balancing of social marketing objectives and firm performance objectives was a constant issue for consideration for the social mission companies' leadership, and the priority accorded to each could be seen as a central defining feature in the operationalization of their missions.

Mission positioning

I have been using the 'campaigning priorities' construct to explain the social mission companies' overall social marketing stance, i.e. the espoused balance between the promotion of cause and product as a strategic marketing goal. My second explanatory construct, mission positioning, relates to how the social mission of the company had been incorporated within the selling proposition of their products and services. That is, regardless of how important the managers said their social cause was as an overall company goal, how important was it to the positioning of the firm's products?

Whilst my main issue of concern here was the natural environment, other social and moral issues were clearly integral to the complete bundle of concerns 'marketed' by the companies. This is not to say that the social mission companies always presented a coherent approach to the treatment of various social issues in their marketing activities. For example, in the case of the principal subject of ManufactureSoc's mission – animal testing – the management repeatedly stressed to me the importance of accurate and fair (as opposed to simply legal) marketing claims. Indeed, this issue had become something of a crusade for the chief executive of ManufactureSoc, and he frequently harangued other firms for their failure to develop honest and verifiable labelling for animal testing. However, where other environmental issues were concerned, his own firm had continued to use the relatively ambiguous term 'environmentally friendly' on company paper and packaging, without specifying why, or in which particular ways, the items could be considered environmentally friendly. These kinds of label had been much criticized in the academic literature (see for example Davis 1992) as well as being widely condemned by environmental and consumer groups (see for example National Consumer Council 1996). However, despite this, and other, inconsistencies in the attention afforded to the social issues addressed by the social mission companies, it was possible to discern distinct approaches among them regarding the role of their mission in their positioning strategies. Basically, this was a question of the extent to which the firm's mission was used to create some form of 'ethical' brand identity for the firm or its products. As Prothero (1990) has argued, if we consider green marketing as an embodiment of a societal marketing orientation, the orientation itself – in this case the social mission of the organization – can provide a powerful appeal to concerned consumers. Indeed, this was recognized by all of the social mission company managers. However, they varied in how pertinent they thought this was in their own particular markets. In fact, the managers indicated a range of positioning platforms for their products, from those where the social mission was central to positioning strategies, to those where the social mission was merely marginal to the central product propositions. Although this might be appropriately regarded as a continuum, three distinct positions appeared to be occupied by the sampled firms, namely mission central, mission prominent and mission marginal. These are considered in turn.

Mission central

Of the four social mission companies, FinanceSoc could clearly be seen to have made the strongest attempt to position its products purely, or at least principally, on the basis of its mission. With an environmental mission, and a core product offering of investment and lending services only for ecologically appropriate properties, it had clearly targeted a niche of green consumers. According to executives, these were likely to be fairly committed environmentalists, perhaps members of environmental organizations such as Greenpeace or Friends of the Earth. To some managers, a proportion of these potential customers could even be relatively 'undesirable' and 'dreamy' consumers with more concern for the environment than for their finances. Corresponding to this targeting of the 'green niche', services had traditionally been priced at a premium (although this had gradually been reduced in line with FinanceSoc's growth), and print advertisements had been primarily targeted towards environmentally oriented media. None the less, it was suggested by the chief executive that FinanceSoc had increasingly been making an attempt to appeal to a wider range of potential customers in order to communicate its environmental message outside its traditional niche and thus avoid simply (as he put it) 'preaching to the converted'.

Mission prominent

Occupying a more moderate approach, but still positioning itself mainly along the lines of its animal welfare mission, ManufactureSoc could be said to have utilized a 'mission prominent' approach. Respondents regarded their customer base as fairly diverse and likely to extend well beyond the 'green niche' targeted by companies such as FinanceSoc. Equally, it was emphasized that products were largely competitive on price and quality criteria against more mainstream competitors, as well as offering the added value of its animal welfare policies. Indeed, the chief executive claimed to me that the charging of an 'ethical' or 'green' premium was not only avoided by the company but would be 'morally questionable' as well. Hence prices were apparently kept to the minimum dictated by costs.

Marketing communications also reflected a mission prominent positioning stance. Print adverts and point-of-sale materials from the company had long emphasized the social mission of the company, although other tangible and intangible attributes such as price and quality had increasingly been stressed as well. Its 1996 poster campaign for example carried the following copy:

Natural Cosmetics
Quality – Performance – Fair Prices
Created for people who care about the earth and the animals

As you can see, the animal welfare aspects were still very conspicuous in this approach, but issues such as 'naturalness', quality and price were actually given greater prominence.

Mission marginal

The remaining two organizations could be regarded as having a more marginal utilization of their social missions as a positioning variable. Despite having an environmental mission, the directors of MarketingSoc suggested that the marketing of the firm's products and services had increasingly moved away from an explicitly environmental platform. In its place, a more 'conventional' approach had been developed which stressed quality, value for money and 'Britishness'. Effectively, as the directors themselves recognized, this meant 'hiding' the social and environmental issues of its mission, and dropping them from their communications platform. This had occurred as a result of a failure to improve sales whilst utilizing the mission, thus prompting a change which was seen as more appealing to their target market, namely retailers. As one director explained:

> I suddenly realized that we were giving them all this stuff about the environment, and it's quite a complex story to talk about . . . and now I realize that they're going: Shit! I don't want to get involved in this! It's a disaster! . . . So now we don't mention anything about anything like that. We just say, we can provide you with x amount of British [product]; it will be packed however you like; this is the price; the quality is controlled; it will be environmentally certified.

RetailSoc was also seen to make only marginal use of its social mission in establishing its market positioning. However, in contrast to MarketingSoc, RetailSoc appeared to be gradually increasing the prominence afforded to its social mission through a newly launched 'ethical branding' initiative. Whilst this development was seen as important in terms of creating some kind of differential advantage for the firm, it was not seen as ever likely to supersede conventional positioning variables of price, quality and store location. This was explained by executives in terms of the limited size of the 'ethical consumer' niche since the company's retail outlets had to appeal to a much wider consumer base within their catchment areas in order to be commercially viable. Hence for managers it was a matter of 'appealing to the majority not the minority'. Social and ethical issues were thus considered to be appropriate, but not central, to the appeal of the company, as this senior manager explains:

> Nobody is ever going to shop with us because we are nice people . . . maybe people will feel warmer about shopping with us, but that won't be the reason why they make the decision to shop in the first place.

In general then, there appeared to be some recognition within the social mission companies that augmentation by 'good ethics' alone would rarely constitute an effective marketing platform, unless a relatively small green niche market could be identified and targeted profitably. However, overall it was clear that the social mission companies had, and indeed continued to, explore and experiment with a range of different positioning approaches. If these approaches are then recombined with the campaigning priorities identified previously, a set of general marketing strategies can be identified in terms of these two dimensions.

Strategies for social mission marketing

Examining the 'mission positioning' and 'campaigning priorities' constructs together helps us to understand the overall marketing strategies adopted by the social mission companies. Taken together, they provide a framework with which to categorize the possible routes through which the mission can be carried forward to various audiences and in various contexts. In this way, greater analytical and explanatory power can be added to the basic assumptions provided by existing concepts found in the literature such as 'social', 'societal', and 'ethical' marketing. Hence, the four sampled organizations, and other similar companies, can be usefully plotted according to their 'scores' against these constructs. This can be seen in Figure 5.1.

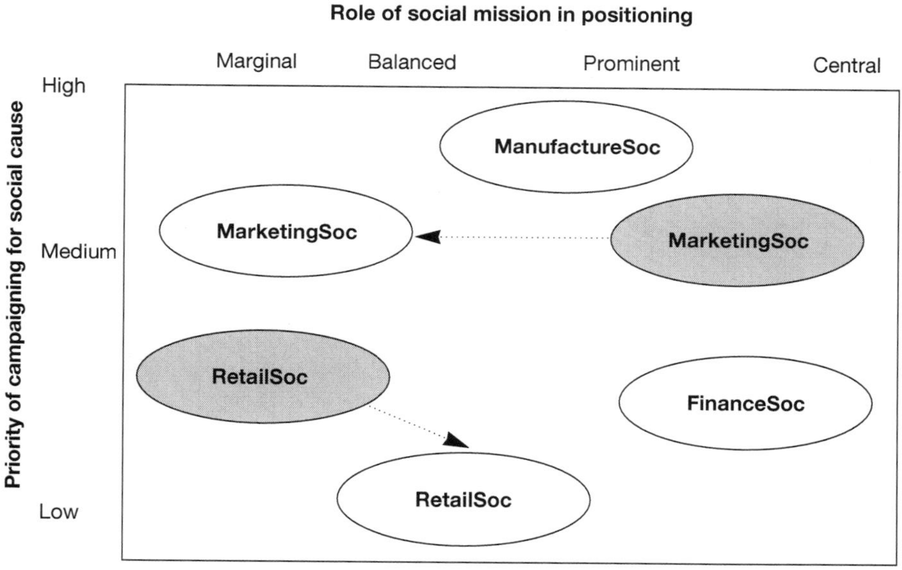

Role of social mission in positioning

Figure 5.1 Strategy map for social mission companies

Clearly there are a number of ways in which marketing strategies can incorporate social objectives for social mission companies. Although obviously the top right hand corner position of Figure 5.1 represents here the most direct approach, and the bottom left the least, it should not be assumed that any particular position is 'better' or 'more ethical' than others. They are simply different approaches to the same problem. However, examining the two constructs together helps us to understand some of the complexities and problems faced by the social mission companies in this respect. With a positioning platform either wholly or prominently based on their social mission, the firm's cause could be promoted more effectively than with a marginal stance. After all, if the company's mission itself is a substantial part of the product offering, there are clear efficiencies (and perhaps synergies) to be gained in promoting both cause and product at the same time. However, if this is not the case, and the firm targets the much larger majority of consumers outside the green or ethical niche, other advantages could be gained. First, such a strategy would almost certainly lead to a wider potential market. This might subsequently translate into enhanced profitability, which in turn could release greater resources for social cause campaigning. It could be argued that there would be certain advantages in this for divorcing campaigning from the necessity of product marketing activity, since the two are in some respects very different practices. Second, by targeting beyond the niche of customers who are already in sympathy with the social mission of the firm, there might be added opportunities for communicating the company's mission to an audience as yet 'unconverted' to the particular cause concerned.

Clearly then, the social mission companies I spent time with were faced with difficult decisions in this respect, as would other similar organizations. In my conversations with these firms' most senior managers, it became clear that the decisions made were likely to be contingent on the type of product concerned, the characteristics of the market, and the strengths and priorities of the company and its leadership. For example, some 'ethical' niches might be more easily and profitably exploited than others. Equally, if a social mission firm sought growth, it might have to consider expanding its target markets beyond those traditionally sympathetic to its mission. Finally, it was evident that some social mission company leaders, such as those at MarketingSoc, saw the goals of the firm as strongly biased towards social impacts, whereas others, such as those at RetailSoc, tended to emphasize economic objectives more. This certainly had a great deal to do with the aspirations and values of these particular managers, but at the same time, these were shaped and constrained by other influences such as the intensity of market competition, the espoused goals of the firms' owners, and the pressures exerted by other stakeholders. It is also important to remember that there was (and still is) nothing to prevent shifts in strategy, and by the same token, movement within the grid shown in Figure 5.1. Indeed some change should be expected given shifts in the market and changes in the goals of senior executives and owners over time. Changes in strategic positioning are represented in Figure 5.1 by dotted lines, with the previous position being indicated by shading.

Having now set out the basic organizational purpose and strategy of the social mission companies, and presented a means of examining these strategies, it is now possible to turn more specifically to the question of green marketing. The preceding analysis obviously provides an essential contextual understanding for exploring the tactical and cultural approaches to green marketing adopted by the social mission companies. Hence, before moving on to examine moral meaning in more detail, I will briefly discuss the processes of green marketing identified in the sampled companies.

Green marketing in the social mission companies

Whilst to some extent the social mission companies could be regarded as pioneers of green marketing in their sectors, they exhibited varying degrees of attention to environmental issues: for FinanceSoc and MarketingSoc it was their main focus; for ManufactureSoc, animal welfare took precedence over other environmental issues; and in RetailSoc the environment was considered a secondary social concern behind issues such as animal welfare, consumer information/labelling, and store access. Such differences were mirrored in the attention accorded to products' environmental performance, and hence in the green strategy adopted by the organization. Hence, as in Chapter 4, the particular orientations manifested in the social mission companies can be addressed using Peattie and Ratnayaka's (1992) typology of green strategies.

In FinanceSoc and MarketingSoc there was an attempt to provide the most radical environmental attributes on the market, suggesting an approach akin to Peattie and Ratnayaka's (1992) 'greening the company' strategy. This means that there was an attempt to integrate environmental concerns throughout the organization, in everything it did, right from the products that were marketed, to the systems of product or service delivery, right down to the reduction and recycling of paper in company offices. In ManufactureSoc, however, managers claimed that environmental issues were largely 'out of our control'. Environmental considerations were not fully explored in the company and processes such as product development remained relatively 'ungreened'. Peattie and Ratnayaka (1992) would refer to this as a 'piecemeal' strategy. Such findings were consistent with Prothero and McDonagh's (1992) results from their wider study of the UK cosmetics industry. In their sample, cruelty-free companies (such as ManufactureSoc) were shown to pay relatively little attention to environmental attributes, and surprisingly, lower degrees of greening were evident in these firms than in conventional (non cruelty-free) cosmetics companies. Finally, in RetailSoc, managers highlighted the importance of offering consumers a wide choice of products (to a certain extent irrespective of their green attributes) and consequently green product and service developments were broadly in line with conventional retailer best practice (such as RetailCo in the previous chapter). Hence, this accorded most with Peattie and Ratnayaka's (1992) 'follow the herd' strategy. Whilst these then were the overall strategic orientations towards green marketing in the social mission companies, it is perhaps more instructive to take a closer look at the particular green marketing strategies and tactics adopted. For this, I shall make use of the traditional 'four P's' mix framework.

Overall, the quality of ostensibly 'green' products offered by the social mission companies was not presented as a problem by managers, at least in relation to their own products. However, it was recognized that negative perceptions of product quality *had* been a problem for suppliers in other product categories, leading to a lack of market success for many green products. Interestingly, similar examples of this phenomenon were presented here as they had been at RetailCo, with cleaning products such as washing powder and washing-up liquid again being repeatedly cited as exemplars of failed green marketing. Hence, managers had recognized that consumer perceptions of potential performance shortfalls might have constituted an important barrier to trial and adoption for their *own* products – particularly in the light of competition from more conventional companies in green product markets. As a result, products had been increasingly positioned as value-for-money, quality alternatives to non-green offerings. In respect to Kotler's (1972) typology of societal products then (see Table 2.1), they could be regarded as having moved from focusing on the 'salutary' aspects of products (i.e. their worthy environmental credentials), towards considering also the more immediate satisfactions of 'desirable' products (i.e. those that satisfy consumers' needs for immediate consumption gratification).

In terms of price, senior executives in the three smaller companies – Manufacture-Soc, MarketingSoc and FinanceSoc – generally felt that they were at a disadvantage compared to their more conventional rivals. This was due either to the limitations imposed by their small size or by their commitment to their mission (entailing higher cost processes/components), or both. There was no indication in any of the social mission companies however that prices had been raised artificially to reap a green premium from concerned consumers. Respondents generally argued to me that prices were set at a 'fair' level, sufficient to maintain survival – an issue of some concern for two of the companies. Despite many green products being new market entrants then, penetration pricing to encourage trial did not seem to have been considered as a viable option. However, where the avoidance of penetration pricing in conventional companies might be due to the marginalization of green products in firm's marketing plans (see Wong *et al.* 1996), in social mission companies it might be more readily explained by either lack of resources *per se* or by the decision to allocate marketing resources instead to social campaigning activities.

For at least two of the social mission companies (ManufactureSoc and MarketingSoc), distribution had remained their most critical marketing issue. The necessity of securing retail space had made them reliant on establishing supply contracts with large retail organizations. However, managers described this as highly problematic, since although retailers were not portrayed as especially hostile towards 'green' or 'ethical' products *per se*, their buyers were depicted as fairly ruthless towards small or new suppliers compared to larger, incumbent ones. Hence, managers identified a dire need for a far greater level of support and commitment from retailers for 'ethical' product suppliers. These problems had provoked different responses. MarketingSoc had moved from a 'mission prominent' positioning strategy to a marginal one, increasingly highlighting conventional product attributes above environmental ones in order to appeal more directly to what they referred to as the 'hard-nosed' and 'conservative' retailer buyers. Conversely, ManufactureSoc – which in the recent past had made substantial staff redundancies due to the sudden loss of contracts with retailers – had moved into retailing itself, thus avoiding contact with what the chief executive regarded as the 'fickle' retail multiples.[2]

Such distribution problems could not be easily offset by communications and promotions policies due to the constraints of limited marketing resources and campaigning priorities. Hence, much of the promotional activity for the social mission companies was focused on public relations and publicity. Whilst interest generated from their particular missions appeared to have engendered considerable, and for their size, disproportionate success through these elements of the promotions mix, several managers expressed concern over the limited effect this appeared to have had on sales. This prompted at least one manager to lament: 'we are the brand virtually everybody has heard of and nobody has ever seen!' It was also stressed to me how this positive publicity had alerted competitors and consumers to the issues that the social mission companies were concerned about, but that this had subsequently helped the industry as a whole rather than aiding the social mission firms in particular in securing customers. This suggests that the introduction of 'new' social and environmental issues into company activities might have the effect of rendering communications activities as 'pioneer promotion' for the issue, rather than promoting the company's particular approach to it. First mover advantages seemed to be limited, especially in the context of relatively conservative industrial consumers.

The environmental content of promotional messages obviously reflected positioning strategies. Interestingly though, all companies in at least some of their environmentally-themed communications could be seen to have stressed a long and consistent history of social and/or environmental concern, often by emphasizing the firm's year of founding. To some extent, this paralleled similar communications at RetailCo, where a long-standing concern for customers and local communities was used to frame certain internal and external green communications. Here, in the social mission companies, it could also be read as an attempt to present a picture of success and stability in what might otherwise be regarded as a radical and unstable area. Moreover, it might similarly be read as a clear attempt by individuals within the social mission companies to distance their company from those of their competitors whom they regularly accused of having simply (even cynically) 'jumped on the bandwagon' (i.e. of social, ethical or environmental issues) in recent years without attendant moral commitment and conviction.

Also in line with findings in Chapter 4, managers stressed the negative impact that misleading green claims by other companies had had on their own potential to make meaningful green claims. Accordingly, it was related to me by a number of social mission managers how they had attempted to describe the 'complex reality' of particular social and environmental issues without resorting to bland slogans. This was seen as requiring an information-led approach, involving the presentation of quite extensive descriptions of company policies or environmental practices in marketing communications. The social marketing priorities of the companies had seemed to elicit a perception that final consumers needed to be informed of the complexities of the issues relating to particular products, rather than simply be persuaded that any particular product was 'best'. This was especially pertinent given that the same managers tended to perceive knowledge gaps on the part of consumers regarding the relative environmental credentials of competing offerings. Indeed, some managers saw this as an issue critical to their own success, since concerned customers were seen as being (in their view mistakenly) convinced by less radical offerings from competitors in the belief that these environmentally labelled products were equivalent in environmental terms to those of the social mission firms.

Green marketing and social responsibility

Green marketing in the social mission companies was then in many ways more developed than in the conventional companies considered previously, but certainly not universally so. However, underlying these greening initiatives were justifications quite different from the 'sound business sense' rationales of executives in the conventional companies. Indeed, in my conversations with managers in these companies, their rationalizations tended to steer away from instrumental notions of enlightened self-interest towards more explicitly moral notions of social responsibility. Indeed, executives were on the whole pessimistic about the prospects for consumer pressure in establishing viable green markets in anything except limited niches. Hence green marketing was often portrayed as emerging out of a drive from within the organization, usually from board level, rather than in response to consumer pressure:

> All the studies show there is concern out there, but that doesn't translate into people voting with their pockets. They will say they are concerned . . . but it's not something you can build a business on easily in mainstream markets. There are only small niche markets where you can build your company on the environmental friendliness of your product . . . and I see the future in terms of corporate responsibility, the company saying we will only stock environmentally friendly products.

Interestingly, among the social mission companies, the strength of managers' claims for this internal drive did not seem to correlate with their companies' positioning policies, as might have been expected. Hence, even where consumers' high concern for ethical or environmental issues had prompted mission-focused positioning by the company (such as in FinanceSoc), an internal cultural impetus was still asserted to be the principal driving force for greening. Moreover, managers also tended to claim that they would not reduce the environmental performance of their products even should customer demand for such green attributes be lacking. In MarketingSoc for example, the lack of customer interest had caused them to play down and marginalize the environmental dimension of their selling proposition (hence, another example of muted greening), but it had not led to any change in the environmental performance of their products.

Overall then, whereas these companies were clearly suggesting that they had incorporated considerations of long-term consumer and societal benefit (as befits a societal marketing orientation), in most circumstances this concern with long-term consumer welfare originated from the moral principles of the firm's leaders rather than as a self-interested response to external pressures. This represents a considerably more explicit moral perspective on the SMC than is presented in the literature (e.g. Kotler 1972; Abratt and Sacks 1988, 1989; Prothero 1990). Thus, any assessment of which products might be in the consumer's and society's long-term interests appeared to be predominantly based on the presumptions of the firm's leadership rather than say Abratt and Sacks' (1989: 33) suggestion that it should be decided 'by all the individuals who together constitute a society'. The exception to this was at RetailSoc where managers claimed that the company's social and ethical policies should directly reflect those concerns identified by market research and environment scanning. Hence, 'we have to take the stand looking at what our customers are concerned about' . . . 'we have to take our lead from what the pressure groups . . . (and) the media (are) going to be interested in'. Critically however, the environment had not been rated in this research as so significant for such groups compared with, say, animal welfare. Hence, managers presented it as more of a 'middling type of issue'. Accordingly, customers should not be 'forced' or 'nannied' into making green choices, since they were seen as largely unwilling to adopt green purchasing behaviour. Hence, in contrast to the smaller social mission companies, managers in RetailSoc argued that giving customers the opportunity to make *informed* choices, rather than making those choices for them, was the socially responsible role for a retailer in competitive markets. As we saw in Chapter 2, this can be regarded as a view of social responsibility based on the protection and enhancement of consumer sovereignty (Smith 1990, 1995), as this RetailSoc manager explains:

> Rather than us making the choice for the customer and saying, 'You are not going to have that product,' we've said: 'It's there, but that one is also there, and you must understand the consequences of purchasing that.' In a way, trying to educate the customer – and leaning towards taking the responsible side – in a way that is trying to strike a balance.

Clearly then, although different marketing strategies had led to differing degrees of societal marketing orientation, notions of morality were integral to some extent to what and how the social mission companies had attempted to accomplish in green marketing terms. This does not mean that they were necessarily *ethical per se*, or even *more ethical* than the conventional companies, but it does suggest that the firms' goals and purposes were more fused with morality and moral concerns than for those in the previous chapter. The question to which this chapter now turns then is: how does this manifest itself inside the organization? If organizational greening is explicitly linked to moral concerns, does this mean that the culture of the organization will be more suffused with a discourse of morality than if it is not?

Cultural dynamics and moral meanings in green marketing

As I have said, social mission company managers generally claimed that the drive for greening in their companies was derived from a cultural impulse from within, mediated in some circumstances by consumer preferences. However, in all of the companies, the social mission tended to be associated with particular individuals or sections whose role it was to manage and interpret the mission in a meaningful way. For these individuals, the environment, and indeed social issues generally, were seen as the daily currency of their workplace roles. Again, they might reasonably be referred to as policy entrepreneurs, much as our protagonists in the conventional companies were. This section identifies and describes the role of such policy entrepreneurs in the social mission companies, and goes on to reveal the implications that their behaviour had for moral meaning within the cultural knowledge of the firms.

Policy entrepreneurs

Overall, the environmental agenda in the four social mission companies tended to materialize in much the same way: that is, centrally and at senior levels. Policy entrepreneurs were located principally in the most senior management positions: in the three smaller companies this was usually at board level; in RetailSoc, the larger social mission company, in the corporate marketing division.[3] It was suggested that such seniority was necessary for successful environmental marketing projects to be initiated:

> If the people at the top think it's important to be environmentally friendly then it will filter down from above. You can never push it upwards. The belief has to come from the top to really get the response from it.

In the three smaller social mission companies, green advocates of this kind had frequently joined (or founded) the company in the first place from a sense of deep personal moral conviction, as these quotes suggest: 'I like to do my own little bit for the environment' . . . 'I have come into this from a sense of responsibility rather than anything else'. In RetailSoc though I did not find this to be so much the case, and reasons for adopting the policy entrepreneur role were broadly in line with the conventional company managers' mixture of personal self-interest and reserved environmental concern.

In contrast to the policy entrepreneurs discussed in the previous chapter, those in the social mission companies did not appear to have much need to utilize political skills in securing support for environmental marketing projects. This was because they already held positions with sufficient power to enable them to impose green initiatives upon their organizations. Moreover, they appeared to place considerably less emphasis on the importance of involving others within the organization. In general, environmental issues were managed centrally so that shop floor employees had little involvement with the environment and could, as a consequence, defer responsibility to their managers. Hence, the possibility of front line employees either contaminating the company's carefully conceived environmental policy or misinforming customers in a complex area, was significantly diminished. In RetailSoc for example, customers were encouraged to use a free-call information line rather than approach store staff for information on social and environmental issues. This connected them directly to head office where customer relations staff could respond from pre-prepared scripts based on the company's fifty-plus page manual which set out the company's position on a range of community, environmental and customer issues.

Constructing the environment

Given such relatively uncontested positions as the principal environmental reality definers within the social mission companies, policy entrepreneurs were fairly free to construct the environment in whatever way they wished. In MarketingSoc and FinanceSoc, a single site, small workforce and focused environmental mission meant that the leaders' concept of the environment was effectively also the firm's. Indeed, these managers could command knowledge of, and interest in, sophisticated environmental concepts and arguments outside the more conventional concerns of recycling and energy conservation characteristic of the individuals described in Chapter 4. This included reference being made to issues of bio-diversity, sustainable living, animal rights, self-sufficiency, decentralization and social justice, among others. Such a thorough construction of the environment left little room for opposing discourses in the firm.

In ManufactureSoc this was less the case, mainly due to a mission more centred on animal welfare than the environment. Consequently, the environment as a concept tended to be overwhelmed by animal welfare concerns, leaving little room for other issues to surface. Also, the need to bridge separate physical locations within the organization meant that the environmental agenda tended to be left to the personal discretion of individual managers to define as they saw fit. Whilst this seemed to provide some scope for environmental policy entrepreneurship, the environment tended to be constructed very much in terms of the practicalities of the immediate location, as this respondent indicates:

> [Policy entrepreneur A] is always picking up boxes and taking them off somewhere. She re-uses everything . . . but I don't like all that mess. I prefer the place clear, you know. So I tend to just throw them out.

Hence, whilst phrases of the kind, 'we do what we can', were commonplace in ManufactureSoc, there was little evidence of a unitary environmental agenda as such.

Finally, in RetailSoc a unitary and sophisticated environmental discourse was beginning to emerge during the time that I spent with the company, although it was not fully developed by the time that my fieldwork concluded. Given the need to communicate environmental issues to external publics, the corporate marketing function had assumed responsibility for defining and communicating RetailSoc's environmental policies and programmes. Understandably, this had resulted in the environment being incorporated within the pantheon of 'consumer issues', which included among other things, animal welfare, store access, bullying, nutrition, food hygiene, and more general customer relations. Hence, the environment tended to be depicted as something customers either wanted or did not want, or could or could not, afford. Indeed, the culture of RetailSoc appeared to be saturated with at least the rhetoric of consumer sovereignty, and few assertions were made without appeal to the exigency of customer needs and demands. This seemed to be the case throughout the organizational departments and hierarchical levels that I had direct contact with, and not only in marketing-related departments. Other conceptions of the environment therefore tended to be relegated as a consequence, suggesting a clear hierarchy of discourses. As one operations manager explained it, 'customer focus' remained the single most important way of presenting an argument seeking to secure commitment and support for environment-related projects:

> When you're selling initiatives to other staff, the one you put first is the customer, because it's good for the customers. That's always number one. This is after all a retail company. After that comes the commercial justifications – the cost savings . . . and only after that you look at the environmental side . . . because at the end of the day, saving the world is not going to keep us in business.

Evidently, the cultural hegemony of the corporate marketing function within RetailSoc had meant that it was here that the doctrine of 'consumerist' green understandings tended to be originated and ossified. For the individuals in the section who had been cast into the policy entrepreneur role, the constructing of environmental meanings within the marketing discourse was not significantly difficult given the lack of an existing frame of reference for the environment. Indeed, to some extent the environment as a concept had remained equivocal and open to localized interpretations. This had generated little consensus over what constituted the environment within the company, and many RetailSoc representatives continued to rely on working definitions which could practicably be fashioned to suit the requirements of a given situation. Indeed, even the incorporation of the environment within the rubric of 'consumer issues' had tended to produce a blurring of social, ethical and environmental issues for many managers and staff, rendering the boundaries of the environment indistinct. For example, my discussions with interviewees on the subject of 'green marketing and management' tended to be steered by the respondent to encompass a whole range of social, ethical and general consumer issues. As far as they seemed to be concerned, I could fit any necessary definitional boundaries between them that I wished, since they had little need or desire to do so.

The notion of the environment as a consumer issue was also cemented more firmly in RetailSoc by presenting it as something of a return to traditional (and to some extend side-lined or forgotten) co-operative values which focused explicitly on fair trading and consumer welfare. Thus, in much the same way as executives in RetailCo had 'surfed' appropriate corporate narratives in order to gain acceptance of green marketing activities, the environment in RetailSoc had been attached to existing corporate narratives of consumer choice and welfare (although, as discussed later, a similar dexterity with narratives was also manifested in other ways among the social mission companies).

Moral framing

Clearly this hierarchical and quite centralized origin of environmental meanings in the social mission companies had significant influence on the sense and form of morality attached to green marketing activities. Since it was senior level respondents who constructed and shaped environmental meanings in the organization, it was they who also set them within a particular, and usually quite explicit, moral context. Indeed, many senior respondents were highly adept at incorporating (at least some) environmental issues within quite sophisticated ethical arguments, and in the main the environment was depicted as one of a range of, or even the central, moral responsibility of the firm. Obviously this was driven by, and indeed reflected, the particular mission of the company. However, it was also apparent that environmental concern was regarded more as an *individual* moral responsibility: for the firms' leaders in the small social mission companies and for the customer in RetailSoc. These positions were manifested as follows.

First, in the three smaller social mission companies, board level executives tended to speak of their *own* personal moral beliefs and convictions on environmental issues, reflecting to a greater extent, a background in active environmentalism of one sort or another. Thus, the founders and CEO of FinanceSoc had been members of the UK Ecology Party (later to become the Green Party), the founders and CEO of ManufactureSoc had been involved in animal welfare work, and of the chairmen of MarketingSoc, one had run the local Greenpeace group and the other had been pivotal in setting up the environmental charity which eventually spawned MarketingSoc. Just as these managers were clearly conversant with quite sophisticated environmental concepts, so too in my discussions with them did they tend to use distinctly moral and emotional vocabularies in relation to environmental issues. This was illustrated with such phrases as: 'it was furthering *my own* beliefs' . . . '*I* think it is morally wrong to torture other creatures in order to seek a benefit for ourselves' . . . '*I've* always been environmental', etc. The environment was therefore presented to me as being incorporated within a personal moral belief system rather than a collective one.

Staff in RetailSoc also tended to regard environmental concern as a matter of individual conviction, with statements such as, 'the environment is very individual' . . . 'commitment is very localized' being common. However, given the prevalence of 'consumerist' conceptions of the environment, this concern tended to be related to me more in terms of the particular preferences of members, consumers and other outside publics than it did to staff, whether they were senior or otherwise. Therefore it was widely argued that the firm's role was to respond to issues of concern for external publics and to ensure high levels of consumer sovereignty by providing appropriate choice and information. None the less, this was also seen as a moral stance, although different to the personal moral conviction exhibited in the smaller companies. In RetailSoc, it was seen not simply as a commercial duty, but as an ethical obligation to respond to, and make a stand on, those social and environmental issues which were highlighted as important for consumers. By the same token it would be irresponsible or 'nannying' to set their own agenda without an adequate mandate from consumers or members. Thus, RetailSoc's consumer welfare mission was translated into a morally relevant frame of reference for the environment by invoking notions consistent with a societal marketing orientation such as society's and consumers' long-term interest. Hence, it was the concept of consumer sovereignty and not the chief executive that was regarded as the principal source of moral rectitude in RetailSoc.

Dexterity with narratives

This setting of the environment within an explicit moral discourse in the social mission companies (at least at senior levels) unquestionably set them apart from conventional organizations. Indeed, this was something that managers were clearly not impervious to. Whilst their status as companies owned either by their members (RetailSoc and FinanceSoc) or by individuals and/or charities committed to their social missions (ManufactureSoc and MarketingSoc) definitely facilitated the incorporation of moral aspirations into the firms' goals, the sense of difference within the firms was broader than strategy alone. Indeed, my overall impression gained during my interactions with the social mission companies was that they exhibited an informality and openness rarely, if ever, evident in other more conventional companies (either those in this study, or in others I had then, and since, come into contact with). Fairly free interaction with staff was allowed to me, and there seemed little if any attempt to present a unified corporate face. Respondents, both at senior and shop floor levels generally depicted their companies as 'friendly' . . . 'like a family' . . . 'like a large corner shop' or at least, 'better than others I've worked for', especially in the three smaller companies.[4]

The companies' social missions were thought by their managers to have had a prominent role in establishing this cultural difference from conventional companies, and narratives of 'difference' were widely alluded to in these companies. Almost all staff commonly assumed that their companies were regarded (particularly externally) as more friendly and more caring than their competitors. One RetailSoc manager described the situation thus:

> I think people do know that we are different. It's that expectation thing again: people expect [RetailSoc] to be responsible. It has a certain ethos. It has a different ring to it than if [Competitor A] or [Competitor B] were doing it.

Such difference was seen as necessitating the construction of new stories to communicate the firm's framebreaking perspective (Menon and Menon 1997), and to distinguish it from those of competing conventional firms (Martin *et al.* 1983). However, this narrative of difference from other companies appeared to be invoked or denied according to the exigencies of the situation. Whilst it certainly provided a convincing explanation for the fairly relaxed working environment in evidence, and to some at least represented a source of pride, it was also clear to me that some executives were concerned that 'difference' might suggest to others outside the organization something of a lack of commercial acumen. In ManufactureSoc, this concern had even been explicitly acknowledged in company literature, as this quote from ManufactureSoc publicity material attests:

> For many years the company has suffered prejudice due to our ethics . . . some retailers, bankers and others in the business world have tended to consider [ManufactureSoc] a 'joke'.

Where the respect of industry peers was thought important, managers suggested to me that they had often played down the difference narrative, emphasizing the importance of a sober appearance, professional manner, and commercial aptitude in dealing with industry peers. In this way, they would not be disadvantaged, either commercially – through being treated as a 'soft touch' – or personally – through being accorded insufficient professional respect. Hence, the construct of 'narrative surfing' developed in the previous chapter might be usefully rounded out here to a more general 'dexterity with narratives' so as to account for the situation identified in the social mission companies. Moreover, whereas in Chapter 4 the intra-organizational attempts at image making by environmental protagonists were considered, we can expand this here to incorporate similar processes at the inter-organizational level.

Clearly then managers in the social mission companies had attempted to mediate the perceived difference with conventional organizations, sometimes emphasizing it, sometimes playing it down. Cultural difference was seen as important in terms of constructing identification with the organization, but it was also seen as a potential threat to personal self-esteem and the commercial fortunes of the company. Indeed, the increase in 'hard-nosed' and 'sharp' business practices, coupled with the hegemony of 'marketing' and 'commercial' discourses into all forms of organizations were cited as important factors in removing differences between conventional profit maximizing firms and those organizations with explicit social goals. At MarketingSoc for example, cultural shifts in the nonprofit sector meant that the transferral of the firm from charitable status to corporate status was seen as relatively unproblematic in cultural terms:

> Certainly a lot of the phrases and a lot of the systems are being introduced into the voluntary sector from the commercial sector . . . so in fact all our work [at the charity] was market-led . . . so we've really been very aware of market forces and commercial priorities at the charity.

Overall then, managers in the social mission companies were increasingly faced with a tension between the nurturing of their uniqueness and of the need for a business culture that matched the sophisticated practices in evidence around them. To some extent, this had to come down to a question of which brand values the organizations were seeking to develop, and whether the mission of the firm could reasonably be a central theme in the overall brand identity. This, as we have seen, was a matter of the strategic priorities of the firm as shaped by the values of their founders and leaders, and mediated by context.

Disseminating environmental values

This inconsistency towards the institutionalization of the narrative of difference in the social mission companies was mirrored by a surprising lack of attention accorded to the involvement of employees in the companies' missions. Very few staff that I spoke to were found to have had any knowledge of their employers' social missions before joining the companies, even though most employees had been drawn from local communities. Some senior executives however did suggest to me that it might be advantageous if employees had 'a natural sympathy' with the company's objectives or 'some knowledge' of environmental issues, particularly at more senior levels. None the less, this was certainly not stressed as a particularly important feature.[5] Equally, I could discern little evidence of company values representing any kind of motivating factor for employees in applying to these particular firms. Indeed, the position was principally seen as 'just a job'. Only at the more senior levels was there any definite indication that social and environmental goals might be 'an added bonus' for managers. However, even here traditional economic and career goals clearly remained paramount, as this ManufactureSoc manager explained:

> I liked what it [ManufactureSoc] stood for, but it was the job I was going for, not the policies . . . You've got to work, and so provided it's not a company that you disagree with, you do your best job. I was pleased to be offered the job because it was a cosmetics company and because it was not tested on animals . . . but if it hadn't had those policies, I would still have joined.

Equally, there was little indication from respondents that the firm's mission or corporate environmentalism of any kind had any appreciable effect on their commitment or job satisfaction once they had joined the companies. More importance was attached to the personal integrity of the firm's leaders, since genuine commitment on their part was seen by some employees as source of organizational attachment. Probably most important (at least in the smaller companies) was company size, and the local, friendly and inclusive nature of the small social mission companies was clearly instrumental in attracting certain staff, and in subsequently enhancing their satisfaction and commitment. More generally, informants could be seen to some extent to have been socialized into conventional feelings of pride and commitment to their organizations, and this had been attached to a range of factors. However, the social goals of the company featured here only to a very limited extent. Hence, all in all there was little evidence that employee commitment was correlated with corporate environmentalism or corporate ethics as suggested by previous theoretical (Hoffman 1993) and quantitative (Hunt *et al.* 1989) treatments. These concerns were perhaps considered too abstract to the employees I spoke to compared with more direct correlates such as the integrity of their employers, or the friendliness of the atmosphere in the workplace.

In general then, little commitment from staff had been sought in ethical or environmental terms and this was reflected in a lack of environmental knowledge and concern in relation to their workplace roles. Indeed, even where the company was actively involved in green marketing projects, comments such as 'I can't think of anything we do on the environment side' and 'there's not an awful lot you can do' were symptomatic of a general feeling of detachment and impotence towards the environment evident in the lower echelons of the companies. There was however some slight – although far from convincing – evidence to suggest that once incumbent, the social or environmental awareness of the company or its managers might 'rub off' on employees. For example, stories were related of how a manager had turned vegetarian since joining one company (Manufacture-Soc), some respondents suggested that the prevalence of green products such as recycled paper and fair trade coffee in the office might influence staff (Finance-Soc), and a number of managers across the social mission organizations considered that the general climate of re-use and energy efficiency was likely to have had some impact upon employee values and behaviours. None the less, employees suggested that even should they desire to, they had little time for environmental concern, reflection, nor advocacy of any kind. The pressures of their jobs were such that 'practicalities' took precedence over 'dreamy' views, particularly in the absence of systems of appraisal and reward that signalled otherwise.

In extreme situations, this might even lead to deliberate sabotage of environmental projects by middle management and rank and file employees due to the additional nuisance or burden imposed upon them. In one example, a group of shop-floor workers related to me how new 'green' packing materials had proved to be so unpopular to them (due to their inferior performance, and their unpleasant texture and smell), that their use had been avoided as much as possible, either by mixing with the old non-green alternative or by avoiding them altogether. In another example, the trial of an internal plastic recycling scheme had been aborted due to the unfavourable reactions both of shop-floor staff ('it was a pain') and middle management ('it cost too much'). Little attention has been directed in the literature towards the potential for such internal resistance to corporate social programmes (see however, Collins and Ganotis 1973), but its existence here, in organizational climates relatively sympathetic towards social concerns, seemed to me to be of considerable significance. The prevalence of centralized value systems, and the avoidance of imposing values on employees appeared to have distanced, and even disenfranchized employees from the moral dimension of the firms' missions. Without sufficient involvement in, or even communication about these decisions, social and environmental programmes had to some extent simply become 'the boss's thing', thus creating a sense of futility among employees concerning their ability to affect social policy (Collins and Ganotis 1973).

Overall then, there appeared to be a general impassivity towards the co-alignment of individual and company values in the social mission companies. The focus in the green business literature on the development of broad, fundamental cultural change (see Stead and Stead 1992; Shrivastava 1994, 1995a; Welford 1995) was not reflected in the practices of the social mission companies. The dissemination of values was rarely a deliberate or managed process, and employees were generally left to develop their own interpretations and meanings in environmental terms. There was however at least some limited evidence of a growing recognition that a movement towards cultural integration of environ-mental values might in some way be desirable. Reasons for this differed between a simple 'because its what we're about' in MarketingSoc, to a pragmatic decision in FinanceSoc to supplement the service offering through employing staff that 'green customers' might more easily communicate and identify with. In Retail-Soc, it was generally subsumed within a broader culture change programme intended to develop greater customer focus and marketing orientation. Hence there was some recognition amongst senior managers in RetailSoc that staff should understand company values, since the importance of these to customers had been verified by market research. Thus, 'getting the company culture down to the people on the bottom' was seen as an important, if difficult, step in establishing any kind of 'ethical' brand building exercise, particularly in a service organization. There were some signals then that attention towards the potential benefits of cultural integration was on the increase, especially in terms of attract-ing more environmentally aware employees, and/or socializing existing staff into awareness or understanding of the firms' environmental values. However this fell far short of Welford's (1995) demands for 'strong' cultures and shared global environmental values, or of Mintzberg's (1989) conception of a 'missionary organization' where the organization's sense of mission is strongly and naturally identified with by members who share intensely its particular ideology.

Mintzberg's (1989) analysis does however provide a framework with which to distinguish between different approaches to the reinforcement of organizational ideology in the social mission companies. For example, attempts in RetailSoc to 'get the corporate message across' to staff might be regarded as indoctrination or 'evoked identification' (p. 226). That is, the firm's leaders attempt to impose their values on existing members. By comparison, ManufactureSoc's attempts to ensure that applicants for vacancies had 'some awareness and concern' for animal welfare might be regarded more as 'natural' or 'selected identification' (p. 226) since this can be seen to expand merely the potential for shared beliefs and values. Such issues of culture change are significant then for developing a thorough understanding of the complexity of the greening process. These are discussed in more depth in Chapter 8.

Conclusion

The analysis presented here provides some important insights into marketing in social mission companies, and in particular on the role of morality in the process of developing and implementing green marketing practices. Five findings in particular are worthy of reiteration.

First, it was found that in some cases, where firms had explicit social missions, environmental issues *could* be integral to this mission, but then so too could they be rather more marginal. Based on conversations with managers, the marketing strategies of such firms appeared to hinge on two key factors: campaigning priorities and mission positioning. Campaigning priorities related to the balance between promoting a social cause or promoting the firm's products, i.e. the tendency towards social or conventional marketing. Mission positioning related to the level of attention accorded to the importance of the firm's mission in attracting customers. Different strategies were evident in different companies, contingent on factors such as product and market characteristics, the strengths of the company and the priorities of its leadership.

Second, a social mission *per se* did not mean that green marketing would be more developed than in conventional companies. Whilst an environmental mission was naturally reflected in the development of radical green products, a focus on other social issues could certainly deflect attention from the environment. In general, similar concerns were raised by social mission company managers in relation to green product markets as they were by conventional company managers, most notably the perceived under-performance of green products, and the effects of misleading green claims on promotional tactics. Here however, the consequences were likely to be more significant given the need to develop coherent social and societal marketing strategies.

Third, two different conceptions of societal marketing underpinned green marketing in the social mission companies. One position held that corporate responsibility was needed to develop greener alternatives in the absence of consumer demand. The other held that the company's responsibility was to make a stand only on issues of concern to customers. To some extent this reflected differences in social missions.

Fourth, notions of the environment within the company tended to rest with key senior executives who employed discourses reflecting their own roles, responsibilities and interests. Therefore there is little or no evidence from these companies to support Prothero's (1990: 95) assertion that 'present companies practising societal marketing are possibly doing so from a bottom-up approach'.

Fifth, within this top-down management approach to green marketing, executives adopted a number of culture management techniques. This involved constructing the environment as a moral issue – either in terms of the personal belief system of the firms' leaders or in terms of establishing a platform for 'genuine' consumer sovereignty; manipulating narratives of difference with conventional companies; and disseminating environmental values. It was somewhat surprising however to discover that managers paid only limited (though possibly growing) attention to establishing some kind of unity of environmental values in their organizations. For the most part, employees experienced only minor socialization in this respect. Therefore, since the main intention of the social mission companies' leadership was clearly to influence external publics rather than organization members, they might be referred to as 'reformers' of outside publics rather than 'converters' of organization members (Mintzberg 1989: 231).

Having then discussed both conventional and social mission companies' approaches to green marketing, and the moral meanings embedded in their attendant cultural dynamics, the next chapter will focus on an approach which was different again: business–NGO collaboration. This looks in particular at one example in which conventional companies, social mission companies and an environmental pressure group had all come together in a single alliance to develop specific green marketing practices. Although there were certainly clear overlaps with the findings already presented, this particular approach was found to be in some important ways, distinctly novel.

6 Business–NGO collaboration

Introduction

In the previous two chapters I focused on conventional organizations (Chapter 4) and social mission companies (Chapter 5). In both cases I was looking at situations where organizations were involved in green marketing programmes where they worked largely independently from other organizations. In this chapter, however, I shall explore a very different approach to green marketing: collaboration between businesses (both conventional and social mission) and non-governmental organizations ('NGOs' or 'pressure groups'). Collaborations of this kind – or 'green alliances' as they are sometimes known in relation to environmental projects (e.g. Mendleson and Polonsky 1995; Hartman and Stafford 1997) – were introduced in Chapter 3. Basically they represent a situation where one or more business organizations and one or more NGOs both commit resources to a single project in order to achieve a common goal. Findings from one such collaboration are reported here, referred to in the text as CollabOrg.

CollabOrg was a UK green alliance focused on the sourcing of timber for wood and wood-based products. Its members were an environmental NGO and (at the time when I conducted fieldwork) approximately seventy-five UK companies involved in the trade of wood, and of wood, paper and pulp products. Company members of CollabOrg included both conventional companies, such as major retailers and their suppliers, as well as (a minority of) social mission companies. For this particular case study, I conducted interviews with seventeen representatives from a sample of thirteen member organizations. These individuals were identified to me by their organizations as their main point(s) of contact with CollabOrg. The findings presented in this chapter therefore relate mainly to the experiences of these particular interviewees in respect to CollabOrg. However, they should also provide considerable insight that is relevant to the total membership of CollabOrg, and also, although only a single case study, to green alliances and business–NGO collaboration more generally.

It has been suggested in the literature that green alliances such as CollabOrg are a relatively new, but potentially important, strategic approach to green marketing (Mendleson and Polonsky 1995; Wasik 1996; Hartman and Stafford 1997). Through them, companies and NGOs might be regarded as moving from their traditional adversarial relationships towards more constructive and collaborative arrangements (Wasik 1996; Hartman and Stafford 1997). However, they have been accorded only limited research attention to date, and there are as yet few case studies of comparable scope to the case presented here in the scholarly management literature. As such, much as the discussion of marketing and strategy in the social mission companies was an attempt to take advantage of an opportunity to explore a much under-researched area, this case represented an important opportunity to develop theoretical insight into a little understood phenomenon. Also, as a new and quite revolutionary means of developing environmental solutions, the study of business–NGO collaboration enabled me to explore some of the limits of contemporary green marketing. Perhaps most importantly though, this case represented for me the possibility of investigating and analysing moral meaning in a very different organizational context to those I had already looked at. This last point is crucial since the involvement of an environmental group in the green marketing process might be regarded as having significant potential to describe a very different moral landscape compared to those considered in the previous two chapters. Hartman and Stafford (1997: 188) even suggest that a 'corporate-wide mindset change' and 'building an environmentally-responsible corporate culture' are necessary first steps for corporations in collaborating with environmental groups, and this has obvious parallels with the discussions regarding culture change in Chapter 2. As the chapter proceeds then, I should like to show the impact of collaboration between such heterogeneous partners on the cultural and moral terrain of green marketing.

The structure of the chapter is as follows. Following a brief introduction into the background and workings of CollabOrg, green marketing issues are considered and discussed at some length. As I have said, Business–NGO collaboration is an unusual and potentially important new means of green marketing, and requires elaboration. Then, in the next section, the cultural dynamics underlying these green marketing practices are set out, with attention focusing again mainly on the form and content of their moral meaning. Finally, in the conclusion these results are summarized and some brief conclusions and implications discussed.

Background to the case study

CollabOrg was an alliance that had been formally established in 1996 (but effectively in operation since 1991[1]). Its two main aims were to improve forest management practices and to develop a market for certified wood-based products. The formation of a green alliance to tackle these problems can be seen as something of a reversal of previous antagonism between environmental groups and business in relation to forest management practices and wood sourcing (Murphy 1996a, 1996b). Indeed, demonstrations concerning retailers' forest sources – particularly the Friends of the Earth 1991 'Chainsaw Massacre' campaign which saw pickets outside DIY stores brandishing defamatory placards and inflatable chainsaws – had clearly been an important catalyst in the creation of the original CollabOrg alliance.

In joining CollabOrg, companies had to pledge themselves to a number of commitments relating to their sourcing of wood-based products, the ultimate aim of which was to phase out all forest sources which failed to meet standards adjudged to be 'well-managed' as defined by an independent body. These pledges required commitment to: a single authorized independent certification and labelling system; the phasing out of wood and wood products not certified as 'well-managed'; a fixed date by which all supplies would be from certified sources; the naming of a senior manager with responsibility for implementing the commitments and targets; the submission of regular progress reports from corporate members to the NGO; and the phasing out of all eco-labels describing the quality of management of forest sources, except the one prescribed by CollabOrg.

'Well-managed' in this context was related to a range of social, environmental and economic sustainability indicators. The role of the NGO in CollabOrg was to manage and co-ordinate the project, to assess the companies' progress towards the targets and to act as a gatekeeper for group membership. Hence its contribution to the collaboration was its environmental expertise and other resources such as administration and marketing expenses. In terms of Hartman and Stafford's (1997: 189) typology of green alliances then, CollabOrg can be regarded as a 'green systems alliance', defined by them as a 'collaborative partnership . . . to implement economically feasible environmental systems or programmes for the greening of business practices'. In this case, the environmental system implemented through the green alliance had principally operated through supply chain management, utilizing vendor questionnaires.[2] These were distributed by member companies to their suppliers, and this in turn triggered a series of supplier assessments right back through the supply chain to the forest of origin. Questionnaires were focused on issues of forest source identification and management with a view to encouraging improved environmental management.

Green marketing in Business–NGO collaboration

In the literature, green alliances have been touted as potential solutions to some of the problems of green marketing alluded to both in the literature itself (see Prothero *et al.* 1994; National Consumer Council 1996) and by many of my respondents. In particular, issues of poor credibility for green marketing approaches, and consumer cynicism and confusion in the face of unrealistic and overclaimed green communications have been identified as possible drivers for green alliances (Mendleson and Polonsky 1995). Although these were certainly important motivations for the formation of this particular collaboration (as discussed later), green systems alliances can be seen to have marketing and management implications beyond communications and promotions policies alone (Hartman and Stafford 1997). Indeed, the present case study suggested to me important issues in relation to marketing strategy, industrial networks, supply chain management, marketing relationships and organizational buying. Therefore, in addition to the emerging green alliance literature, the findings that I present build upon two important recent studies: Drumwright's (1994) investigation of green organizational buying in the US, and Lamming and Hampson's (1996) exploratory work into the greening of supply chain management in the UK.

Marketing strategy

Essentially, CollabOrg was depicted by company respondents as a mechanism enabling the long-term marketing of credible and environmentally appropriate products. The strategy was long-term in the sense that although the alliance itself was intended to be of limited duration (four years each for both the original group and CollabOrg), the processes and procedures set in place were considered to be on-going. As one manager suggested to me:

> I don't think it finishes. All that happens is that it will bring these things so far ... and make this a normal part of working practice. As soon as we get to the stage where we are buying from just certified forests then the forestry management will become a monitoring process.

The project was presented by respondents as providing for credible green marketing because it was seen as a proactive response to the plethora of what my informants suggested were 'meaningless', 'unsubstantiated' and 'rubbish' claims relating to forest management and sustainability in the marketplace. The independent certification of forest management practices provided by the initiative was therefore described as an effective route for developing a credible eco-label for these particular types of product. However, in this situation, the eco-label only related to a single environmental dimension of the product offering, namely the source of wood, paper and pulp components. Since other issues such as the content of recycled/recyclable material, product processing, product disposal, etc. were not incorporated into the scheme, I'm using the term 'environmentally appropriate' here in a strictly limited sense.

Industrial networks and supply chain management

Given the goal of identifying and improving forest sources, CollabOrg clearly centred on issues of supply chain management. However, in a broader sense, the management of environmental issues through collaboration within and around supply chains can be thought of within a context of industrial networks (Cramer and Schot 1993; Shrivastava 1995a, 1995b). Accordingly, I would suggest that critical importance can be attached not only to the individual firm and how it manages its supply chain, but also to the pattern of relationships and interdependencies of which the firm is part (Hakansson and Snehota 1997a, 1997b).

Indeed, the overriding impression given by respondents of the prevailing networks in which the member firms were operating was of considerable scepticism, apathy or even hostility towards the work of the collaboration. Actors within the surrounding networks (and those in the timber and paper industries were particularly highlighted), were commonly portrayed as determinedly unreceptive to environmental overtures. Group representatives suggested that this was generally as a result of conservatism and a wariness towards what were regarded as the environmental 'fads and fashions' in the industry which had not subsequently been translated into increased sales. Moreover, respondents also identified a marked spirit of entrenchment amongst these network actors concerning established industry practices, particularly in the face of unwanted outside/NGO interference. Effective supply chain management was therefore presented as a demanding, even 'tortuous' and 'horrendous', task by respondents, particularly given the complexity of the prevailing networks. Individual chains of custody were shown to run to as much as fifteen to twenty different organizations from the forest of origin to the customer.

My respondents also reported little indication of an overtly positive or proactive response from their networks of suppliers in the face of such increased environmental concern and assessment. Whilst some suppliers were characterized as clearly hostile to the initiative, most common appeared to be an acceptance of, or at least acquiescence to, their customers' wishes and demands, as this production manager suggested:

> Working in partnership with suppliers: I think we kind of thought we might be up against a tricky one there . . . but so far they've actually been pretty co-operative . . . I'm not saying that they are necessarily happy with it, but they are co-operating.

This generally passive, reserved, and commercially attuned response from suppliers supports Lamming and Hampson's (1996: S58) findings from their exploratory study of supply chain management and organizational greening:

> In general, the response of suppliers to initial customer proposals to make improvements in environmental soundness was reported to be cool. . . . Broadly, suppliers responded to problems only in so far as the customer companies required them to.

Evidently more striking to some managers, however, was the apparent ignorance on the part of their suppliers concerning the source and type of the timber involved in their products, particularly as this constituted the 'meat and drink' of their business. One quality manager for example offered the following opinion:

> The thing is a lot of them are not aware how vulnerable they are. It's ignorance. You ask them where their wood comes from, what species it is, and they can't tell you! It's been a surprise to me really how much they don't know about their business. Any manufacturer should know where his raw material comes from and how much he gets from there.

None the less a number of respondents who had been involved in the alliance for some time also gave some indication that supplier responses improved and quickened over time as a consequence of their increasing familiarity with the issue, and a refinement of questionnaire formats by their customers. This might be regarded as indicative of the emergence of stronger marketing relationships being developed within the collaboration.

Marketing relationships

An important contribution of the networks perspective on business–NGO collaboration is its consideration of inter-firm relationships, as well as the placing of these relationships within wider industrial interactions. The notion of relationships was acknowledged by respondents, both with respect to immediate marketing relationships with their suppliers and customers, as well as their strategic relationships with other CollabOrg constituents. Indeed, most interviewees spoke of 'working with' and 'consulting with' their alliance partners and with their suppliers to achieve the aims of the alliance. For example, the co-ordinating role of an independent NGO in the initiative appeared to assist in enabling companies to interact with their competitors on issues of mutual concern:

> We went out for the first time to Sweden and Finland. I was consulting with other members of [CollabOrg] . . . getting together and saying: 'OK I'm going out there this week, what stage are we at with the process?'

In this way, the potential communication and information flow problems associated with managing environmental issues through supply chains, such as those highlighted by Lamming and Hampson (1996), could be overcome. Also, informants suggested to me that long-term and consistent supplier relationships represented an easier context than 'spot market' trading in which to trace the chain of custody for their products. Most managers, however, put even stronger emphasis on the value of 'partnership sourcing' in lubricating the channelling of environmentally certified products through the supply chain. This necessitated the 'nurturing' and 'supporting' of supply relationships to encourage vendors to adopt greener sources. The question of maintaining existing supply relationships or switching to newer 'greener' suppliers, however, was a critical one within this context (see Lamming and Hampson 1996). In general, the former rather than the latter seemed to be preferred, probably due to a mixture of inertia and uncertainty reduction (Ford 1980), power seeking (Frances and Garnsey 1996) and/or managers' interpretations of corporate social responsibility within their companies (Drumwright 1994). For example, a senior manager at one supplier member of the group described this mixture of rationales underlying his customers' purchasing strategies thus:

> Basically you can't get them to change their buying philosophy. They . . . said to me something like: 'We have a very strong ethical buying policy.' And I said: 'Oh really?'. 'Yeah,' he said, 'so you won't be able to persuade the buyer to buy your product just because it's environmental.' It was extraordinary!

A few respondents (including the one above) did, however, offer a few clear examples of supply relationships evidently more based on buyer support and assistance. More frequently though this discourse of 'partnership' marketing relationships conflicted with corresponding accounts of the need for 'buying clout' on the part of member firms in their purchasing role in order to 'pressurise', or at least 'encourage' suppliers into acquiescence. An environmental technologist from one of the large retailers in CollabOrg described the situation thus:

> Simply [the suppliers'] business acumen tells them they should often beg, bow and scrape to [respondent's company]. But you know the kind of customer–supplier relationship that often exists: where the customer has such a large value to the supplier that they'll do anything they can to please them? Not anything, but within reason. And that is the way it works.

It was clear then that much of the espoused desire for partnership sourcing tended to be either wishful thinking on the part of respondents or a rhetorical device that masked less equitable supplier relationships based on compulsion and persuasion from (in particular) the large retailers (see also Frances and Garnsey 1996). The length, frequency and response rate for questionnaires also appeared to reflect resource dependence and the purchasing power of the buyer relative to the supplier (Pfeffer and Salancik 1978). Hence, those members less able to mobilize buying power clearly settled for shorter questionnaires, slower turnaround times and more chasing up for questionnaire responses. Resource dependencies of this type were also compounded by the concentration of group membership in particular industrial networks, thus effectively locking in a sizeable majority of individual firms' potential suppliers/customers.

At the level of individual marketing relationships, executives in this study tended to suggest to me that the most effective way to encourage those further back in the value chain to embrace the alliance's certification route was through the invocation of commercial arguments rather than moral ones. Indeed, executives from subordinate (in power terms) suppliers of member firms indicated that there were immediate commercial paybacks from joining their customers in the alliance, making them, as one respondent put it, 'instantly one of their best suppliers'. Equally there was some recognition that subordinate suppliers expected to be played off against each other on environmental criteria just as they would be on economic criteria. For example, an executive from one supplier suggested that the gaining of the group's official accreditation by one company would be 'used as a stick to beat the other suppliers with'. Accordingly, it could be argued that some suppliers simply felt under pressure from customers (and potential customers) to switch to certified products, even though they did not always believe the customers were fully committed to the process, and nor did they necessarily offer corresponding support.

Buying centre

The nature of industrial networks, supply chains and the marketing relationships within them were clearly of importance in tracing the particular marketing dynamics of CollabOrg. Moreover, it was apparent that the relative importance of the moral or environmental dimension within these relationships was dependent upon where within the member companies these relationships were initiated and maintained. Certainly there was a marked lack of procurement executives as company representatives in CollabOrg.[3] This, combined with the lack of formal involvement of buyers generally in the alliance, might be regarded as a significant problem, given that the project was centred on organizational buying and supply chain management. Hence, the role of company respondents as environmental protagonists within their companies frequently allowed them only to initiate and influence the buying decision process rather than make the final purchase decision (Drumwright 1994). Indeed, although some of the company representatives had been instrumental in their company approaching the NGO in the first place, for many of them it was simply a job that had been assigned to them. Thus, their role was primarily about having an input into existing supply relationships rather than initiating new relationships with new ostensibly 'greener' suppliers. Equally, a number of CollabOrg representatives were not themselves responsible for sending out and chasing up supplier questionnaires, only the collation, interpretation and presentation of responses. Their main role in the buying process then was that of attempting to inform, advise and encourage the final decision-makers along the path of timber certification.

Green marketing and social responsibility

Whilst the alliance itself might be regarded as an environmentally responsible project along certain dimensions, my respondents tended to suggest that the organizations within it had various rationales for joining, some more rooted in notions of corporate social responsibility than others. Indeed, different orientations towards social responsibility within organizations can impact significantly on green purchasing strategies and tactics (Drumwright 1994). Hence, in order to distinguish between different approaches, such marketing activities can be usefully categorized in terms of their economic, non-economic or mixed objectives (Drumwright 1996).

Economic objectives

Several respondents expressed a clear conviction that their organization's involvement in CollabOrg was purely on account of economic objectives associated with adding value, maintaining or improving sales, and/or building corporate/ brand image. A few respondents even suggested to me that *all* companies could be subsumed within this category. However, purely economic objectives were particularly evident for those members of the collaboration either totally or principally located within industrial marketing networks, and who had joined in response to the 'recommendation' or 'pressure' applied to them by their customers (principally retailers) who were already members of CollabOrg. Therefore, for many of the industrial marketing companies in the alliance, membership was presented as a strategy aimed at securing distribution channels for company products, driven in the main by a desire to guarantee and retain *existing* customers through current channels rather than attracting new business and/or developing new channels.

Non-economic objectives

A few of my informants (and not only those from the NGO and social mission companies) were emphatic in their conviction that their organization had joined CollabOrg as a result of social purpose or moral conviction, usually on the part of particular senior managers. The issue had usually already been a major concern for the company, and the alliance simply represented an obvious tactical route forward. Whilst these claims for purely social objectives could potentially be interpreted as a disguise for other more commercial motives, respondents themselves at least appeared entirely convinced. The following two examples, from a production manager of a publishing company, and a safety manager of an operations company respectively, illustrate this well:

> When [respondent's manager] asked us to look into it, we actually asked to see him on his own for a bit and said: 'Look, why do you want to do this?'. And it was when he said, well he wanted to be doing the right thing for his children and his children's children, and really that is what it comes down to, that we felt comfortable with what he was asking us to do. At least we knew that it was being done for the right reasons, not for some kind of PR scoop.

> We are doing it because we want to. There's no real advantage to us. For instance, the [CollabOrg certification] logo: the only time one of our customers would see the logo would be if they were committing suicide, because then they're face-to-face with the [product].

Although, for these companies, non-economic objectives could be seen to have driven the project, this does not mean that economic benefits were necessarily absent altogether, only that when they were in evidence, they were perceived to be merely 'spin-offs'. None the less, of those respondents citing their companies within this category, none of them actually suggested to me that they had adopted what might be regarded as the extreme ethical position, namely that they deliberately would *not* take advantage of such 'marketing spin-offs'.

Mixed objectives

The largest group of respondents cited mixed objectives for joining CollabOrg, stressing the alignment of economic and non-economic goals similar to the enlightened self-interest position adopted by the conventional companies in Chapter 4. This was particularly true of the consumer products companies, especially the retailers in the alliance, given their direct contact with the public. Interestingly however, respondents from these companies tended to under-emphasize direct marketing *advantages* and any positive brand augmentation afforded by membership of the group, and preferred instead to articulate marketing dimensions in terms of avoiding commercial *disadvantages*. Such disadvantages might be either through price increases, quality shortfalls, or reputation problems. Hence, companies had joined 'because we wouldn't be at a commercial disadvantage by doing it', rather than for obvious marketing advantages. This environment manager stressed the point to me in the following way:

> Well yes, I guess there are some [advantages] . . . but the general public probably don't know anything about it, but then that's not the prime reason we are doing it.

Respondents emphasized to me in particular their refusal to accept cost increases from suppliers, or price increases on their own products, as a result of joining the alliance. Indeed, one of the principal attractions of the initiative for many organizations appeared to be the possibility of passing on, or at least sharing, the costs of appraisal, verification and certification with other firms in the same supply networks. The principal reasons forwarded for the relatively peripheral concern with marketing benefits for the mixed objective companies were in line with those discussed in Chapter 4. Thus, respondents again related to me issues of consumer scepticism for green claims, the relatively small number of highly concerned green consumers, and the continued dominance of price and performance product evaluation criteria over green concerns. Accordingly, many respondents indicated that environmental certification would only provide a significant positive product or brand benefit if all other product criteria were equal with respect to competing offerings. Hence, it was considered unlikely that environmental certification would have a substantial impact on sales or market share.[4]

Interestingly, some respondents from other alliance members (particularly those specifying their objectives as non-economic) tended to perceive some of the large retailers as actually rather more concerned about positive marketing benefits than the retailers themselves suggested was the case:

> I get a bit fed up when I'm at the [NGO] seminars listening to the supermarket squabble . . . they are trying to score points over each other for a start; and also they seem to want to almost hijack the process. They're in it for the commercial side of things, primarily because they believe that they'll get an advantage to their company by being able to say, well our products come from certified sources. OK fine, but [respondent's company] doesn't really have that motivation behind it.

None the less, long-term or 'strategic' objectives, particularly those centred around the building and consolidation of corporate reputation, and the achievement of 'industry best practice' were frequently cited as important. However, this appeared to be driven more out of a desire to be 'squeaky clean' in environmental terms (i.e. avoiding negative publicity) than it was a desire to publicly extol their own virtues. Again, this was akin to the 'muted greening' strategy already identified in Chapter 4. Hence, it was the mixed objectives evident in the avoidance of potentially negative media exposure (as encountered by several companies in advance of the formation of the original alliance) and the moral obligation to back up marketing claims that had motivated their entry into CollabOrg. This environment manager explained to me the story of their firm's entry into CollabOrg as follows:

> At the time, [some of our competitors] were being targeted by [an NGO], with great blow up chainsaws outside their stores saying you know, 'Destroying Tropical Rainforests!' which was having . . . an impact on their business. So that's why they joined. We joined because it wasn't being highlighted as an issue for us but we were uncomfortable with making those claims.

Cultural dynamics and moral meanings in green marketing

In general then, respondents from alliance members suggested to me that social responsibility might be a factor in their organizations' involvement in the project, although this not only varied in its extent, but also in the meaning and significance applied to it by the organizations and individuals involved. Whilst the previous section sought to provide some description of the different organizational contexts in evidence within the collaboration, it is more useful to explore these different interpretations by looking at the cultural dynamics underlying the operationalization of the project within these contexts. My analysis of managers' responses revealed some common themes that appeared to illustrate exceedingly well how moral meanings were constructed within the alliance. I have categorized these as subcultural divisions, cultural mediators, managing symbolism and moral circumscription.

Subcultural divisions

The specific network of relationships created by CollabOrg, in combination with the nature of the buying centres in member companies, could be seen to have precipitated significant subcultural divisions within the domain of the alliance. Remember, my respondents were those individuals indicated by member organizations as their main representatives in the alliance. Now since these individuals were charged with fostering the project's development and driving it forward, they might be regarded as environmental policy entrepreneurs, in much the same way as those environment protagonists discussed in the previous two chapters. There was little doubt though that many of these respondents felt substantial cultural difference between themselves (either individually or as a group) and those vested with the responsibility of putting the policy into practice at a day-to-day level, i.e. company procurement managers and staff. For example, many of the company representatives interviewed were specialist environmental staff. Now these individuals tended (not unnaturally) to stress to me the importance of their having substantial environmental knowledge and expertise, as well as the ability to employ sophisticated environmental management techniques in order to expedite the project within member organizations. Even non-specialist representatives tended at least to express *some* interest or concern for the environment, presenting themselves, as one respondent put it, as 'enthusiastic amateurs'.

In contrast to these environmental policy entrepreneurs, company buyers were predominantly described by my interviewees as 'hard-nosed' business people, driven by concerns for margins and costs rather than for environmental considerations. This was evidenced in statements of the kind: 'all they are interested in is screwing down the current supplier another 5 per cent', . . . 'they're not environmentally conditioned', etc. In many ways this kind of representation was similar to Drumwright's (1994: 13) findings in the US. In her study of green procurement, purchasing executives were shown 'to ignore opportunities for socially responsible buying and resist the initiatives of others'. However, in my case looking at CollabOrg, this was especially pertinent since it was the area of procurement that provided the essential mechanism through which the collaboration could operate and succeed, i.e. the purchase of wood products by organizations.

These kinds of subcultural division evident in the alliance also extended beyond the member companies and into the NGO itself. In particular, the project team responsible for the running of CollabOrg was presented as culturally distinct from other sections of the organization, especially with respect to their commercially attuned frame of reference for environmental knowledge. One of the NGO project managers for CollabOrg, described the situation to me as follows:

> [A fellow project manager] is . . . extremely credible, obviously the sort of person that can interact well with business. He's an ideal person for the job . . . realizing you can effect change by working with some of the forward thinking industry. And how deeply that culture goes beyond [CollabOrg project team], I don't know. But I think it's quite good you've still got people like [a fieldworker in the NGO] with a huge big bushy beard lost in the rainforest because that's the other side of what the organization is doing. And I don't think [the NGO] would have complete credibility without having that other side.

Clearly within these subcultures, individuals might in many respects display a healthy diversity. However, substantial unity was certainly evident in terms of the cultural knowledge of these groups, particularly since individual roles, goals and systems of assessment tended to reflect subcultural divisions. Perhaps the best example of this was provided by informants' descriptions of the differing under-standings of notions of 'competition' and 'co-operation' within the two main corporate subcultures involved in the workings of the alliance (buyers and environmental policy entrepreneurs). This I have referred to as the 'co-operation–competition paradox'.

Co-operation–competition paradox

As we have seen, a network perspective on industrial marketing and purchasing highlights substantial interrelation and exchange contingencies among firms not directly connected through dyadic relations (Anderson *et al.* 1994). However, a broad alliance such as CollabOrg went yet further than this. In fact, the situation experienced by member firms was such that many companies found themselves in the relatively unusual scenario of working *with* some of their main competitors as well as *against* them (see also Varadarajan and Rajaratnam 1986; Hamel *et al.* 1989; Jarillo and Stevenson 1991; Bucklin and Sengupta 1993). Indeed, a few of the alliance members had clearly been at least partially instrumental in their competitors joining CollabOrg early on in its development, even to the point of 'recruiting' some of these other companies. Moreover, many respondents expressed a certain satisfaction in working with their alliance counterparts in com-panies that might more usually be regarded as fierce competitors. This technical manager for example, even found the situation quite humorous:

> It's comical actually because I phone up my competitors . . . and say, 'I want to speak to so and so, it's [respondent name] here from [respondent's company].' And you hear them go: 'What?! What are you doing?' Ha ha. They say: 'Are you sure? Or are you taking the mickey?'. . . . so I've got to know them personally; and when I joined [CollabOrg] they [competitors] said, 'If there's any questions you've got, get in touch.'

At the time that the fieldwork was conducted many of my respondents indicated that the size of the collaboration's membership was sufficient for the project to succeed. However, member companies were still presented with something of an anomaly in that: (a) the collaboration was likely to operate more successfully (by having greater 'clout') the more of a company's competitors joined the project; but (b) this was likely to erode any marketing advantages that membership might bring in terms of creating a differential advantage against these same companies. As one marketing manager put it:

> From a business perspective . . . anything that gives me competitive advantage is going to be welcome . . . so from that perspective I'd be happy if everybody stays away and gives us a free run. On a broader scale, ultimately it's got to become better if more people become involved and committed to it.

Consequently, policy entrepreneurs were faced with competing preferences with regard to encouraging alliance membership. Even more significantly, however, there was a paradox in how such individuals defined their companies' relationships with other members of the collaboration. They were at the same time both collaborators and competitors:

> Our competitors . . . are competitors in terms of selling [products], but they are allies in terms of reducing environmental impacts.

In one sense this apparent paradox may have generated conflicting 'network identities' among the firms concerned (Anderson *et al.* 1994). That is, certain companies' perceptions of themselves and of other companies may have lacked any overarching unity and consistency. Whilst alliance representatives appeared to have recognized this, the cooperation–competition paradox was successfully rationalized in terms of the subcultural divisions within their organizations and how these appeared to have diffused throughout the network. In particular, alliance policy entrepreneurs could be seen to be representing themselves as sharing environmental orientations and a common environmental goal. Equally they were not personally in direct competition with each other. In contrast, those personnel seen as most in competition with each other, the company buyers, were rarely involved directly in the machinations of CollabOrg. Hence respondents could stress their companies' co-operation on environmental issues (what the policy entrepreneurs themselves did) within an overall context of intense market competition (what the buyers did):

> Us and our competitors . . . come together. You haven't got buyers there, you've just got environment people, so it's a lot less competitive atmosphere, more co-operative. . . . When [CollabOrg] members go over to visit the forests, they all go over together because our aims are common. You wouldn't get a bunch of buyers visiting a supplier together because they're in competition together.

In short, respondents did not see network organizations as monolithic entities, but as micro-collections of cultural groups. Each of these groups was perceived and presented as having its own role to play, and with its own particular network bonds. Hence, the success of those actors directly bonded by the alliance (in this case company representatives), might be said to be strongly dependent on those not bonded by the alliance (here, the corporate buyers). Why? Because it was these non-bonded groups of buyers that actually conducted the marketing exchanges. Therefore it was they, and not the CollabOrg representatives, who had control over the linking of critical network resources, i.e. the products themselves (see Hakansson and Snehota 1997b).

Cultural mediators

The existence of such subcultural divisions could be seen to have had important ramifications for the cultural dynamics of the alliance, and in particular for the moral framing of the environment within this context. Most notably, certain individuals and cultural groups within the alliance were thrust into the role of what I have called *cultural mediators*. What I mean by this is that they were required to bridge gaps in cultural knowledge between disparate groups within the alliance. Hence, their role was to act as depositories of specific environmental knowledge, interpreters of environmental meanings, and architects of appropriate, and ideally shared, frames of reference.

CollabOrg project managers in the NGO were cultural mediators in that they had to translate the relatively radical environmental concerns of their organization – sustainability, biodiversity conservation, etc. – into a business issue with business objectives, business opportunities, etc. Their success in this respect was demonstrated by the generally positive views of corporate respondents' with respect to the aims and structure of the project, as this middle manager attests:

> They [the NGO] have been able to set some practical goals. They've set up some tangible steps in that they have this specification standard for getting certification for the forests and there are people that will do the certification. They will do the check. So they will deliver to us effectively somebody that is as sound as you can get in terms of the source forest.

Not all company respondents, however, were as sanguine. Although generally considered supportive and approachable, several individuals depicted the NGO as sorely lacking business acumen and 'too short-sighted business-wise' to be able to 'appreciate commercial pressures'. Indeed, these perceived shortcomings were further considered to potentially threaten the smooth running of the collaboration. For example, this environmental consultant, working on behalf of one the CollabOrg corporate members, was fairly scathing about the NGO:

> In terms of how that works with the companies, you are not dealing with a competent strategic alliance partner, the [NGO]. They are under-resourced, they've been running at a standstill and they are not as clear thinking as they purport to be, in my view. Things keep changing . . . and it is quite difficult.

Perhaps surprisingly, those respondents least convinced of the NGO's commercial credentials and most aggressive in their castigation of the organization's lack of commercial-mindedness tended to be (although not exclusively) environment managers and external environmental consultants. However, I had initially assumed that these particular individuals would be more likely to have had especially pronounced environmental orientations, and would therefore be *more* in support of the NGO rather than less. It is probable then that this dynamic resulted from some kind of role competition. That is, the companies' environmental experts may have either consciously or unconsciously seen the NGO as competing with them in the role of cultural mediation. This may have resulted in a subsequent playing down of their NGO partner's credentials in understanding the position of the commercial partners, because that is how they saw their own role.

Indeed, company policy entrepreneurs could themselves be seen to be cultural mediators between what they regarded as the commercially reasonable, but still relatively 'idealistic' demands of the NGO and the 'commercial priorities' of their companies. In this way they could be regarded as helping both sides to see the position of the other in what might otherwise be a relationship between incompatibles:

> Pressure groups are in the business of campaigning and they are not in the business of making other people's lives easy. I'm not in the business of being good to pressure groups. And the businesses are selling what they sell . . . so it's a constant tension between everybody's needs. And we try to smooth the waters – I'm not sure successfully, but we try.

Most respondents seemed to attest then to a process of mutual learning, facilitated it seems by this series of cultural mediators whose role emerged from the particular organization and relationships which typified the group. These mediators – be they NGO employees, external consultants or company employees – reinterpreted and reframed the environmental problems at the heart of the alliance in order to involve and motivate those who were more commercially oriented and in more competitive positions than themselves. Essentially then, individuals within the alliance can be thought of as occupying positions on twin scales of business– environment orientation and co-operation– competition orientation. Accordingly, both competition and business orientations can be said to gain in strength as communication proceeds from the NGO to the buyers who implement CollabOrg policy for their companies in the marketplace. The role of cultural mediators is to facilitate the smooth communication and meaning transferral between these culturally disparate groups within the alliance.

Constructing the environment

It was apparent that this process of mediation had significant implications for the construction of the environment within the domain of the alliance. Most notably, there was strong evidence to suggest that the effect of serial reinterpretation of the group's purpose, objectives and importance was to successively remove layers of moral meaning from the notion of forest conservation. The moral imperative so clear in the conservation mission of the NGO thus tended to be stripped away in order to make the project more meaningful for factions within the alliance with more advanced commercial and competition orientations. For example, buyers were perceived by the more environmentally oriented representatives as needing commercial arguments with clear directives and performance incentives, and not moral arguments, in order to act upon the policy on a day-to-day level. One technical manager explained his approach as follows:

> How I go about it [motivating the buyers] – all I can do is try and make the case . . . show how it relates to customers and how . . . there's a danger of

losing business ultimately if we don't actually come up with . . . the [certified product] that those people are going to want to buy.

This process of reinterpretation and reframing was abetted by range of cultural and symbolic activities across the member organizations. Given the varying orientations and goals of collaboration members, those keen to ensure its success sought to render the image and associations of its members as compatible, or at least acceptable, and this necessitated a substantial degree of manipulation and management of various symbols (Mendleson and Polonsky 1995).

Managing symbolism

A number of elements within the alliance appeared to be managed at the symbolic level, and I perceived these to have profound implications for the moral meanings established and communicated within the group. First, many informants suggested that the particular environmental subject of the alliance had to be seen to have wide appeal to various alliance constituencies. There were a number of ways in which this was communicated. One is that the issue of forest certification was shown to have clear commercial resonance, and the symbolic potency of forests, trees, and hardwoods as dangerously 'emotive' and 'sensitive' public relations issues was widely acknowledged by executives in this study. Also, there was some recognition that the erosion of forest reserves was clearly detrimental to commercial expansion (basically, if you chop down all the trees you won't have a business anymore). And finally, given that the narrow focus of the project prevented any need to reflect at length on wider (and more challenging) issues of reducing timber consumption and increasing recycling, the issue was relatively easily translated from a moralistic, 'emotive', environmental issue into a compelling, 'rational', business argument.

A second area of managing symbolism was around the issue of senior management support. Here respondents emphasized the symbolic importance of top management endorsement and support for the alliance. In this respect, the task of mobilizing support for the initiative in member organizations was expedited by the obligation within the alliance to secure board-level patronage. Thus, whilst the direct and tangible involvement of senior managers was rare in the larger organizations,[5] the *signature* of board members on internal memos, or particularly on correspondence to suppliers, provided an important symbol of the project's significance and weight for otherwise recalcitrant factions within the domain of the alliance:

> When we sent out the questionnaires, it wasn't coming from me or from [the firm's other CollabOrg representative], it was coming from . . . the boss. We . . . wrote the letter for him to sign, so you've got these [suppliers] getting something from the top man – they can't ignore it. They'd be very foolish if they did!

Third, the importance of constructing a correct and unchallenging image for the project meant that an appropriate vocabulary had to be established and accepted. Therefore terminology for appropriate forest management was steered away from the semantically suspect 'sustainability' towards the more agreeable term 'well-managed'. Discussions with respondents were indeed littered with references to the term 'well-managed' and to other even less environmentally explicit terms such as 'managed' and 'certified' whereas the use of 'sustainability' terms was rare.[6] In addition, company respondents tended to stress the issue of maintaining forest resources (with its obvious commercial resonance) to the virtual exclusion of other principles of good practice laid down by the accreditation body such as conservation and diversity of forest fauna and indigenous people's rights. Executives in mediator roles then had clearly adopted a vocabulary with little obvious moral or environmental symbolism and which exhibited little semantic baggage that might have been considered inappropriate or challenging to business interests. Whilst this may have been seen as important in terms of managing the image of the project in order to lubricate the challenging process of meaning transferral and reinterpretation, it may also give some indication that fundamental environmental values were either being suppressed or exorcised by these individuals and groups.

Finally, the role of cultural mediator also involved a considerable amount of personal image making, similar to that described for the conventional companies in Chapter 4. For example, attempts by individuals in the NGO to create an overall impression that was as acceptable to business as possible prompted an approach much like the 'professional management' approach of the policy entrepreneurs in RetailCo. As one NGO respondent put it:

> There is an attempt to be extremely professional. I wasn't formally a shorthaired, suit wearing person. I was a longhaired forest ecologist who knew all about trees.

Also, extra staffing needs at the NGO were satisfied by bringing in external consultants who, according to my informants, were apparently selected as much for their business credentials as for their environmental skills. The professional image and commercial approach taken on by the NGO as a consequence did not go unacknowledged, or for that matter unappreciated, by the commercial partners:

> [The consultant] . . . has a commercial background. They are aware that they can't afford to have a stereotyped environmentalist approach. They can't be woolly and indeterminate on things. They can't have high moral principles and ideas but not have actually any degree of a sense of reality with it because there's no way they'll get to tie business in.

Essentially then, for the most part, the adoption of a cultural mediator role was seen as important for the success of the collaboration. However, the acts of symbol manipulation and image management associated with this role tended successively to strip emotional and moral meaning from the issue of forest sustainability. This for them was a perfectly rational response to the need to make the project an attractive and workable proposition for other network members, and in particular for the groups and individuals who were actually required to implement the project on a day to day level in commercial organizations. Clearly, there was as a consequence some contesting of discourse in and around CollabOrg. However, there was considerable evidence to suggest that commercial or enterprise discourses had tended to gain some degree of privilege above moral discourses during the course of the collaboration. Despite this, there was at least some evidence of moral meanings remaining attached to the environment, and to forest conservation in particular. However, it is fair to say that this was highly circumscribed into particular moral arenas, as we shall now see.

Moral circumscription

Whilst certainly not the only possible route, some respondents suggested that the alliance itself, and formal meetings in particular, could act as an important forum that allowed (or in some cases perhaps compelled) individuals to consider the environment as a moral issue, and as an end in itself rather than as simply instrumental to business goals of long-term survival and profit. Congregations of representatives from those organizations involved in the collaboration were as one earlier respondent described it, characterized by a 'less competitive atmosphere, more co-operative'. This was seen by some as a result of a congruence of values and moral convictions concerning the environment and environmental protection amongst many of those involved in the project. As a result, this environmentally supportive context could act as a catalyst for the resurfacing of sidelined or forgotten personal values, as this NGO respondent argued:

> When they join the group and they have someone to talk to who has got a like-mind (or it might be a like-mind like they were when they joined the company fifteen years ago) then it can get their enthusiasm going again. But it can work both ways as well. . . . There's people I know in companies that are really serious, totally serious, totally committed, as committed as I am about what we are doing. And it is enormously heartening. I love it from that point of view!

Therefore, it would appear that moral meanings were not completed eroded in the acts of constant reinterpretation by the cultural mediators since a favourable climate could resurrect, or even create, an enthusiasm for greening which might otherwise be submerged under the socialization processes associated with more conventional cultural norms and behaviours in firms. None the less, a distinctly moral conception of the environment was relatively rare in CollabOrg and to some extent appeared to be circumscribed into particular limited arenas where it might arouse less hostility or suspicion. Therefore, although the discourse of the environment in this case was to some extent amoralized in the need to establish a common and acceptable frame of reference within business organizations, this did not mean that moral meanings could not be translated in certain contexts. It would appear, however, that this moral circumscription was fairly limiting and generally became more so as communication moved away from the NGO partner and towards more morally antagonistic factions such as the procurement function. Overall then, amoralization was probably more in evidence than in the social mission companies, but less so than in the conventional companies.

Given the potential scale and scope of green alliances and supply chain management approaches, it also became evident to me that forums such as CollabOrg could also have impact beyond their borders. This might be, for example, through educating consumers (Mendleson and Polonsky 1995) and/or suppliers (Lamming and Hampson 1996). In the present case, many thousands of questionnaires were (and have continued to be) distributed throughout wide-ranging industrial networks, reaching people and organizations where before there may have been little knowledge or interest, let alone concern, for forest management. This might be regarded as providing greater potential for the activation of personal reflection on the morality of corporate policies and practices:

> There . . . have been several hundred thousand questionnaires gone out all over the world. So that wherever you go, wherever you meet a forest manager, they've probably had – or somebody they sell to has had – a [CollabOrg] questionnaire. And it really makes people sit up and take notice when it's somebody they've got a commercial relationship with asking them about their environmental performance.

Moreover, this reinterpretation and circumscription of morality in relation to green marketing activities may also have implications for how such under-standings are communicated to consumers. However, with so few products certified by CollabOrg on the market at the time that fieldwork was conducted it was too early to investigate this empirically with this particular case. None the less, since one of the requirements for inclusion into the alliance was the removal of all claims relating to forest management from firms' non-certified products, it could be said that the presence of an NGO collaborator in companies' green marketing practices at least had the effect of censuring ostensibly 'unethical' claims. Correspondingly, it might be seen as adding credibility to 'ethical' or at least 'more appropriate' ones. Hence the circumscription of moral meaning may potentially be extended to include consumers and other publics external to the alliance.

Conclusion

This chapter has provided considerable insight into the practice of green market-ing through business–NGO collaboration, and also to some degree through supply chain management. Moreover, my analysis of the particular moral landscape that such an approach was found to describe in the case of CollabOrg might be seen as contributing significantly to an understanding of the way in which notions of morality are handled and transferred in settings characterized by such cultural heterogeneity.

Green alliances are based on an assumption of mutual dependence amongst businesses and pressure groups in relation to the environment. The evidence of the CollabOrg case study, however, was that this dependence can also be extended to incorporate wider network interdependencies between firms and their chains of suppliers/customers. Hence, it is reasonable to suggest that alliances widen the scope and domain of green marketing, bringing it into broader strategic and industrial policy debates. Critically, the importance of environmental criteria in industrial marketing exchanges appears to be, for the most part, contingent on the nature of existing relationships, characterized primarily by issues of loyalty, power differentials and resource dependencies. Hence, the environment remains a subordinate issue in industrial marketing networks (or at least those centred on the timber and paper trade), highlighting the important role for rigidities in industry attitudes in dampening green marketing projects, irrespective of the concerns of individual firms or managers.

Despite being termed here a green alliance, the case of CollabOrg has also illustrated the range of motivations behind individual firms choosing to collaborate with pressure groups. Clearly, some of these motivations are more centred around social and environmental responsibility than others. For many organizations there was found to be an overriding economic rationale for collaborating, for a few there was a convincing moral justification, and for the largest number, a combination of the two appeared to provide the necessary impetus. Again, as in Chapter 4, the avoidance of potentially negative publicity and other disadvantages rather than an explicit search for competitive advantage appeared to drive firms towards environmental initiatives.

Moral meanings were also relatively understated in the organizational and cultural dynamics of the alliance. Its domain embraced substantial cultural diversity both within and between organizations. Broadly speaking, this diversity could be categorized in terms of subcultural divisions representing differing personal and group environmental beliefs and orientations. It was found that the need to bridge these divisions resulted in certain individuals and/or groups being thrust into the role of cultural mediators. Their role was apparently to translate appropriate environmental and moral frames of reference between subcultural groups. The cultural mediator can be thought of as a complementary role to that played by the policy entrepreneur as shown in Chapters 4 and 5, and in some instances, they appear to be analogous.

As a result of the manoeuvres of the cultural mediators, moral meanings were successively stripped from conceptions of the environment such that it could be presented in an appropriate guise for acceptance by important factions within the alliance network. This was found to be particularly due to the strategies employed by the cultural mediators, many of which were similar in form and execution to those revealed as part of the policy entrepreneur's weaponry in Chapter 4. Most notably, the management and manipulation of symbolism was found to be central to the phenomenon in this case.

In the final analysis, however, the amoralization of the environment in the case of CollabOrg was not as complete as in the conventional companies in Chapter 4, but considerably greater than in the social mission companies in Chapter 5. First, it was stripped away through *successive* reinterpretation, suggesting that some (probably decreasing) elements of moral meaning remained attached to concepts of the environment as they were traded throughout the alliance network. And second, distinctly moral discourses clearly prevailed in certain circumscribed arenas, suggesting parallels with the social mission companies, given their strong concentration of moral meaning in the upper echelons of the organization.

Whist I have made a few contrasts and comparisons, it has been my intention in these last three chapters to set out each of the three organizational approaches to green marketing largely in isolation from the others. My rationale for this was that it allowed me to tease out the full richness of analysis of each case, thus taking full advantage of the exploratory research approach. Attempts to standardize the reporting of results into set categories and constructs at an earlier stage may have stymied the emergence of some of the more important insights and findings revealed here. Having explored these different contexts in some depth then, it is now possible for me to draw some of these findings together, to locate them into existing scholarly literature, and to suggest what implications might be drawn from these results. These are the aims of the final three chapters.

7 Green marketing and morality

Evidence from three approaches

Introduction

As stated near the beginning of this book, the main aim of the empirical study reported here was to analyse whether, and in which ways, morality was given or denied meaning and expression in green marketing practices. In the previous three chapters I have provided descriptive accounts of the green marketing process as observed and articulated by organizational informants in the three organizational contexts – conventional, social mission and business–NGO collaboration respectively – as well as setting out the cultural dynamics through which moral meanings were identified. Various elements pertaining to the moral dimension of these processes and dynamics have been identified, leading to some preliminary construction of theoretical categories, constructs and propositions regarding moral meaning in marketing. In these next two chapters the results presented in Chapters 4, 5 and 6 will be brought together in a more integrated manner. My intention is hence to summarize, compare, contrast and explain these results, and ultimately to examine their possible implications.

This subsequent discussion is organized around four key themes, two of which are considered in this chapter, and two in the next. These are: green marketing practices and processes, and morality in green marketing (this chapter); and moralization and amoralization in green marketing (the next chapter). It is my belief that these four themes capture the main findings provided by the study with respect to the basic research questions set out in Chapter 3. They also provide a focus for developing further on these findings and locating them successfully within the extant organizational and management literature.

This chapter will proceed then with a discussion of contemporary green marketing practice as perceived and presented by respondents in the case organizations. This covers both tactical (marketing mix) and strategic issues, before going on to set out a more grounded theory of green marketing. This is followed by an examination of where and how I found morality to have impacted upon green marketing. Here, the classification of moral arenas in marketing which was introduced in Chapter 2 is utilized (i.e. macro and micro moral domains). Implications are also drawn for different views of organizational greening. Finally, the main points in the chapter are summarized and some brief conclusions set out.

Green marketing practices and processes

Environmental considerations had impacted upon marketing, in one form or another, in all of the organizations I visited. In some firms, products with environmental attributes were being developed or were currently marketed; in others, environmental considerations were less directly product-related and impacted more on packaging and distribution systems, or communications policies. Let us briefly examine these developments, as perceived by my informants, in terms of the marketing mix.

Green products

Respondents' definitions of 'green' products showed little consistency across the sample. However, in a general sense, for most respondents the concept of a green product was taken to imply either explicit green brands or products with green attributes of some kind. None the less, it was widely recognized that the grounds in this respect were constantly shifting. What were once green attributes (e.g. zero-CFC propellants or recycled packaging), and therefore worthy of green claims, had in many instances become industry norms, sometimes even legal requirements (National Consumer Council 1996).

It emerged that product strategies most commonly focused on gradually improving the environmental performance of existing products, such that various discrete elements of individual products were incrementally greened through continuous improvement over time, rather than going through any kind of fundamental environmental overhaul or transformation. Therefore, although environmental considerations were found to be entering the product development process, they were 'seldom a factor in determining whether a product is made or which product is made' (Schot and Fischer 1993: 11). This pattern was not repeated, however, amongst the three small social mission companies where senior executives claimed that the firm's social mission had to be mirrored by their products. Indeed, if the green product attributes offered by the social mission companies were more radical than those of the two other organizational types, it was not because it was something that customers demanded, but because it was what the social mission company leaders themselves wanted to produce. According to most marketing textbooks, this might be thought of as representing a product orientation as opposed to a true marketing (still less societal marketing) orientation (see for example Kotler *et al.* 1996). Still, only two out of the four social mission companies (FinanceSoc and MarketingSoc) were observed to be really offering product attributes which took account of a far greater number of environmental impacts than was considered normal for the industry. Hence, the inclusion of certain social or environmental attributes into a firm's product offering should not be assumed to indicate a general predisposition towards incorporating a greater range of environmental features into products (see also Prothero and McDonagh 1992). Moreover, it was also apparent that the assessment and measurement of the social and environmental impacts of products were often more formalized, and in some respects better developed and more sophisticated, in the conventional and collaborative organizations than in the social mission companies.

Packaging could be seen to have been a prime initial target for greening in most organizations, both in terms of reducing product packaging and re-using or recycling transport packaging.[1] In the majority of cases this had brought with it cost savings as well as environmental benefits, with informants representing these as clear examples of win–win solutions. The larger companies such as RetailCo and RetailSoc had focused mainly on limiting the negative impact of impending legislation, particularly in the context of the targets for packaging reductions, recycling and recovery set by the 1994 EC Packaging Waste Directive. As one RetailCo manager commented:

> We started with packaging. One, because of the Packaging Directive; and two because it was a very easy target to make gains on.

The prospects of the introduction of a landfill tax (eventually introduced in October 1996) which set levies according to the amount of waste going to landfill had crystallized the importance of the issue to managers. And with new packaging regulations imminent, these firms had recognized the importance of developing more sophisticated assessment systems for 'auditing' packaging usage, as well as logistics systems to manage its flow more effectively. To this end, respondents spoke of the importance of creating long-term contracts with trade recyclers in order to facilitate the flow of packaging and packaging waste, and to buffer the firm from rapid fluctuations in prices for its recyclable materials. In this way, the threat of regulation could be turned into a steady, if small, income. Thus, even where recycling and re-use initiatives had been originally motivated by environmental concerns, they were often quickly crystallized into economic costs and benefits. For example, the following account from a RetailSoc manager describes the firm's decision not to introduce recycling of plastic transportation packaging:

> We trialed plastic recycling for two weeks in (store A). We were very careful and diligent in making sure that all the right plastic went in there . . . and in one week's turnover of say £1,000, all we got was 1lb or 1/2 kg of plastic. Multiply that by the total turnover, say £4m – that's 2 tonnes of plastic! £14 of landfill levy! And that's after all the efforts by staff, say £1,000 in personnel costs, plus all the problems of getting balers and getting the plastic back from the stores. It's just not worth it.

In the smaller companies, informants suggested little more than that packaging was simply 'minimized' and 're-used where possible', rather than claiming that it was systematically managed. Regulation was, if anything, perceived as a positive step forward since it curbed some of the excesses of their larger competitors. Where they experienced most problems though was in failing to attract trade recycling companies to collect packaging due to their lack of size.

Pricing

The majority of respondents identified a general antipathy on the part of consumers towards paying premium prices for greener products. Only relatively small segments of the market were seen as prepared to pay for green attributes – a phenomenon mirrored, and in some cases amplified further, in the case of industrial markets. None the less, this did not appear to have been seen by many firms as a signal that their marketing mixes were inappropriate, but rather that consumers wanted 'something for nothing'. Accordingly, the use of aggressive penetration pricing to build initial demand had been eschewed, leaving new green brands somewhat unappealing in relation to conventional offerings (Wong *et al.* 1996).

Promotion

In terms of promotional tactics, only those firms with an explicit environmental mission continued to favour an approach which called considerable attention to environmental features, and even this was observed to vary according to the prominence of the firm's mission in its positioning strategy. In general then, strong green claims were avoided. Indeed, there was considerable evidence to suggest that executives even regarded these as potentially *harmful* additions to the marketing effort given consumer preconceptions of performance short-falls (National Consumer Council 1996; Wong *et al.* 1996), problems of poor credibility (Kangun and Polonsky 1995) and the prospect of increased scrutiny from pressure groups as a result of public declarations of greenness (Fineman 1996).

There was widespread concurrence from managers with the National Consumer Council's (1996) findings (following an extensive study of green claims on consumer goods) which showed a shift since 1991 away from green advertising to on-pack claims and logos. At times, it was clear that green claims might even only be implied through the design of product packaging. Moves to increase the regulation of such claims were only really welcomed by the social mission companies, who saw it not only as a good thing in itself, but also as a potential prop to their otherwise ailing 'ethical' competitive advantage, as this manager from ManufactureSoc suggested:

> I'm with it (the EU labelling directive). I support it. Animal labelling has been abused beyond recognition . . . this could mean other companies will have to consider the replacement of meaningless slogans with factual statements . . . which we've being doing all along of course.

In addition to legislation (and as a means to forestall it), the growth in business–NGO alliances during the 1990s can also be seen as indicative of a parallel movement away from self-endorsement towards external certification and validation of green claims (Mendleson and Polonsky 1995; Hartman and Stafford 1997). The CollabOrg alliance, as one such initiative, was certainly seen by most of its members as a positive and significant step towards redressing consumer confusion and cynicism regarding green claims. None the less, for those companies dealing in a wide range of products outside the remit of the alliance, it remained an experimental approach in one product area rather than one which was to be introduced across all ranges. As such, it did not appear that the 'bewildering' number of claims and logos identified by the National Consumer Council (1996) would actually be reduced in any substantial way, even if the number of unsubstantiated ones might. For the consumer then, the responses of managers in this study suggested that their overwhelming perplexity towards green claims seems only likely to be diminished as a result of further legislative amendments (see National Consumer Council 1996).

Green communications can also be seen to be part of a wider move by businesses to restore and/or consolidate legitimacy in the face of increased public environmental concern (Patten 1992; Tombs 1993). The need to convert other constituencies to the environmental worldview of the organization appeared to be a significant force in driving various communications efforts for the firms in this study. This was most explicit in the case of the social mission companies where the relative commitment to campaigning was seen as a critical distinguishing feature of their marketing strategies. However, *all* of the sampled organizations were observed to have communicated their environmental position at some point to some external (and to a lesser extent, internal) audiences, usually in the form of public relations and publicity campaigns. In the main, such communication appeared to be aimed at legitimation of the form and scope of environmental management at the organization, focusing primarily on information provision and persuasion of the 'truth', 'responsibility' or 'rationality' of the organization's approach (see Tombs 1993). For example, an executive at RetailCo explained the development of environmental material for schools thus:

> You've got to get right back to educating – or getting involved in the environmental education of children – at an early age to try and help them understand and get rid of some of these fallacies that are around with regard to environmental issues. So that if environmentalists are coming through, and coming into our stores and deciding whether to buy our products, they do it on the basis of some of the facts, rather than what they might read that's more emotive sort of journalism.

This construction of discourses of rationality and irrationality, 'facts' and 'fallacies' clearly had the purpose of excluding critical constituencies, and might be regarded as an attempt to deny the possibility of critical voices (Puxty 1986; Tombs 1993). A more progressive strategy, however, might involve engaging in more open, participatory and trust-based dialogue with various audiences (Tombs 1993; Prothero *et al.* 1994; Peattie 1995; McDonagh 1998). Indeed, there was some evidence from the findings reported here, as well as elsewhere (see Schot 1992; Simmons and Wynne 1993), that some conventional and social mission companies might, for various reasons, have been increasingly willing to engage in dialogue with stakeholder groups, as was happening with CollabOrg. However, the extent to which this actually manifests itself in practice as open and participatory remains to be seen.

Distribution

Finally, the role of distribution has been shown here to have played a critical role in the green marketing process, despite remaining relatively underresearched to date (Simintiras *et al.* 1997). In one case (MarketingSoc), distribution systems were at the heart of the environmental strategy. However, MarketingSoc managers not only perceived environmental issues to be *not* valued positively by potential resellers, but even valued *negatively* by them. Consequently, managers in this firm had been compelled to seek competitive advantage elsewhere. Indeed, the willingness or otherwise of channel members to accept green products, or even the principle of greening in itself, has been shown to be a key concern for many firms (Wong *et al.* 1996). For the social mission firms in this study, retailer reluctance to switch from favoured suppliers to greener new entrants was experienced as probably the major stumbling block for marketing success and for the diffusion of green innovations more generally. In other cases of course, the opposite was true: green marketing initiatives of re-sellers (such as those at the forefront of the CollabOrg initiative) had driven pro-environmental change on the part of suppliers.

Fineman's (1996) in-depth account of the reaction to environmental issues in the UK grocery multiples reveals the importance of different cultural styles in determining the particular response of retailers. His picture is one of conservative adaptation to green concerns in retail organizations where managers have been well socialized into feelings of commitment to the well drummed culture of social responsibility, and clear hostility in those less so. In my study, it was apparent that although the relative approbation of the prevailing culture of industrial purchasers was an important determinant of the success of green product distribution, the role of environmental protagonists in the buying decision was also critical (Drumwright 1994). The mediation effected by such individuals between sub-cultural interests within (and around) the firm, and their relative influence within these constituencies, was found to have significant impacts upon channel behaviour.

Representing green marketing

Clearly then, some degree of greening was taking place in the sampled organizations, although perhaps much of this activity would not be regarded as 'genuine' green marketing by writers such as Peattie (1992, 1995) and Charter (1992). Indeed, it would be true to say that few people I spoke to in these organizations themselves actually laid too many claims that their organizations were conducting anything called 'green marketing'. In fact, the discovery that some even vigorously denied that this was what they were doing can be construed as evidence that the term itself carried some apparently unpalatable connotations.

This seemed to be particularly driven by the perception of green marketing having to some extent 'failed' in the 1990s. Certainly, the hopeful prognoses which characterized the green marketing zeitgeist of the early–mid 1990s (e.g. Ottman 1993; Peattie 1992, 1995; Wasik 1996), where a 'green tide' (Vandermerwe and Oliff 1990) of consumers was expected to rush to buy environmentally-friendly products from responsible and ecologically-sensitive firms did not seem to be matched by organization members' perceptions of what had subsequently 'actually' happened. Indeed, the dramatic growth in green product introductions at the beginning of the decade (see Vandermerwe and Oliff 1990; Ottman 1993) had, by the time I completed my fieldwork, subsided into a trickle; many of the groundbreaking green products produced by specialist green 'boutique' firms had either left the market or been absorbed or copied by mainstream competitors; and companies had clearly become increasingly cautious about launching environmentally-based advertising and other communications campaigns for fear of receiving unwanted attention from pressure groups, such as Friends of the Earth's derisory Green Con of the Year Award.

A green marketing backlash?

Wong *et al.* (1996: 278) have written of these developments in terms of a consumer 'backlash' against green marketing. Essentially, their claim was that under-performing green products, overzealous promotional claims, inexact science and inconsistent legislation had conspired to discredit the practice of green marketing, such that by the mid-1990s (when my fieldwork was conducted), consumers were left confused, relatively alienated from green marketing firms and apparently reluctant to engage in green purchase behaviour. This is very much also the picture presented by my informants, most of whom indicated a knowledge of survey evidence reporting strong environmental concern on the part of consumers, but juxtaposed this with their own impressions and experiences of relatively limited pro-environmental purchase behaviour manifested in the marketplace. As such, evidence of the greening of consumers was either viewed with suspicion, or else seen more as a indicator of a potential *future* demand for green products, as these managers from social mission companies attested:

> All the studies show there is concern out there, but that doesn't translate into people voting with their pockets. They will say they are concerned, although the actual percentage of people concerned has fallen since the 1980s.

> Environment comes into what I call my secondary programmes. It is not a high issue in the forefront of the consumer's mind at the moment; it may be again next year, or the year after, but at the moment it tends not to.

Such a backlash against green marketing has been argued to be a feature of a wide range of markets in various industrialized countries (see Simonian 1995), including the UK (National Consumer Council 1996; Wong *et al.* 1996; Peattie

1999), the US (Carlson *et al.* 1993; Kangun and Polonsky 1995; Schrum *et al.* 1995; Ackerstein and Lemon 1999) and Australia (Kangun and Polonsky 1995; Mendleson and Polonsky 1995). In the current study, much of the blame for this unimpressive performance (at least in the UK) was laid on miscreant firms who had confused consumers with inappropriate and misleading labelling. This was even seen as sabotaging any possible attempts by firms to highlight environmental product attributes. There was agreement on this from managers in all three types of organization, illustrated by these quotations from managers in RetailCo and ManufactureSoc respectively:

> There's been a lot of confusion about all the spurious environmental claims that were made in the early nineties. Consumers got confused: they didn't believe that green products worked as well as standard products, and they were suspicious of claims made by manufacturers on their own products. So what with that and the recession, people believe that the environment has gone off the agenda a bit, off the boil.

> One of the aspects that's queered the market, and may have betrayed the whole campaign for a generation, has been this free-for-all on labelling.

None the less, it was evident that even these very same firms often continued to make questionable claims themselves, at least within some product ranges. However, as the National Consumer Council (1996) reported, such claims had increasingly become more low key since the early 1990s, and were usually relegated to on-pack labels and logos rather than advertising messages.

Blame was also laid on maladroit attempts by competing firms to introduce green products that had clearly failed to convince consumers of their efficacy. Over and over, respondents at all levels across the range of sampled organizations repeated the same cautionary tales of doomed green product introductions by niche firms which had failed to match the perceived performance of conventional offerings. These 'salutary' products (see Kotler 1972) were seen as having achieved environmental benefit only by sacrificing the immediate appeals and satisfactions sought by consumers. In particular, the case of green detergents and washing-up liquids appeared to be an important story in shaping organizational perceptions of consumer preferences for conventional performance standards over environmental benefits. This story, in its various tellings, crossed organizational as well as industrial contexts. This was one conventional company manager's version:

> They produced product that was inferior and hoped to sell it to the fanatical fringe . . . If you look at the washing powders that came out – the so-called green powders – I don't think there is one left on the market. Because they did not perform in the way that the non-environmental powders did . . . People thought they could get away with it; the public's expectations were considered to be less for an environmental product.

This story was widely used throughout the sampled organizations to justify a number of assertions, in particular: consumer dislike of green brands; performance problems of green products; and irresponsible or inappropriate green marketing from competitors. In fact, few other examples were ever offered to support these contentions. And indeed, at the same time as emphasizing these inherent problems with green products, some respondents even confirmed that these apparent green trade-offs were frequently more perceived than real, since they were based on inaccurate perceptions on the part of consumers (see Peattie 1995). For example, the manager above later commented:

> It's like washing powder, or detergents, to be fair. Detergents do not produce soapsuds; the manufacturers of detergents add a 'sudser' so that when you open the door, you see frothy soap bubbles on the top. It doesn't help clean the clothes – but it makes you think it's washing clothes properly . . . But what is more environmentally friendly? Detergent without froth in! We spend a fortune in treatment plants taking the froth out that we put in just to satisfy the customer!

Essentially then, the green detergent story can be regarded as a widely accepted *myth* which helped to create and sustain meaning about the marketing of green products. Myths can be regarded as 'unjustified beliefs, often enshrined in stories, and which influence how organizational actors understand and react to their social situation' (Brown 1995a: 15). In this instance, the detergents myth was used to help in explaining the failure of green marketing under conditions of incomplete knowledge, regardless of whether it was factually true or not (Boje *et al.* 1982). Such a myth was important for it established that the 'fault' for the green marketing backlash could be successfully externalized: either it was due to the poor marketing of 'other' firms, the confusion and irrationality of consumers, or the negative effect of recessionary forces on consumers' demands for non-essential 'extras'.

Strategic responses

So what strategic postures did managers suggest that firms were adopting in a context represented by them as largely unfavourable to the growth of green marketing? Amongst my three organizational types, informants presented four general approaches that could be used to address the proposed green marketing backlash. These I have labelled passive greening, muted greening, niche greening and collaborative greening. I shall briefly explain each in turn, and in so doing, present empirical evidence underpinning the development of a more grounded theory of green marketing.

Passive greening

The strategy of passive greening was essentially a reactive one whereby the firm did not actively seek out green markets, nor actively seek to improve the environmental performance of its products across the board; rather, its approach was to tackle those environmental issues which it felt pressurized to respond to by key influential stakeholders. These were identified by respondents as important customers (for industrial products firms such as ManufactureCo), regulators, corporate parents, pressure groups or the media (in the case of some of CollabOrg's less enthusiastic members, as well as arguably, RetailSoc). For example, a RetailSoc manager claimed:

> We have to take our lead from what the pressure groups are going to be doing next year, what the media is going to be interested in.

> [Environment] is more in the minds of the legislators at the moment, so the things that I am working on are those things where there will be a legislative impact upon us in the near future – particularly thinking of waste management concerns, landfill tax . . .

Hence, green marketing at these companies was seen by respondents to be fragmented, unmanaged and reluctantly compliant to significant and immediate changes in the marketing environment. However, where particularly significant pressures had been forthcoming, respondents at these firms did acknowledge that a more structured environmental policy would have to be part of their response. Indeed, overall there was virtually no confidence in an approach that completely ignored the environment; it was just that it was felt to have little to do with marketing as such. It is significant also that the majority of respondents involved in these strategies did not perceive their passive greening position to be unusual. Indeed, it was inconceivable to many that the environment would feature in *any* firms' marketing policies unless driven to it by external pressure – and this included those of their own customers who were expending pressure on the sampled firms. This strategy was presented then as a quite logical position to adopt in industry environments generally seen as unsympathetic to green concerns, and where environmental features did not appear to figure significantly in the purchase decisions of consumers. Here, the costs of greening were widely regarded as exceeding the benefits, unless that is, the benefits were made eminently tangible by the immediate demands of powerful customers, legislators or other stakeholders.

Muted greening

The muted greening strategy appeared to be particularly common and differed from the passive greening strategy in the sense that although specific green markets were again not explicitly sought, environmental product improvements were – even in the absence of palpable external pressure. According to the arguments presented by respondents, this approach appeared to have been adopted by RetailCo, several of the social mission companies, and by CollabOrg and many of its members. In the main, developments in these organizations were focused on achieving incremental improvements, such that products would be gradually modified to become more environmentally benign over time. In the most advanced firms, this had translated into intra-functional efforts to improve environmental quality, indicative of an attempt to move from a 'tactical' to a 'quasi-strategic' mode of green marketing (Menon and Menon 1997). Often this would rely on the energy and drive of politically adept environment champions who would need to engage recalcitrant factions across functional, even organizational, divides (Drumwright 1994). Generally, however, this meant avoiding any kind of fundamental environmental overhaul or transformation, and hence, environmental considerations would rarely be a factor in determining *which* products would be made, or *whether* particular products were made at all (Schot and Fischer 1993). None the less, respondents emphasized that this did not mean that significant advances in green marketing were not achieved, but rather that these might not be immediately apparent or particularly visible, such as the setting up of lifecycle assessment procedures, 'auditing' or reduction of packaging and product inputs, and environmental assessments of suppliers. This generally conservative and behind-the-scenes approach to green marketing in the muted strategy firms was particularly evident in the understated role ascribed to the environment in positioning and communications policies. This RetailCo manager describes their understanding of why environmental themes were avoided in product marketing:

> [Product A is] not marketed as green and recycled which I can assure you would cause the sales to bomb . . . unfortunately that's still the case that the UK consumer thinks that green or recycled or whatever means lesser quality. So I think that the way to go for marketing is . . . putting out information like that [indicates information pack] . . . instead of just slapping a green label on the product.

Indeed, in some firms, such as MarketingSoc, managers suggested that they had increasingly played down the environmental attributes of their products out of concerns that it might predispose consumers to avoid purchase altogether. Thus, rather than attempting to use the environment to present an overtly *positive* corporate image and thereby motivate favourable purchase behaviour, if the environment was to have any strategic role at all in the development of corporate reputation, it was as a 'hygiene' factor (see Herzberg 1968), i.e. one which needed to be managed in order to avoid the development of any *negative* corporate associations, or stakeholder dissatisfaction.

Niche greening

A third strategic route identified as a viable option in the context of the green marketing backlash was that of maintaining a narrow strategic scope focused almost solely on the green niche. A strategy well documented in the green marketing literature (e.g. Peattie 1992, 1995), essentially niche greening represents a situation whereby the firm targets consumers with strong environmental preferences, and hence positions its products as green alternatives to conventional competitive offerings. According to green marketing logic, products should therefore offer unique environmental features, and communications should be based on emphasizing these green benefits. However, despite the sample including a number of social mission firms, only one (FinanceSoc) actually claimed to be specifically and primarily targeting a green niche, as these quotations from its CEO illustrate:

> Most of our savers are probably environmentally committed; actually traditionally they probably had to be because of the lower interest rates we used to pay out. So they did pay a premium.

> The environment does tend to be the main marketing platform . . . sometimes we actually lose prospective customers because they don't consider themselves green enough!

For this firm then, the problem of reaching the committed green consumer had largely been addressed, and indeed it had successfully defended its green niche for some fifteen years, i.e. before the major growth in green marketing in the late 1980s, during it, and even throughout the backlash period. In the main this had been made possible by aiming for steady, measured growth, and operating in a niche which had, until very recently, seen little if any serious competition. There had been no other niche greening firms competing in the same market, and according to the CEO, mainstream competitors were largely unwilling or unable to target committed green consumers:

> [Competitors] are inherently conservative, and even if they lent on ecological criteria, then [FinanceSoc] would always be attempting to seek out and support the more radical approaches.

However, for growth to continue, it was seen as necessary for the firm to expand its customer base beyond the green niche. Targeting less committed consumers not only allowed for greater market penetration, but also provided the opportunity to effect social change in some way and avoid 'preaching to the converted'.

Significantly though, two of the sampled social mission firms had actually moved progressively away from this kind of niche strategy, particularly given the changed context presented by the backlash. Indeed, the niche greening strategy was widely seen as increasingly vulnerable in most markets. The niche had been gradually squeezed by the incremental improvements offered by the muted greening firms, and the absence of expected growth in the green segment meant that such a strategy was only viable for small firms. As a director of MarketingSoc (which had shifted from a niche greening strategy to a muted greening one) commented:

> There has been a drop off in environmental concern. And it's not something you can build a business on easily in mainstream markets. There are

only small niche markets where you can build your company on the environmental friendliness of your product.

The green niching strategy then was still a viable alternative in the context of the backlash, but an increasingly less attractive one, particularly if growth was a key strategic goal. And certainly for larger, mainstream firms, the emphasis in the prescriptive green marketing literature on targeting the green niche might be seen as carrying little weight in the context in which they were placed. It appears to rely rather too much on managers' faith in the growth of this segment, in the face of embedded perceptions of discomfirmatory evidence in the marketplace. New strategic alternatives might therefore be required, such as the fourth and final strategic response identified, collaborative greening.

Collaborative greening

The collaborative greening response represented an acknowledgement by some organizations that the problems of the green marketing backlash were such that solitary approaches by individual organizations might have only limited potential to provide an effective strategic route forward. Thus, many green marketing problems were often located outside the boundaries of individual organizations:

> We were aware that unsubstantiated claims were a problem. We realized that a lot of the things that we were saying the *suppliers* couldn't substantiate (*emphasis added*).

In particular then, although product supply and distribution chains contained value-making activity, it was often here that environmental problems might be identified (Lamming and Hampson 1996; Hartman and Stafford 1998). Organizations had sought to experiment with joint efforts to ameliorate these problems, for example by working with suppliers to develop products with more fundamental environmental improvements than those previously supplied. Although the power relations in these relationships tended to be resource dependent, with 'persuasion' and 'pressure' on suppliers commonplace, there was certainly a realization that credible green marketing could only move forward if firms were willing to be supportive of their suppliers. This manager from a small supplying firm in CollabOrg commented:

> At the stage that we are at with things like certification in environmental issues, generally there needs to be, from a supplier's point of view, well you can't just turn on the tap and have *x* thousand certified products available overnight. So one issue is supporting suppliers and taking some of their products slowly and building it up for them.

Moreover, collaboration also with competitors, purchasers or environmental groups has been identified in the literature as a potentially important means of developing and/or accessing green marketing resource and competence not otherwise readily available (Hartman and Stafford 1997, 1998; Polonsky and Ottman 1998). In the case of alliances with environmental groups, managers from CollabOrg generally emphasized the high degree of consumer trust in charities and pressure groups, given their own credibility problems in the backlash period. Therefore, as Mendleson and Polonsky (1995) have argued, programmes based on securing certification from environmental groups might be seen as an effective response to consumer cynicism and mistrust. This marketing manager from a corporate member of CollabOrg for example explains the benefits derived from collaboration with their NGO partner:

> We could determine our own policy about what we believe is an acceptable [component] source, but there isn't the same degree of credibility there. So if you like, [NGO partner] adds an element of credibility: a body that is recognized perhaps as having, in the eyes of end users, the consumer, some degree of detachment to it; and [customers] saying, 'Hang on, if they're part of it, if this is an approved thing being endorsed by [NGO partner], obviously they're not going to be swayed by commercial interests.' Whereas if we came up with our own label . . . then it wouldn't carry any weight.

Such groups were also presented as a good source of environmental skills, as even were competitors. In fact collaboration with competitors on environmental issues was seen as rather less problematic in the context of the backlash, since green issues had become more about guarding the corporate reputation than seeking a differential marketing advantage. Accordingly, collaboration could help in establishing a stronger voice with which to present defensible environmental positions and arguments to other stakeholders. Moreover, when organized into some kind of buying group, it could also help to provide the requisite 'clout' with which to effect some degree of greening within the product supply chain, as this CollabOrg respondent suggests:

> [Suppliers] have actually been pretty co-operative, considering we are to some extent changing the way that they choose to do things . . . Why? They know who buys the [product] . . . and you've got some very significant buying power in [the buying group] already, and that is buying all the time. They can't ignore it. They can't afford to ignore it.

Finally, it should be noted though that rather than being a corporate-wide strategy in itself, for the firms sampled here, the collaborative greening response tended to be overlaid across one of the other three strategic orientations. Hence, it might be seen as a means by which: a passive greening firm could respond to the demands of key stakeholders; a muted greening firm could work gradually and guardedly towards improved environmental solutions; or a niche greening firm could retain and promote its green credentials.

Towards a grounded green marketing theory?

Given such approaches to green marketing as represented by informants from the organizations studied, there appears to be a strong case for reframing green marketing theory in the light of these empirical findings. In this way it might be possible to move towards a more grounded understanding of the phenomenon. For example, Fineman and Clarke's (1996) empirical study of industry responses to green stakeholders revealed that consumers generally tended to have less impact on the environmental responses of firms than did campaigners, regulators and internal champions. The evidence in the current study was generally supportive of this finding, with green marketing programmes apparently being more substantially motivated by a desire to minimize the threat or impact of environmental legislation or pressure group attention (especially in conventional or collaborative organizations) or to reflect the ideals of the leader/powerful factions (especially in social mission companies) than to take advantage of explicit market opportunities. In fact, the market as presented in terms of a consumer backlash, was actually perceived to be just as much a *barrier* to green marketing as it was a driver. In this sense, prescriptive, non-empirical models of green marketing strategy and marketing such as those presented by Peattie and Ratnayaka (1992) and Simintiras *et al.* (1997) are correct in their attention to describing the range of green driving forces, although perhaps overly emphatic in the role accorded to green consumers in pushing forward the issue. Moreover, although useful as a starting point in understanding possible approaches, off-the-peg typologies as presented by Peattie and Ratnayaka (1992) among others, appear to fail in mapping the complexity of green strategy in practice as represented by organizational members. Clearly, informants saw green marketing strategies as changing, evolving and emerging as their firms experimented and learned about the complexities of various issues, and about the role and reactions of various stakeholders. Therefore, organizations can probably be better understood as operating more than just a single strategy, but rather experimenting with a number of approaches as they attempt to adapt to the shifting business environment (Mintzberg 1990, 1991).

Overall then, it was evident from this study that managers saw the key strategic decisions of green marketing to be not so much locked within the marketing department itself, but within interactions with other constituencies, particularly those in other organizational functions, those in the product supply chain and powerful stakeholders external to the organization. In the case of the former, the perceived strategic importance of the environment was found to be highly dependent on the championing of certain policy entrepreneurs across organizational divisions, particularly in the absence of unequivocal support from the market (Dillon and Fischer 1992; Drumwright 1994; Fineman 1996, 1997; Fineman and Clarke 1996). Such internal selling of green initiatives might only rarely be initiated from those in marketing functions, often rendering the task highly formidable, unless activated from the executive suite or other powerful centres in the organization.

A second issue of importance regarding organizational interactions is that of value chain constituents. Since environmental value and/or costs are likely to be associated with various different stages in the value chain, consideration of the full environmental impact of any given product needs to extend beyond the boundaries of the individual firm (Peattie 1992). Hence, environmental management practices such as cradle-to-grave stewardship and lifecycle analysis inevitably involve the individual firm in taking account of upstream and downstream activities in the supply chain (Lamming and Hampson 1996). This suggests a significant extension of the green marketing decision-making domain beyond the individual firm and its marketing department (Fuller 1999).

This seemed to suggest to many firms that alliances might be an important strategic option, either with other supply chain members (Cramer and Schot 1993; Shrivastava 1995a, 1995b) or with competitors (Varadarajan and Rajaratnam 1986; Hamel *et al.* 1989; Jarillo and Stevenson 1991; Bucklin and Sengupta 1993). Whilst radical greening initiatives appeared to be impeded by a mixture of apathy, inertia, uncertainty-reduction and conservatism, the incremental development of environmental products by existing industry members was argued by respondents to provide the stability for long-term and gradual environmental improvements (Cramer and Schot 1993; Lamming and Hampson 1996). The adoption of an alliance strategy to address such issues might then be a reasonably efficient and effective manner of generating leverage through the supply chain, although this is clearly reliant upon existing inter-organizational power differentials, as well as the level of influence of environmental protagonists upon the industrial relationships (Drumwright 1994). Effective response to powerful green stakeholders appeared to be seen as an important factor in driving firms to collaborate with NGOs, as in the CollabOrg initiative. As with other forms of alliance, this could provide access to environmental expertise (Hartman and Stafford 1997) and in addition, perhaps more importantly, help to co-opt what might otherwise be sharp and very public critics of the firm (Fineman and Clarke 1996). Indeed, there appeared to be some consensus amongst the sample of corporate respondents that working with powerful stakeholders – especially regulators and pressure groups – in a proactive manner might be preferable to a responsive strategic mode since it allowed for some possibility of shaping the business context (Sethi 1979; Freeman, 1984).

On the basis of these observations, interpretations and insights, it would appear then that from a theoretical perspective, the practice of green marketing is perhaps most appropriately conceptualized in terms of a network of internal and external interactions. This assertion, however, stands in sharp contradiction to most of the existing green marketing literature which tends to focus on the atomized organization (denying external interactions), and treating it as a monolithic entity (denying internal interactions). However, not only does an interactionist model appear to best reflect the reality of green marketing practice as observed in this study, but it also accommodates well 'deeper' green perspectives on organizations which highlight such issues as systems structure, interdependence and reciprocity (see Stead and Stead 1992; Shrivastava 1994, 1995a, 1995b). Hence, I would suggest that the best theoretical perspectives on green marketing are likely to be those such as the networks model of marketing exchanges and stakeholder theory, both of which accommodate such interactions fairly successfully.

The central proposition of the networks model is that firms' marketing exchanges can best be studied within the context of the broad pattern of interrelationships of which the individual firm is but a single element (Easton 1992; Hakansson and Snehota 1997a, 1997b). This model, however, has been accorded only limited attention in the green marketing literature to date, reflecting perhaps both the continued focus of marketing theory on individual transactions rather than relationships (Gummesson 1987) and the fact that the theoretical foundations of the networks model have little or nothing to say about the role of the environment in these relationships (McDonagh 1996). It does, however, help to conceptualize green marketing issues as pertaining not simply to individual firms but to whole systems of interrelated exchanges. Environmental impacts are not simply the result of individual exchanges, but of the behaviour of input and output chains (Cramer and Schot 1993; Peattie 1995; Shrivastava 1995a; Lamming and Hampson 1996; Fuller 1999) and of competitors (Schot 1992; Peattie 1995; Shrivastava 1995b), among others. Indeed, executives in this study repeatedly stressed that the intensity of green marketing policies was dependent on the extent of supplier and customer support, 'competitive pressures' and whether or not there was 'a level playing field' in the marketplace.

There are, however, relationships which are critical to green marketing and which the networks model does not appear to accommodate very satisfactorily. These are those within the organization (especially those including parties not integral to the exchange itself) and those with organizations involved in non-economic exchanges and other relationships with the organization (e.g. pressure groups, regulators, the media, etc.). In this respect, the stakeholder theory of the organization is a more appropriate model with which to conceptualize green marketing. Although the stakeholder model has been most commonly associated with the social responsibility and social performance literatures, there is a growing body of literature associated specifically with organizational greening (e.g. Stead and Stead 1992; Fineman and Clarke 1996). However, the usefulness of this theoretical framework to green marketing in particular is still noticeably underdeveloped beyond some consideration of the pressure for greening associated with these groups and exhortations to involve (at least some of) them in the green marketing policy process (see Charter 1992; Peattie and Charter 1994; Mendleson and Polonsky 1995; Wasik 1996).

Perhaps the greatest strength of the stakeholder model though is that it not only allows for consideration of formal and informal relationships between constituencies internal and external to the organization, but can also take account of the relative power, influence and expectations of these constituencies on the behaviour of the organization and its managers (Donaldson and Preston 1995; Fineman and Clarke 1996; Johnson and Scholes 1997). This offers considerable conceptual space for green marketing theory since, as has been shown, green marketing practice as experienced by organizational members can largely be explained in terms of the influence of internal and external stakeholders, and the ability of the former to mobilize and mediate the latter to further particular goals. Hence, it can be reasonably argued that stakeholder theory provides a good descriptive model of a range of green marketing behaviours.[2]

Whilst it is a relatively uncontroversial assertion to suggest that the networks model of marketing and stakeholder theory appear to offer significant promise for advancing green marketing theory, the implications are significant. First, it means that the scope of green marketing is considerably greater than often envisaged by practitioners and researchers, providing enormous opportunity (and also not inconsiderable problems) for further work in the area. Second, it means that much of the existing literature is rather limited in its relevance to much of what appears to be going on in contemporary organizations. And third, it is clear that future research efforts should endeavour to develop much more around and within these models. Saying that, by reframing green marketing in this interactionist way, it may even be possible to use elements from these frameworks to devise an entirely new theoretical dictum. However, it is not my intention to do so here. After all, I have but provided a snapshot of contemporary green marketing practice in order to develop insights into its moral dimensions. Hence, it is sufficient for my ends to leave that particular discussion at this juncture, and to return to it in more detail in Chapter 9 when I go on to discuss possible directions for future research. For the time being, it is more important to move on to discuss the central concern of the book, morality.

Green marketing and morality

In Chapter 2, I introduced and discussed two principal domains of morality in marketing, namely macro- and micromarketing. These are returned to now in order to summarize and assess the moral dimension of green marketing as observed in the sampled organizations, and as perceived and presented by respondents. Particular attention is paid to providing insight on societal marketing, and to assessing findings in the context of 'shallow' versus 'deep' perspectives on green marketing. Such a distinction is derived from the two broad traditions within the environmental ethics literature of 'shallow' (or 'reform') ecology and 'deep' ecology. According to Naess (1989), the basic distinction between these two schools is as follows. 'Shallow ecology' tends to reflect a concern with fighting against resource depletion and pollution (the symptoms of environmental decline) for human-centred reasons (i.e. it is *anthropocentric*). Alternatively, the philosophy of 'deep ecology' contends that the environment has a right to exist and flourish in its diversity irrespective of humans and human needs (i.e. it is *ecocentric*), and that the structural and systemic causes of environmental decline should be tackled. Translated into green marketing, these ethical positions centre attention on: a promotion of environmentalism in the context of continued commitment to profitability, consumption and market growth in the 'shallow green' movement; and more fundamental ideological change, new values, sustainable goals and a transformed corporate morality in the 'deep green' movement.[3]

It should be remembered also that this study has taken an analytical perspective on morality in green marketing, centred around the notion that morality can be examined in the sense that it has or does not have meaning for organizational members. Therefore, it is timely to reiterate here that this has entailed some bracketing of my own normative frame of reference in order that the conceptions and interpretations of my respondents might be better foregrounded. Hence, I have attempted as much as possible to allow respondents to apply notions of morality to green marketing as *they* saw fit, rather than introducing my own categories, definitions, or judgements.

Green marketing as a moral subject

In the main, I approached questions regarding the morality of green marketing as a practice in itself through establishing how individuals and organizations integrated green marketing programmes within concepts of social responsibility, i.e. to what extent was the provision of environmental benefits through marketing activities presented as a moral duty or role for the organization? Substantial variations were observed in this respect. First, respondents in a number of organizations (particularly managers in some CollabOrg members and in ManufactureCo, as well as a number of shopfloor employees) saw the marketing of green products as divorced entirely from notions of social responsibility. Here, the environment was not presented in terms of being a social concern for the business or a moral dilemma to contend with, but merely as another element in the daily routine of supplying timber or sewage treatment technologies, or whatever (see Jackall 1988). Hence, only if customers demanded environmental attributes, and/or they could be delivered at a greater profit than would be forthcoming otherwise, would they be supplied. Protestations of ethically-driven greening (e.g. by colleagues or other organizations) were often seen by these respondents as attempts to hoodwink a gullible public, and 'to jump on to a bandwagon' of environmental concern. This might be regarded as consistent with the Friedman (1970) position, namely that it is only through pure self-interest that the firm satisfies its social responsibilities of profit maximization. Questions of ethics beyond the standard 'rules of the game' are thus merely diversions, and ultimately unethical in themselves.

The Friedman argument, however, does not capture the whole breadth of this type of response. Articulating a different ideology, but ending up with curiously similar conclusions, a minority of these respondents (all from shop floor positions) presented a different argument. This centred on the claim that environmental problems were either not properly, or not realistically, within the remit of businesses and of the market, and therefore should be handled at a governmental or even at a personal level. These self-avowed 'sceptics' or 'pessimists' might be generally equated with some of the 'deep' green politics writers who see green marketing as essentially an oxymoron (see Gorz 1980, 1989; Irvine and Ponton 1988). The fact that these informants were of low hierarchical status might be seen as indicative that such employees tend to be sceptical of the corporate green line. Managers in contrast might progress through some degree of socialization process whereby role and organizational attachments begin to impact upon their green moralities (Fineman 1996).

In the case of RetailCo, and a large proportion of CollabOrg members, enlightened self-interest positions were articulated by respondents, such that it was argued that environmental benefits should only be pursued when associated with economic benefits. Central to this position, however, was the contention that the financial interests of the firm and its social responsibilities were unlikely to be in conflict (see Abratt and Sacks 1988, 1989). Whilst in general this centred on denying that costs were likely to increase through 'responsible' greening programmes, there were also suggestions that pragmatic responses to green stakeholders would be sure to benefit the firm in the long run through brand building, reputation enhancement, stakeholder satisfaction, etc. However, this ignored any recognition that the costs of environmental programmes might spiral once the limited number of cost-reducing, win–win solutions were exhausted (Walley and Whitehead 1994), as well as green arguments that current costing procedures fail to internalize true environmental costs (Bebbington and Gray 1992; Gray *et al.* 1993). As we have seen, this very upbeat and positive view of the commercial benefits of greening was closely associated with the need to legitimatize environmental projects in the eyes of otherwise reluctant and suspicious organizational constituencies.

Respondents from a number of other (particularly social mission) organizations were more comfortable with ascribing the introduction of green marketing programmes to ethical motives of social responsibility. These were probably closest to the visions of 'deep' green marketing presented in literature (see Kilbourne 1995), although in most cases a strong 'shallow' element prevailed. In the main, this distinctly moralized green marketing appeared to correspond with strong signals from the top of the organization, indicating that the adoption of a firm voluntary stand on the environment was defensible without concomitant commercial justification (Fineman 1996). Indeed, to some extent, for these respondents the vagaries of customer demand were seen as an unstable platform on which to build green strategies compared to a moral impulse from within, particularly given the distortions in the market brought on by the backlash. This social mission company manager sets out his view:

> We recognize that environment is a very low priority for most people . . . and most consumers will opt for the cheapest, or what gives them the right combination of quality and price, and won't take much notice of environmental criteria . . . although there is a lot of scope for corporate responsibility in that [retailers] put out on the shelves what they want to sell . . . in many cases it's just as a company that's what we stand for – to do things in a certain way, to have a regard for environmental principles. And I'm sure we lose orders on that basis.

Organization size, bureaucratization and professionalization appeared to be important factors here, for these brought with them the need to couch greening in more formal, dispassionate discourses rather than in personal, emotional and informal terms (Jackall 1988; Fineman 1996, 1997). Hence in RetailSoc, the largest social mission company sampled, increasing professionalization as a retail organization had meant that social responsibility was increasingly presented in terms of a brand value rather than as a moral principle. For example, environmental initiatives would be justified on grounds of positioning rather than ethics, as this quote from an internal management briefing testifies:

> Through the provision of customer bring-to recycling points and internal recycling schemes, [RetailSoc's] positioning as the responsible retailer is enhanced in the eyes of the consumer.

Therefore, managers emphasized how, rather than deploying resources for social objectives according to any ethical decision, the decision should principally be based on prevailing stakeholder demands – and in particular consumer tastes – much as resources for economic objectives were. Respondents in the other companies claiming social responsibility meanwhile continued to explain such decisions in terms of the personal moralities of their leaders, and not responsiveness to customers and other stakeholders.

If, as has been argued, the main point of departure for the radical critiques of green marketing is a rejection of the pursuit of ever-expanding consumption (see Schumacher 1974; Irvine and Ponton 1988; Kilbourne *et al.* 1997), it is clear that only very few of these examples where green marketing was presented as a moral subject (perhaps only MarketingSoc and FinanceSoc) corresponded with a true 'deep ecology' position. Even the valuable effort to explore sustainable options represented by CollabOrg still had a long way to go before it could be considered as a means to sustainable growth. Its focus on a single product attribute (timber sources) meant that there was no attempt to consider the sustainability of end products as a whole since this would also have to include other components, production methods and distribution systems, etc. Hence, we might regard these other more common positions as distinctly 'shallow' in their conception.

Societal marketing concept

I claimed earlier in the book that one of my intentions was to attempt to flesh out the notion of the societal marketing concept (SMC). Although some discussion was presented in relation to the social mission companies, I shall widen the discussion here to explore the extent to which any of the approaches analysed had embraced the SMC. Certainly of the sampled *firms*, only perhaps the small social mission firms MarketingSoc and FinanceSoc (and to a lesser extent Manufacture-Soc) might be in a position to argue that *all* of the goods and services provided by them had taken into consideration their overall social impacts and the long-run welfare of consumers and other citizens. This was clearly due to the personal convictions or conscience of their leaders, informed as they were by previous (often continued) engagements with environmental groups and organizations.

Certainly these were not simple marketing orientations since the managers involved freely asserted that these positions would be maintained *regardless* of immediate consumer needs or wants. Environmental product attributes were in the main non-negotiable and thus open only to selling (or even hiding) rather than marketing. The element of long-run consumer welfare that is added by the SMC therefore was introduced here in a very different manner than that of short-run or immediate satisfaction. The small social mission company managers had decided that it was they (by dint of their wide experience in the area) who could adjudicate on what in fact was in the best long-run interests of society.

In contrast, RetailSoc, the largest social mission company, had also taken account of long-run consumer interest, but did so by canvassing the opinions of these customers, as well as to some extent those of pressure groups and other external constituencies. Thus, the SMC in this context was given a more distinct marketing emphasis since the social concerns that were incorporated were customer-driven. This is close to Prothero's (1990) position on the SMC and green marketing, where the 'metaneeds' of increasingly sophisticated consumers are seen as driving the SMC. Also, Kotler's (1972) original formulation of the SMC stresses the need to focus on those issues highlighted by consumer groups in order to maintain the firm's legitimacy.

Deciding what exactly is in the long-run interests of consumers or of society, and what constitutes a 'salutary' or 'desirable' product as opposed to merely a 'pleasing' one (that is, products which are in consumer's long-term interests rather than satisfying only their short-term desires) is not, however, a straightforward task (Kotler 1972; Abratt and Sacks 1989). The efforts in the social mission companies to focus either on the beliefs of managers or of customers represent two means of attempting to do so, but clearly the business–NGO collaboration route discussed in Chapter 6 represents a third. Indeed, this approach might more readily accommodate the SMC, due to the way in which it opens up the firm to dialogue and participation with non-economic stakeholder groups. Stakeholders such as pressure groups can act as an important moral voice or social control for corporations and therefore can play a critical role in determining and effecting the long-run interests of consumers and society (Smith 1990; Fineman 1997). This can not only counteract corporate hegemony over discourses of rationality and truth (Tombs 1993) but also can avoid the wholesale capitulation to (real or rhetorical) short-term consumer desires.

In the end though, the adoption of a societal marketing orientation must lead to the firm imposing some restriction on the choice of products available to consumers according to perceived social and environmental consequences (Prothero 1990). As Kotler (1972) himself contends, merely 'pleasing' products should be phased out despite their appeal to consumers. Certainly the restriction of consumer choice was an element intrinsic to the CollabOrg initiative, as some respondents (albeit a minority) attested, e.g.: 'being in the group isn't about offering choice'; 'customers won't have a choice', etc. However, corporate respondents other than those in the small social mission companies chose not to articulate issues of consumer choice in this way, contrasting as they did with embedded discourses of consumer sovereignty, evident both in the present sample and elsewhere (see Du Gay and Salaman 1992; Knights *et al.* 1994). Hence, if prompted to consider the impacts on consumer choice, they would fall back on any available evidence suggesting that in fact they were driven by 'customer pressure' from 'out there' despite the general perception of limited green purchase behaviour. This 'pressure' might be as little as a few letters. 'If we saw ten letters on the same subject, we would respond to that', one manager claimed to me. Even this quantity, he suggested, could be mobilized to represent an important and growing consumer trend. However, at other times, and for other managers, such 'pressure' could also be interpreted as an insignificant but bothersome campaign co-ordinated by one of the 'fanatical' pressure groups. It was clear to me that in many respects this reluctance to acknowledge the full implications of the SMC owed much to the impoverished role of morality embedded in green marketing practices. It is to this that the discussion now turns.

Morality in green marketing practice

As was stated earlier in the book, the main concerns of this study with respect to green marketing practice were in terms of the moral meaning experienced, understood and communicated by organization members. I examined this issue mainly by assessing whether individuals involved in the green marketing process experienced any sense of morality, and if so, what form this might take and to what subject it was applied. Overall, my findings revealed that in relation specifically to the environment, the personal moralities of those involved in the green market-ing process were, on the whole, understated and pragmatic. Respondents were found to bear much more similarity to Fineman's (1997) 'unimpassioned' UK automotives executives than Drumwright's (1994) 'evangelistic' and 'crusading' US middle managers. This lack of moral engagement crossed most organizational categories and hierarchical levels, with the most notable exception being, perhaps unsurprisingly, at the top of the small social mission companies. Here managers appeared to have moved towards a more 'principled' level of moral development (see Kohlberg 1969), where the environmental welfare of others was seen as a powerful motivating force and where organizational decision making was ruled by their own personal ethical principles. Despite such strongly moral positions, these personally committed executives had not, however, tended to adopt a 'strong' culture approach which rested upon disseminating their green values through the organization (see for example Peters and Waterman 1982). Consequently, individual members were thereby allowed to develop relatively dispassionate and detached moralities of their own. Hence, to a large extent, greening in these companies was significantly meaningful in a moral sense only to a small slice of the organizational membership (in this case the top). Equally, in the conventional companies, only small pockets of moral engagement with the environment were in evidence, such as where individuals had direct contact with green pressure groups, since this could prompt feelings of unease or guilt in relation to the environment (Fineman 1996).

Overall then, few individuals amongst the total sample of respondents presented the process of marketing environmental products (compared to non-environmental products) as distinctly moral in character, beyond conventional standards of acceptable behaviour. In this sense, they were to some extent exhibiting what Bird and Waters (1989) refer to as a 'moral muteness' both within, and towards, their work. That is, they tended to avoid any description of their work in terms of 'idealistic' or 'emotive' moral talk, and spoke instead of the environment as a technical or functional area of individual expertise or corporate cost/value, such that individuals involved were 'just doing my job' in much the same way as those in other areas. Whilst for a minority (mainly social mission company managers), the involvement of their organization in providing products with green features was an 'added bonus', most were relatively untouched. As one manager from ManufactureCo summed it up: 'I don't think that making environmental products will make you more environmentally conscious . . . you do tend to get blasé about it.' Clearly this represented a situation broadly in line with the 'shallow' as opposed to the 'deep' green marketing paradigm – a not altogether surprising finding. But if individuals themselves were not morally engaged in green marketing, where were notions of morality observed to impact upon the green marketing process? According to my investigations, it was communications, codes, and products that were the main subjects of moral meaning in this respect.

Communications

At a basic level, green communications were the most common issue to which moral considerations of both a positive and a negative nature were considered relevant. In the case of positive moral considerations, the incidence of distinctly moral themes appearing in green communications was in evidence, but was far from extensive. Where it did occur – such as in the couching of environmental programmes in terms of a philanthropic gesture of the organization – this tended to be where corporate morality was perceived to be of importance to the particular audience. Similarly, where it did not appear to be occurring, either the audience was perceived as being uninterested (or even antagonistic to ethical protestations) – such as with internal communications to corporate colleagues – or a significant possibility of subsequently attracting unwanted attention from more hostile stakeholders was identified. Hence, it appeared that organizations had generally opted to develop different communication vehicles for different audiences, allowing for careful control of the moral claims and perspectives carried by them. Where moral themes were used, the most common strategy was to focus on the corporation rather than on individual products, a finding consistent with major studies of green communications in the US (see Iyer and Banerjee 1993; Iyer *et al.* 1994; Banerjee *et al.* 1995). Indeed, to the extent that green communications might be regarded as part of the wider process of maintaining legitimacy with, and/or fostering trust amongst, various stakeholder groups, this was much as expected. Specific products might well represent good examples for the organization to use in justifying its legitimate status in society, but it is at the level of the organization (Gray *et al.* 1993), industry (Patten 1992; Simmons and Wynne 1993; Tombs 1993) or institutional framework (Puxty 1986; Jennings and Zandbergen 1995) that self-legitimation is likely to be primarily centred.

In terms of 'negative' moral concerns over questionable green claims, many individuals highlighted the importance of being 'ethical' in this respect, although most organizations appeared to exhibit little real consistency. Some claims were obviously being policed far more vigilantly than others. Indeed, the attention accorded by managers to the ethics of certain claims appeared to some extent to be a function of the level of attention given to the organization by those stake-holders perceived as the most important and powerful. Hence, questions of morality again entered the marketing process in response to threats to legitimacy. As a result, however, ostensibly 'ethical' questions were frequently experienced as exercises in appeasement or conciliation. One particularly graphic example of how the truthfulness of green claims tended to be viewed in terms of legitimacy rather than ethics emerged in an environment-related meeting at one of the sampled conventional companies. It had been discovered that the company's environmental policy statement had been printed on paper that contained an incorrect, and by all accounts accidentally printed, claim. This stated that the paper used was of '100%' recycled material when in fact it was actually of a lower percentage. The small, but in PR terms potentially very dangerous possibility that the mistake would be discovered put the managers responsible into a position where there was perceived to be no choice at all but to destroy the originals and re-print them; this despite the obvious environmental (and economic) cost. However, so critical was the issue of perceived credibility, that questions of right or wrong hardly even surfaced in the discussion.

Codes of practice

In addition to claims, most of the organizations in this study had adopted (or were in the process of adopting) some kind of code of practice in relation to the environment – CollabOrg itself representing one particularly significant example of such codification. Some managers spoke proudly to me of having introduced environmental criteria into standard product development procedures, supplier assessment, or even product managers' job descriptions, suggesting a successful dissemination of environmental responsibility and duty. Whilst this most certainly had given rise in some instances to pro-environmental marketing behaviours, in many cases this represented little more than another box to tick, or another form to fill in. In practice then, these codes and criteria appeared to have had limited, if any, affective impact, in that they failed to provoke any palpable sense or feeling of environmental responsibility on the part of individuals (see Desmond 1998). As psychologists such as Kohlberg (1969) and sociologists such as Bauman (1989) have shown, the adoption of codes reflects a cognitive morality based on social accord and system maintenance rather than personal engagement, belief and/or moral impulse. In fact, in the main, deontological moralities of duty, responsibility and obligation were apparently directed not towards the environment, but towards the organization, profession, individual leaders or to those with whom the organization participated in economic exchanges (Watson 1994a). Accordingly, the most compelling normative behavioural standards were those such as 'responsible management', a 'professional approach', 'quality', and 'customer service' or 'customer expectations'. In the case of marketing exchanges, this was centred around notions of loyalty, reciprocity and trust between customers and suppliers – although as was argued in Chapter 6, such rationales were often used to justify or even mask power differentials and resource dependencies (Pfeffer 1981b; Frances and Garnsey 1996). Overall then, the attitudes and emotions associated with the working moralities of organization members (at least as presented in their discussions with me) appeared to be most genuinely centred on job-related and cultural characteristics that impacted upon personal and organizational performance. This was in preference to more abstract social issues, such as the environment, which were perceived to be divorced from the immediate economic realm of the organization, (Jackall 1988; Dahler-Larsen 1994; Watson 1994a).

Products

Finally, products themselves also appeared to be a terrain for some kinds of moral meaning. Certainly any lessening of the lifecycle environmental impacts of products through recycling, waste minimization, packaging reductions, energy efficiency, etc. was generally presented as a 'good' thing by most, if not all, of my respondents. However, it was mainly only in the top ranks of the small social mission companies that there was any clear assertion that this subsequently established these products as morally superior in the way that 'ethical' consumers might see them. In the majority of cases, such products were seen as no different conceptually from other product offerings: their green credentials were simply a matter of quality, differentiation or added value in the same way as other product attributes might be. Moreover, it was generally regarded as important that products with green attributes were not even depicted within the company as 'green', still yet 'ethical' products, because of likely resistance from various subcultural interests, particularly in the context of the perceived green marketing backlash as detailed earlier in this chapter.

For most respondents then the 'good'-ness of marketing outcomes was mainly good in the sense that all improvements in product quality were good. However, even this was dampened somewhat by respondents' resigned acceptance that few measures were beyond criticism in some respect. This equivocality regarding environmental impacts and the nebulous nature of the 'best' environmental solution was a cause of concern for many interviewees, particularly since they hampered organizational efforts to communicate in a positive fashion to external stakeholders. Analysis of the environmental impacts of products and processes in the larger, more bureaucratic organizations weighed heavily on techno-rationalist, utilitarian approaches such as environmental impact assessment and cost–benefit analysis, where 'measurability' was the critical issue. Indeed, for these companies, development of mechanisms for the measurement, or 'auditing', of environmental impacts was the basic first step in a so-called 'responsible' approach to green marketing. Ambiguity over outcomes was seen as clouding any consideration of right or wrong, perhaps unsurprising given embedded utilitarian frames of reference. Hence, much faith (and in many cases, resources) was invested in the development of more sophisticated assessment instruments and analyses, such as product lifecycle assessment, etc. Clearly, for policy to be decided, not only did lines have to be drawn somewhere, but they also had to be defensible to various stakeholders. Indeed, evidence suggests that lifecycle assessments have been very much used primarily to defend *existing* products against regulatory and competitive pressures rather than to actually develop greener processes or products (ENDS Report 264, 1997: 20).

In contrast, the social mission companies could be seen to have rather less faith in rational, quantified analyses of environmental impacts, stressing more deonto-logically based arguments of what was, or was not, acceptable in principle. As one manager from MarketingSoc argued:

> We're trying to demonstrate the principle . . . calculation [of environmental impacts] would be a bit meaningless, even if you could work it out.

None the less, CollabOrg was widely seen as presenting an attractive model since it removed the inherent ambiguity of assessment altogether by transferring the responsibility (though also the control) over to an external organization much trusted by the public (see Mendleson and Polonsky 1995). As many of my CollabOrg interviewees commented, the appeal of the alliance to businesses was that it set measurable and achievable targets and it provided the means by which clear statements of fact could be made and defended. Thus the inclusion of less quantifiable issues into the remit of the alliance, such as indigenous people's rights, etc., did not have to become a concern of corporate managers since it was covered by the guarantee of the quality of 'management' at source forests.

Conclusion

In this chapter, the findings relating to the three organizational approaches as presented in Chapters 4, 5 and 6 have been developed in order to present a clear analysis of green marketing practice and of its moral dimensions. The case study research strategy adopted in the study has allowed for a fairly detailed exam-ination of these issues in a diverse, albeit limited, series of contexts. A number of important conclusions can be reached.

First, the picture that emerges in relation to green marketing practice is principally one of adaptation in the face of continuing change. At the time that fieldwork was conducted, the environment had clearly fallen down the economic, political and social agendas since its peak in the late 1980s/early 1990s, and yet firms were still experiencing continued (and in aggregate terms, increasing) internal and external impetus towards greening. Also, the past strategies and tactics of firms – and the success or otherwise of these – were observed to have had substantial impact both on the market and on the current strategies pursued by the sampled organizations. The so-called 'backlash' to green marketing had led to the emergence of a range of strategic reorientations. Probably the most popular of these was 'muted greening', a strategy whereby environmental impacts were addressed, but products were positioned according to conventional product attributes. In some cases, 'passive greening' prevailed, although complete antipathy to greening appeared to be diminishing. A focus strategy of 'niche greening' that targeted small green niches was also increasingly seen to be problematic, although could be sustained in certain contexts. 'Collaborative greening' approaches were clearly increasing in importance and seemed to offer significant promise in the context presented by the backlash.

Second, it was mainly only in the small social mission companies that very profound green attributes were offered, and where environmental credentials were a crucial determinant of whether a product would, or would not, be marketed. In other cases, however, improved environmental features were found to be gradually introduced, often accompanied by increasingly sophisticated systems of assessment. These might be regarded as constituting a 'deep' green and a 'shallow' green approach respectively. Third, it can be argued that green marketing strategies and tactics might be best conceptualized from an interactionist perspective, i.e. with the organization viewed in terms of internal and external relationships. In particular, the stakeholder model of the firm, and to a lesser extent the networks model, have been shown here to provide effective frameworks for locating green marketing theory. These might be usefully brought to bear on future research, as discussed in Chapter 9.

Fourth, by adopting an analytical position on green marketing moralities, I was able to identify a range of moral positions adopted by respondents and organizations. This suggests certain limitations, even dangers, in assuming that the existence of green marketing behaviours is strongly linked to any particular ideological position. There could perhaps though be an association between the types of behaviour, or the manner in which they are conducted, and some combination of the organization's moral stance, the working moralities of its managers, existing cultural knowledge, and the enacted power and influence of stakeholders. Specification of this model might also be a fruitful avenue for research in the future, as discussed in the final chapter. The fifth significant finding is that the implementation of aspects of the societal marketing concept could take a variety of forms. Firms taking greatest consideration of social issues did so with an approach that appeared to bear little relation to conventional marketing theory, i.e. their orientations were principally of the 'product' or 'selling' type of orientation. The approach most in touch with Kotler's (1972) original SMC conceptualization then was that which concentrated on transparency and enhancing consumer sovereignty. However, it was shown that a more appropriate approach to societal marketing might be that which, in addition to transparency, was also based on more open dialogue and participation with polities (such as government and non-government organizations and special interest groups) without direct economic stakes in the firm.

Finally, moralities in the green marketing process were shown to be understated in relation to the environment itself, but less so in terms of procedures more directly related to personal and organization performance. The most compelling normative standards appeared to be qualities such as professionalism, responsibility, quality, customer service, and trustworthiness, etc. Even marketing elements such as communication, codes of practice and products were shown to be subject to only limited moral engagement. None the less, the ambiguity of the morality of marketing outcomes in relation to the environment remained a thorny problem, particularly for those companies attempting to utilize utilitarian ethical rules. Assessment by independent external organizations appeared to offer considerable promise in this respect – again something that will be returned to towards the end of the book.

In the next chapter then, the somewhat morally penurious picture of green marketing that I have presented here will be examined in more detail, with attention focused on how and why this might have occurred. In order to do so, the concept of *amoralization* is revisited and its dimensions are set out more explicitly. Following this, the possibility of the opposite process of *moralization* is considered, and the potential for a rather more 'moralized' green marketing will be discussed.

8   Amoralization, moralization, marketing and the natural environment

Introduction

In the last chapter, I described how morality in the green marketing processes within and around the case organizations tended to be considerably understated in respect to the environment itself, and was more strongly associated with procedural norms and practices that were directly job- and performance-related. I also suggested that this cultural dynamic could similarly be translated into marketing artefacts – policies, products and promotions, for example – under the mediating influence of both real and constructed stakeholder influences. Overall, this certainly represented something of a denial of moral meaning in the case organizations, at least as far as green marketing was concerned. This phenomenon I shall refer to here as *amoralization*. Basically, what I mean by amoralization is the removal of moral meaning from the green marketing process, or from the objects of green marketing; essentially it concerns the phenomenon whereby something (here, green marketing) is rendered an amoral subject.

In framing this discussion around the concept of amoralization, I may, I have to admit, be at risk of introducing a term which not only does not figure in most people's academic vocabularies, but which may also appear to have only limited association with debates couched more usually in terms of 'ethics' and 'social responsibility'. The decision to employ this particular term though has been a considered one, since it helps to communicate not only the essence of the phenomenon to which I am referring, but also the distinction I am seeking to draw between this and more conventional views of business ethics. As I explained in the introduction to this book, my intention has been to develop an interpretive and descriptive approach to understanding moral meaning, rather than normative or prescriptive insights into ethically 'good' or 'bad' decisions and behaviour.

Notwithstanding these points, since the crux of my discussion rests upon some kind of shared understanding of novel terminology, it is clearly worthwhile before proceeding further to set out a concrete definition of amoralization. The following is derived from the entry for 'moralize' in *The Shorter Oxford English Dictionary on Historical Principles* (vol. II, third edition, p. 1355). Amoralization can be thought of as the action or result of amoralizing:

Amoralize *v.* **1.** To interpret amorally; to point to the moral neutrality of; to not make (an event, etc.) the subject of moral reflection. **2.** *intr.* To refrain from moral reflection. b. *trans.* To change the condition or aspect of (a person or thing) by amoral discourse or reflection. **3.** To make amoral.

In many respects then, as I acknowledged in Chapter 3, amoralization is strongly related to Bauman's (1993) notion of adiophorization, i.e. the process whereby bureaucracy renders decisions 'adiophoric', or 'of a kind on which ethical authorities do not feel it necessary to make a stand' (p. 30). However, the two terms are not directly analogous and it would be inappropriate to appropriate Bauman's terminology here. Specifically, Bauman (1993) presents adiophorization as an inevitable and absolute process: the only logical consequence of bureaucracy is moral indifference to all organizational goals, since it is the techno-rationalist process of the organizational system which is viewed as the arbiter of right and wrong. In contrast, by presenting green marketing in terms of amoralization, my intention is not to suggest that morality is *completely* denied in the modern organization, but rather that it is frequently marginalized from the environment in particular, or else enacted in a selective, contextual fashion. These issues shall be explored in more detail as the chapter proceeds.

I would suggest that the identification and examination of amoralization is probably the most significant finding of this study, and in many respects its main contribution to the literature. Therefore, the principal purpose of this chapter is to set out and explore the amoralization phenomenon in considerable detail. However, although I have not explicitly discussed it in any depth thus far, there is also a case for spending some time analysing the opposite phenomenon, namely *moralization*. Perhaps obviously, this might be regarded as the process whereby morality might be *given* meaning in the context of green marketing. Thus, the cultural dynamics and activities with which we are concerned might conceivably have positive or negative effects on the morality as perceived, experienced and understood by organization members.

In this chapter, the analysis of the results presented in Chapters 4, 5 and 6 will continue with an examination of these two constructs – amoralization and moralization – as they occurred in the context of green marketing in the case organizations. My main aim is to explain how and why each might have occurred in the specific organizational contexts examined, and to set out what the consequences for organizational theory and practice might be. Following this, some of the broader implications of amoralization and moralization will be discussed in order to build up a picture of whether, and how, morality in marketing (in its more general sense) might be managed. Finally, the main findings of the chapter are summarized and some conclusions are set out.

Amoralization and green marketing

One of the principal findings of this study is that the underlying cultural dynamics of green marketing, as enacted in the issue selling and impression management activities of green protagonists, can conspire to reframe the environment as an amoral subject. Hence, the majority of organizational actors were found to be rendered largely morally indifferent to the process and goals of green marketing, except where it impinged upon existing, job-related, working moralities (see also Fineman 1996). These working moralities contained within them implicit notions of what was right or wrong to do and think in the organization, centring on accepted, though often unstated, normative standards (Jackall 1988; Bird and Waters 1989; Watson 1994a; Fineman 1996). Hence, referring to this phenomenon as 'amoralization' is not meant to imply that it renders organizational life morally neutral overall, but rather that it removes any possibility of the environment and environmental product attributes *in particular* being accorded any moral meaning over and above other organizational issues which may lack such explicit social import.

There was evidence of this phenomenon, in various guises and to varying degrees, in all three of the organizational contexts examined. It was most pronounced in the case of the conventional companies since green marketing here appeared to be almost entirely castrated from moral meaning. In the collaborative organization, morality tended to be successively stripped from green marketing as communication proceeded from the pressure group through to the subcultural groups with greatest market interaction; as such it remained in certain small areas. In the social mission companies, amoralization was evident, although far less complete than in the other cases; in the main it related primarily to rank and file employees. Although these aggregate differences were perhaps not surprising given the differences in governance and espoused goal sets, there were important and quite striking similarities and variations in the manner in which amoralization appeared to be occurring. It is my intention to use this section then to examine the amoralization phenomenon as observed in the three contexts with respect to four considerations: agents (*who* is involved?); processes (*what* is involved?); explanations (*why* does it occur?); and implications (what are the *consequences* of its occurrence?).

Agents of amoralization

In almost all cases, the process of amoralization was observed to occur partly as a result of the behaviour of those individuals and groups who were the principal environmental reality definers in their organizations. These might therefore be reasonably regarded as 'agents of amoralization'. Such agents could be seen to abet and sustain this process either by active participation through horizontal (Drumwright 1994) and upward (Dutton and Ashford 1993) issue selling tactics (in conventional and collaborative organizations), or by passive acquiescence to individual sensemaking activities (Weick 1995) and the subsequent failure to disseminate moral frames of reference across subcultural divisions (in the social mission companies). Either way it was not entirely clear whether all of those involved were wholly conscious either of the process, or of their role in it.[1]

In Chapter 4, it was shown that the main agents of amoralization in conventional companies were policy entrepreneurs, or environmental champions.

Whilst it could be reasonably claimed that these individuals had taken on their role of establishing the environment within the marketing process more for career advancement than for satisfaction of personal green commitment, of more interest were the recipes for success associated with such protagonists. With greening in their organizations generally viewed as a potentially 'radical' introduction into the corporate milieu, with its associations of anti-corporatism and distinctly 'alternative' worldviews, it was suggested that the likelihood of successful selling generally relied on protagonists' abilities to manage new, uncontroversial understandings. My argument is that these tactics sustained processes of amoralization, since the policy entrepreneurs clearly regarded a more moral conception of the environment, and of green marketing, as a serious handicap in advancing the green agenda within their organization. Generally shallow and instrumental environmental values were thus disseminated through the organization.

A similar picture emerged in the case of business–NGO collaboration in Chapter 6. In this case though, the process of amoralization was not so much associated with a single set of individuals but with series of such groups, or subcultures, involved across the range of organizations in the alliance. It was shown in the previous chapter that this feature can be regarded as a consequence not only of marketing being inherently a boundary spanning function, but also of green marketing being an interactionist phenomenon. Accordingly, I have suggested that the role of these agents in shaping amoral conceptions of the environment can be ascribed to a more general process of cultural mediation. Successive iterations of such mediation were shown to gradually strip away layers of moral meaning. Again, this was seen by those involved as a necessary process in order to implement the alliance and to thereby develop greener marketing practices and procedures. In this instance, the process of amoralization did not appear to be complete, and moral conceptions of the environment were observed to remain to some extent in certain quarters.

In the social mission companies considered in Chapter 5, environmental reality definers were observed to occupy more senior positions. Whilst this might be expected given the greater historical preoccupation with social issues in these organizations, it could also be partly a result of their smaller size and hence less extensive division of labour (i.e. they would not be in a position to employ a lower ranking specialist). Here, the agents of amoralization did not necessarily deliberately enact the process which led to amoralization in the same way as in the other cases. However, their focus on individual moralities did have the effect of failing to morally engage other organization members with respect to the environment. In RetailSoc, this occurred due to the prominence given by policy entrepreneurs to consumers' environmental convictions rather than those of staff. Hence, the moral imperative was to respond to consumer desires rather than engender internal green commitment. In the other social mission companies, explanations could be found in the strong attachment of environmental guardianship to the companies' leaders, provoking little moral commitment (and even sometimes resistance) from the lower ranks.

Processes of amoralization

Having identified who was driving the amoralization dynamic, it is possible now to turn towards considering the processes in which it was manifested. In Chapters 4, 5 and 6, I presented various cultural dynamics of green marketing as contributing to this phenomenon. Because of the exploratory nature of the study, thus far I have set these out so as to maximize their utilization to the analysis, or story, associated with the particular approach considered in each of the chapters, rather than to develop one single line of theory. However, from the point of view of developing more general and integrated theoretical insights, it is important now to group these dynamics into the more coherent superordinate categories and constructs which have emerged from second-order analysis of the data, and from more abstract reasoning. In all, I would suggest that four principal processes of amoralization can be identified. These are: *morality boundaries* – the construction of barriers limiting the moral status of the environment; *appropriation of discourse* – the use of, and value attached to, certain discourses in communicating greening; *mobilization of narrative* – the application of different narratives to make sense of green marketing; and *depersonalization* – the avoidance of personal moral responsibility for the environment. Table 8.1 is a summary table of how each of these elements was manifested in the three organizational types. The findings presented in the table are elaborated upon in more depth in the discussion which follows.

Table 8.1 Elements of amoralization across organizational types

Element of amoralization	Type of organization		
	Conventional	*Business–NGO*	*Social mission*
Morality boundaries	Functional	Situational	Personal; hierarchical
Appropriation of discourse	Privileged and hierarchical	Contested and mediated	Pluralistic
Mobilization of narrative	Borrowed	Evolved	Novel
Depersonalization	Depersonalization	'Split'	Personalization

Morality boundaries

In each of the three organizational contexts, there was substantial evidence of morality boundaries being constructed around what was or was not considered to be open for 'ethical' or 'moral' reflection, consideration, debate or decision. Thus, each organizational type provided evidence of what Bauman (1993) would call adiophorization, i.e. the creation of moral neutrality. By the same token though, since this was achieved through constructing understandings of exclusion and inclusion into the moral realm, this also meant that the opposite was achieved, i.e. the creation of moral meaning, albeit in marginal areas or in those deemed non-environmental and/or non-marketing. Overall then, the construction of morality boundaries had two main strands: the circumscription of distinctly moral conceptions of the environment into certain (minority) polities or arenas; and the construction of the environment as manifestly different from ethical issues amongst other (majority) polities.

Whilst these two strands could to some extent be identified in each organizational context, there were differences in the form that morality boundaries took. In the conventional firms, morality was presented as *functionally* specific. That is, whilst 'the environment' was perceived as one functional area, 'ethics' were ascribed to another. Morality then was presented as bounded or circumscribed into particular 'other' organizational functions, effectively representing a denial of moral status by the principal environment reality definers. Instead, corporate greening was constructed as a 'technical' issue that demanded 'technical' solutions (such as lifecycle analysis and auditing systems) rather than moral reflection and discussion (Fineman 1998). Ethical questions were usually presented as the responsibility of someone else (usually more senior) in the organization, another organizational area altogether, or else 'imponderable', and hence beyond the purview of businesses altogether.

In the collaborative organization, morality boundaries were drawn on *situational* grounds. That is, collaboration meetings with other environmental staff and NGO representatives presented a relatively rare situation, or forum, for surfacing or re-surfacing individual environmental commitment which might otherwise be stifled back in the conservative corporate climate. Finally, in the social mission companies, *personal* and *hierarchical* morality boundaries were identified. Here, only some individuals were perceived as legitimately committed in an emotional and moral sense to the environment through their roles, and these were invariably senior managers. There appeared to be no attempt on the part of these individuals to impose their own frames of reference on others, or to go to any significant lengths to seek 'converts' among their organizations. Changes in the values of green converts might, though, be regarded as an important element in developing forms of green marketing based upon personal moral conviction and cultures of social responsibility (Drumwright 1994; Menon and Menon 1997). In this sense then, these environmental protagonists were content with eliciting pro-environmental behaviours from others rather than seeking more fundamental attitudinal change.

Appropriation of discourse

Just as organization members were found to perceive and construct boundaries around what could be deemed morally significant, and where and who and in what situation this might relate to green marketing, so too were particular discourses found to be appropriated in order to frame understandings of green marketing. Techno-rationalist discourses of 'commercial logic' were widely used to describe environmental issues, whereas emotional, ethical or otherwise 'woolly' discourses were more rarely uncovered. Again, this varied in the way in which it occurred in the three organizational contexts, but in each case clearly played a key role in supporting aspects of amoralization.

In the conventional companies, it was widely understood that only 'rational', 'business' arguments of customers, profits and costs were considered useful in promoting the green agenda. Not only did this mean that rational–instrumental discourses of commercial logic, costs and/or customer satisfaction were appropriated to communicate environmental issues, but also that such discourses were privileged over what were referred to as the 'emotive' discourses utilized by the media or pressure groups. In particular, respondents emphasized that only arguments couched in terms of instrumental self-interest were considered useful in selling green marketing internally, and were generally proud to explain how they had ensured that corporate greening and economic efficiency went hand in hand in their organizations. This prevailing rhetoric of 'win–win' solutions overshadowed the potential for discussing competing motives for greening, such as moral conscience, social responsibility or ecological duty. It also reflected a denial that greening might eventually have to incur increased costs, or that the savings achieved through greening were not linked with greater expense elsewhere, e.g. the labour and administrative costs associated with the environment team (Walley and Whitehead 1994).

Some managers spoke of this in terms of 'dressing up' environmental discourse in language more appropriate to the marketing (and other organizational functions) context. An upshot of this was the wholesale avoidance of various *semantic suspects*, i.e. words and phrases which were perceived as likely to be regarded with suspicion by power interests within the organization. Here, words and terms with implicit connotations of morality were clearly suspect in this way. Accordingly, terms such as sustainability, biodiversity, ecology, etc. were shrewdly omitted from the management lexicon in order to avoid alienating important marketing constituencies. Occasionally they would surface in marketing communications to certain stakeholders, although usually in a form which promised little in practice, and invited little real emotion work from internal audiences, e.g. claims to be 'committed to the *principle* of sustainable development' (as opposed to the substance). Bird and Waters (1989: 73) refer to this as the 'moral muteness' of managers, such that:

> (Managers) talk as if their actions were guided exclusively by organizational interests, practicality, and economic good sense even when in practice they honour morally defined standards codified in law, professional conventions and social mores.

This appropriation of commercial discourses in the conventional organizations was supported by considerable symbolic action on the part of environmental protagonists. Much of this centred on attempts at image making and impression management (see Ashford *et al.* 1998) so as to ensure that there was congruence between the commercial themes of the green message and the 'responsible management' image of the messenger. In the main, cultural norms dictated that successful green marketing project management relied on a 'professional' and 'businesslike' manner, untainted by the stereotypical image of the environmentalist 'crank'. Hence the discourse-based amoralization required other cultural cues, such as dress, appearance and manner, in order to garner authenticity and credibility.

As for the collaborative organization, it might have been expected that amoralization would have been tempered by the presence of a green pressure group, since they are to some extent a moral conscience of corporations (Smith 1990; Fineman 1997). Certainly in field interviews, CollabOrg respondents from the NGO member used highly moralized language in relation to the environment, frequently framing their responses in terms of 'responsibility', 'integrity', 'duty', etc. However, the corporate respondents from CollabOrg suggested that this 'idealistic' representation had to be reframed in order to garner business credibility. Indeed, the NGO's attempt to maintain legitimacy as an alliance partner meant that perceptions of organizational identity had to be shaped in line with the perceived expectations of corporate partners (Pfeffer 1981a; Elsbach and Sutton 1992; Elsbach 1994). Accordingly, environmental discourse was to some extent contested in the collaborative organization, with the moralized language of the NGO and the amoralized language of the corporate partners representing distinctly different frames of reference.

Overall, however, it was clear to me that it was the utilitarian, techno-rationalist discourse typical of the corporate members which was ultimately predominant. Occasionally there was some evidence of a more moralized discourse being used by the corporate members, but at the same time, respondents emphasized how the need to secure vital project support from internal marketing and procurement constituencies meant that this had to be further dampened. Thus, the green marketing discourse was contested, though dominated by commercial themes, and mediated between different subcultural constituencies. Again, what this meant was that impressions had to be carefully managed in order to sell the greening issue, both internally and externally (Gardner and Martinko 1988; Ashford *et al.* 1998). Hence, green protagonists tended to expediently adjust their image in line with the perceived expectations of the selling context.

In the social mission companies, there were considerable variations in moral discourse. The moralized and emotional vocabularies used by leaders were not generally shared by other staff, and overall there was less evidence of a single common discourse attending green marketing activities. However, this apparent plurality of discourse was accompanied by some acknowledgement that, increasingly, privilege tended to be accorded to commercial themes characteristic of the conventional companies. In RetailSoc for example, the discourses of strategic adaptation and marketing orientation had begun to overwhelm the social agenda of the firm, such that it was presented as legitimate only to respond to those social issues identified as important by customers and other external stakeholders, rather than internal constituencies. Thus, a clear hierarchy of discourse had begun to emerge.

Mobilization of narrative

The third mechanism of amoralization concerns the way that green marketing protagonists tended to frame understandings in terms of organizational and marketing narratives. In the conventional companies, this took the form of borrowing existing and accepted organizational narratives. Both in internal and external communications, narratives such as the introduction of total quality and the paternalism of the firms' founders were used in order to apply 'normal' and uncontroversial meaning to greening. In this way, green marketing protagonists could negotiate the collective sensemaking and shared meanings which framed organizational interpretations of the environment (Boje 1991; Boyce 1995; Weick 1995), thereby steering organizational frames of reference away from the identification of greening as an unconventional, inappropriate or radical corporate activity. Indeed, it was apparent that different narratives would be mobilized according to particular contextual and political exigencies (Boje 1991). Such 'surfing' of multiple narratives allowed for some degree of control over organizational interpretations of events in order to reduce uncertainty, increase control, manage expectations or otherwise achieve political advantage in the organization (Boje 1991; Brown 1994, 1995b; Brown and Ennew 1995).

In the case of the collaboration, the appropriation of existing organizational narratives was also used to support the smooth facilitation of greening. Here though, the narrative would tend to be extended, developed or evolved in some way to acknowledge that collaboration between traditional adversaries was a break with the past, but at the same time, a break which was a natural next chapter in the story (Wilkins 1983). Again, the emphasis appeared to be mainly on presenting greening as a rational and linear development of existing corporate policies of customer satisfaction, total quality, etc.

In the social mission firms, some dexterity with narratives was also evident on the part of the principal environment reality definers. Often green marketing would be presented both internally and externally within a narrative which illustrated how novel and distinctive their organization and their particular approach was. Such difference was seen as necessitating the construction of new stories to communicate the firm's framebreaking perspective (Menon and Menon 1997) and to distinguish it from those of competing conventional firms (Martin *et al.* 1983). As suggested in Chapter 5, managers at these companies also suggested that they had often quelled these difference narratives, emphasizing instead a certain 'normality', much as with the conventional firms. Hence the mobilization of the novel narratives tended to be used judiciously in order to support different readings of the moral culture of the organization by various stakeholders.

Depersonalization

Finally, amoralization was also driven in part by the extent to which greening initiatives were constructed as being owned by, or a personal campaign of, particular individuals. In the conventional companies, there was a marked tendency to under-emphasize any personal interest in the environment. By denying owner-ship or guardianship of the environment, individuals could avoid difficult, even dysfunctional, interpersonal confrontation which might have been viewed as inefficient, inappropriate and far removed from the 'rational' decision making model (Bate 1984; Bird and Waters 1989). The key message that came from informants then was that advancement of the green agenda certainly required substantial 'championing' (Drumwright 1994), but to avoid personal marginal-ization or potential stigmatization, this had to be disassociated from any overtly moral personal agenda (Dutton and Ashford 1993). Personal convictions then were, on the whole, understated, pragmatic and aligned to espoused corporate policy. Thus, depersonalization, and its attendant denial of personal responsibility for the environment, was effectively shaped by the perceived context in which greening was to be 'sold' (Dutton and Ashford 1993; Ashford *et al.* 1998).

In the collaboration context, depersonalization was also significant, with company representatives in the alliance keen to avoid personal ownership of the project back at their host organizations. However, there was also evidence that whilst actually engaged with other members of the alliance, greater degrees of personalization *could* be fostered. A number of informants spoke of their co-operation with alliance representatives from other companies, and in particular of their own shared environmental goals. Participation in the collaboration could even bring forth more intense personalization, in large measure due to the relatively rare opportunity to interact with environmentally-committed others outside the usual workplace. Therefore, the collaboration respondents could be said to exhibit both depersonalization *and* personalization towards the environ-ment, supporting rather different forms and degrees of moralization: the former, pragmatic, and apparently empty of green feeling; the latter, emotional, even impassioned. Such a 'split' in personalization meant that respondents would sometimes offer apparently contradictory assertions of their own environmental beliefs, similar to Meyerson and Scully's (1995) 'tempered radicals'. Interestingly, this seemed to be accepted as an intrinsic part of the ambivalence and theatre of corporate life rather than a source of emotional or 'moral stress' (Bird and Waters 1989). The particular personal green orientation adopted seemed then to depend very much on the situation concerned and on the particular role which individuals felt expected to play.

Finally, in the social mission companies, such depersonalization was much less in evidence. In fact, in the three smaller companies (ManufactureSoc, FinanceSoc and MarketingSoc), senior managers generally spoke in depth of their own moral beliefs and convictions on environmental issues. Even in RetailSoc, whilst lower degrees of personalization were in evidence, the company's mission was generally seen to be very strongly tied to the ethical drives of certain key senior executives. These findings were in stark contrast to the levels of depersonalization observed in the previous organizational types – but crucially, this personalization also appeared to contribute to some degree of amoralization. Here, the perceived attachment of morality issues to the crusades of senior executives appeared to some extent to prompt those further down the hierarchy to morally disengage, and even at times to sabotage, what they saw as disruptive incursions into their established working practices (Collins and Ganotis 1973). Overall then, it could be said that depersonalization contributed to amoralization by denying the possibility of personal moral responsibility for the environment at all, whilst personalization contributed by attributing moral responsibility too narrowly.

I have argued here that morality boundaries, appropriation of discourse, mobilization of narrative, and depersonalization are all significant dimensions of amoralization, and more importantly, can be seen to operate in subtly different ways in different organizational contexts. In the next section I want to turn my attention to examining the impetus or roots of amoralization, and to explain both why it might have been occurring at all, and why it might have been occurring in the different ways observed in the three organizational types.

Explaining amoralization

To some extent, during the course of the preceding chapters, I have already attempted some discussion of the forces underlying amoralization. As discussed in Chapter 3, bureaucracy itself is likely to squeeze out moral meaning from organizational life. It not only distances the individual from the moral consequences of their actions, but may also prompt him/her to conspire to remain so, in order to avoid any 'unnecessary' obfuscation of their much valued (and rewarded) 'rationality' in decision making (Jackall 1988). Bauman (1989, 1993) for example has been important in showing how morality in bureaucracies can be driven by obedience and abidance to rules (a 'technocratic morality'), rather than by moral autonomy, reflection or impulse. This, he argues, is due to a number of intrinsic features of bureaucratic organization, namely: the imposition of moral distance ('denial of proximity'); dehumanization ('effacement of face'); and the reduction of total persons to traits (e.g. customers are reduced to their needs, workers to their productivity, etc.). The upshot of this is that morality becomes instrumentalized with respect to the goals of the organization, rendering a complete disregard of the moral substance of the actual goals themselves (ten Bos 1997).

Clearly, these arguments present important theoretical insight into the causes of amoralization in green marketing. Bureaucratic systems in themselves tend to render marketing goals – whether environmental or not – beyond moral concern, since it is the techno-rationalist *process* of marketing which is viewed as the arbiter of good and bad. If due marketing process (signifying 'commercial logic') has been observed – that is, if customers have been researched, products tested and sold, and sales data analysed – then the bureaucratic ethic has been followed. This extends also to more societal marketing orientations whereby the social concerns of customers (e.g. RetailSoc) or pressure groups (e.g. with CollabOrg) are simply incorporated into this process, without questioning the moral basis of the process itself, or of its goals. Accordingly, the processes of amoralization described above can be said to constitute attempts by green marketing protagonists to expedite their projects into this process, thereby legitimatizing them in the eyes of their colleagues, superiors and certain other stakeholders. However, the fact that this phenomenon was observed across organizational forms, and in quite subtly different ways, suggests that other factors might also have been at play.

Indeed, evidence for the amoralization dynamic was most strongly evident in respondents' depictions of the cultural, political and sensemaking processes accompanying the selling and institutionalization of green marketing initiatives into the organization. Broadly, I have suggested two main themes in this respect. First, in the conventional and collaborative organizations, the building of bridges of understanding between environment protagonists and vital marketing constituencies in and around the organization (e.g. company buyers, brand managers, etc. as well as suppliers and customers) could be seen to necessitate tactics of amoralization in order for green marketing projects to be seen as a legitimate part of corporate activity. Indeed, the impression management behaviours of green protagonists, and concomitant attempts to engineer collective sensemaking, focused on establishing green meanings with as little of the undesirable baggage and obfuscation of morality as possible (Bird and Waters 1989; Fineman 1998). This was, however, mediated to some extent by perceived audience characteristics (Gardner and Martinko 1988), as well as any legitimacy challenges experienced by managers (Elsbach 1994). Hence, the amoralizing effect of impression management behaviours was therefore at least partially dampened in the context of business–NGO collaboration. The second theme relates to the social mission companies where the focusing of moral sensibilities regarding green marketing at very senior levels was observed to have occasioned processes of amoralization in respect to less-senior employees.

I would suggest then that in the latter context, green protagonists wielded substantial power, and greening was, to varying degrees, a 'strategic contingency' (Salancik and Pfeffer 1977) – i.e. it was essential to the achievement of the firms' prominent social goals. In the former contexts, however, the opposite appeared to be true: not only was the environment viewed as contributing to increased uncertainty, but also lacked any centrality or critical dependence for other functions or activities (Salancik and Pfeffer 1977). Accordingly, the social mission company managers could manipulate organizational language and symbols (Pfeffer 1981b), and were thus observed to construct green meanings that supported and reinforced their own goals (e.g. framing the environment as a matter of personal moral conscience). Moreover, the need to legitimatize organizational actions through symbolic action was less significant here given the extant power base of green protagonists (Pfeffer 1981a). In other contexts though, low power corresponded with a low degree of influence over accepted organizational frames of reference (Pfeffer 1981b). Hence political machinations predominated, with various constituencies contesting the necessity and/or appropriateness of green marketing, as well as negotiating the form and level of its potential impact on organizational activities (Fineman 1997). Political activity here was centred on the manipulation of symbols and language to play down any 'undesirable' associations (Meyerson and Scully 1995; Ashford *et al.* 1998), but with only limited organizational power, environment protagonists had little choice but to reframe the environment such that it was consistent with *existing*, accepted, organizational symbols, narratives and discourses (Pfeffer 1981b). Since these provided little purchase for morality to be accorded any meaningful status, an interpretation of greening as distinctly amoral *had* to be constructed in order to render it a legitimate corporate subject (Fineman 1998).

Power though not only allows for the manipulation of language and symbols but is further consolidated by it (Pfeffer 1981a, 1981b). Since language carries with it accepted norms and their implicit value implications (Pettigrew 1979; Watson 1994a), the privileging of certain discourses means that organizational and cultural knowledge can become institutionalized and legitimatized by creating a 'way of seeing' which reproduces its own truth effects (Pfeffer 1981a; Knights and Morgan 1991). Therefore, as powerful groups begin subjectively to characterize green marketing in a certain (largely amoral) way (or are perceived as doing so), this particular interpretation tends to become institutionalized over time as objective truth (Fineman 1998). Indeed, such 'frozen' cultural knowledge (Schein 1992) was perceived and presented as a significant obstacle to change in the conventional and collaborative organizations, and norms tended to be observed rather than transgressed (Bate 1984). Environmental values would be absorbed into existing cultural certainties of techno-rationalism and utilitarianism rather than elicit any kind of moral transformation of these (Fineman 1996, 1998).

In general then, environment protagonists in these contexts would present a kind of 'learned helplessness' in the face of established cultural norms (Bate 1984). Hence, the possibility for moral autonomy and reflection in the green marketing process would become suffocated by the instinctive adherence to routinely declared and reiterated corporate values as presented in formal company communications and literature (Dahler-Larsen 1994; Fineman 1996, 1997). Even at the subcultural level, where stronger, informal and non-unitary working moralities might be expected, environmental duties and obligations appeared to be traded, suppressed, or at least bracketed, in the face of more powerful normative impulses associated with personal success, existing relationships and, above all, the dictates of 'commercial logic' (Jackall 1988; Fineman 1996, 1997).

The apparent failure of business–NGO collaboration to significantly moralize the greening process beyond narrow situational boundaries can thus be explained in terms of powerful subcultural rigidities coupled with the power implications of NGO resource dependence on their business partners (Pfeffer and Salancik 1978; Pfeffer 1981b). Threats to the perceived legitimacy of NGOs in market-based initiatives can therefore propel the construction of personal and organizational images insufficiently moralized to penetrate the boundary-spanning subcultures of corporate partners (Elsbach and Sutton 1992). For the social mission firms, however, managers may have felt less need to rationalize their actions in economic, utilitarian terms not only because they did not need to co-operate with corporate partners (indeed, they were frequently in competitive conflict) but also because of their different missions and governance structure. Diacon and Ennew (1996) for example have shown how mutual ownership can provide a more ethically-attuned context, and the symbolic, legitimating, action of management is clearly shaped by the felt need to maintain and accommodate accountability (Pfeffer 1981a).

Implications

The evidence and arguments presented here suggest quite strongly that despite fairly concerted environmental action, most corporations and their members remain largely distant from the moral imprecations of pressure groups and green business writers. As Fineman (1998) suggests though, this is not surprising: of course corporations respond conservatively to environmentalism, and of course the majority of their members are not the moral leaders of a green revolution. The self-sustaining order of the modern organization is one of utilitarian-based techno-rationalism, a social architecture where the moral code is constructed around growth, consumption, profitability and personal success. However, despite this apparent pervasiveness of amoralization, there do appear to be important variations across different organizational types. In the main, these differences appear to be driven by variations in: the power and accountability of issue sellers; perceived context favourability; audience characteristics; cultural rigidity and unity; and perceived threats to organizational legitimacy.

It could be argued that from an environmental point of view, provided greening can be continued, this lack of moral engagement in large numbers of green marketing actors is not really problematic. Indeed, this study shows that some level of greening is possible without emotional and moral attachment to the environment on the part of organizational members, and that even fairly advanced greening is possible without a cohesive 'ethical' culture of shared environmental values. However, the limits of voluntarism in this respect should not be under-emphasized (Newton and Harte 1997). The results here indicate that motives of ethics and social responsibility for greening initiatives are rarely claimed by executives other than those from social mission companies. This suggests that coercion from powerful stakeholders, such as pressure groups and regulators, mediated by politically adept and professionally ambitious internal champions, is more likely to encourage corporate greening than any voluntary moral impulses or principles (Fineman and Clarke 1996; Fineman 1996, 1997, 1998). Indeed, there is concern, as many of the respondents here indicated, that once the firm has been prompted into greening, the introduction of 'emotive' moral arguments as opposed to 'rational' technical ones can hinder rather than facilitate its institutionalization. Hence, even where greening is *not* viewed as contingent on personal moral engagement, understanding of the role and importance of morality in the cultural knowledge of the firm is critical to the advancement of the green agenda.

For the most part then, it could be argued that to initiate fundamental greening initiatives, a distinctly moral engagement may only perhaps be necessary on the part of the strategic leader, providing they have sufficient power to do so, and the requisite political skills and dexterity with symbols to render the process legitimate. This clearly calls into serious question 'deep ecology' prescriptions which suggest that only through a fundamentally moralized business culture can radical greening possibly take place. Thus, according to this view, significant voluntary advances towards greener products, production processes and communications would require companies to embrace 'ethical' core values, and principles of social responsibility and sustainability into the fabric of the organization (e.g. Stead and Stead 1992; Peattie 1992, 1995; Shrivastava 1994, 1995a, 1995b; Welford 1995). Certainly the senior managers of those social mission companies which marketed products to other organizations were clear in their conviction that only on the basis of a deep and distinct moral conviction would these reselling organizations offer the kind of support necessary for them to develop their radical green product and process innovations. It was argued to me that without such values in place, organizations would always take the simplest route, which entailed the least amount of change. In contrast, what the social mission companies actually suggested they needed was some degree of assistance, flexibility and patience to allow them to progress in new and unique directions.

Of course, there are also important arguments from the 'deep ecology' school of thought that an ecocentric approach to greening should *by definition* involve not only the participation of internal and external stakeholder groups, but also their moral and affective engagement (e.g. Shrivastava 1995a). From this point of view, the findings reported here might be seen as distinctly disappointing, since even the social mission firms exhibited little success in promoting and sustaining a company-wide environmental ethic. However, arguably of even more concern in this respect is the possibility of amoralization extending into other stakeholder groups and polities. Given that even in the context of collaboration with an environmental pressure group, moral dimensions of green marketing were largely interpreted in terms of corporate self-interest, such groups might be regarded as limited in their potential to act as a moral conscience for corporations, or as a form of ethical control in themselves (see Smith 1990; Fineman 1997). Moreover, the avowed intention of many sampled companies to focus communication efforts at converting external groups to the organization's environmental world-view might be seen as attempted hegemony, or railroading, of the environment debate. For example, the development by a number of the firms in this study of environment education material for schools could be viewed as a barrier to developing a more pluralistic green agenda which recognizes and encourages a diversity of views and perspectives, rather than simply that of commercial organizations. The proclivity of managers in this study to construct discourses of 'rationality' and 'irrationality' and 'facts' and 'fallacies' clearly effected some exclusion of critical constituencies, and might be regarded as an attempt to deny the possibility of critical voices (Puxty 1986; Tombs 1993). Indeed, it is the prospect of this excrescence of environmental amoralization on the part of economic institutions that has prompted critical green politics writers such as Gorz (1980, 1989) to argue for the need to limit the scope of the economic system and to liberate environmental questions from it altogether. For the 'deep ecology' writers then, the results presented here might be either further grist to the arguments for non-market, non-voluntary solutions to the environmental problem, or for those seeking to articulate a utopian vision of ecocentric business, an indication that in order to develop more practical and realistic prescriptions for green marketing they need to better accommodate the political and cultural realities of modern corporate life.

Towards moralization?

Having to date described something of a morally penurious view of contemporary green marketing practice, the final section of this chapter seeks to explore how morality has been, and potentially could be, injected into this practice. To continue in a consistent lexicography, this is essentially a question of how marketing *moralization* might be effected. In particular, I shall examine proposals for programmes of culture change (as introduced in Chapter 2) in the light of the findings reported here. This is then used as a basis to discuss the potential for moralization in the three organizational approaches.

Moralization through culture change

This study has been based on the assertion that marketing morality, and more specifically green moralities in marketing, can be examined through cultural phenomena, knowledge and artefacts. As shown, though, the more common perspective in the business and marketing ethics literatures, as well as in the green business literature, is that the group of elements which comprise the organization's culture can be *changed* in some way to effect greater morality in marketing practice. Whilst the data collected here only related in a fairly minor way to explicit culture change programmes, they do suggest that rather than culture being a platform for marketing moralization, it commonly acts as a significant barrier to such. Indeed, in the conventional and collaborative approaches, widespread perceptions of cultural immutability had prompted little attempt at culture change, such that where positive green values were in evidence, they were not disseminated more widely through the organization. Green behaviours had though in some cases been encouraged within these organizations, both at a corporate level (e.g. greening of products and processes) and at a more local level (e.g. re-use and recycling of office supplies), although the values articulated to legitimatize such activities were in the main of an instrumental nature. Hence, 'in practice, enacted "ethical" moralities are essentially pragmatic, well-attuned to the organization's profit interests, and expediently adjusted to different subcultural interests' (Fineman 1996: 492). Culture change then, where it was apparent, might be regarded as relatively superficial and symbolic rather than representing fundamental shifts in organizational values, beliefs and assumptions. Even where green marketing was seen to be supported by socially responsible cultures, these tended to be *existing* and *stable* cultural forms rather than changing ones (Drumwright 1994; Fineman 1996)

In the social mission companies, more attention had apparently been given to green cultural change, although it was recognized that cultural uniformity in this respect would be extremely difficult and potentially even undesirable. The arguments relating to the difficulty of changing cultures are by now well rehearsed in the organization and management studies literature (e.g. Martin 1985; Nord 1985; Siehl 1985; Ogbonna 1992; Anthony 1994). Indeed, there has been precious little empirical evidence in the literature that provides wholesale support for the claim that culture can indeed be managed. Cultural pragmatists who do support the proposition tend to conceive of culture in relatively superficial terms – i.e. in relation to behavioural change – whereas those that refute it tend to define culture in deeper and broad terms – i.e. in relation to values and beliefs (Martin 1985; Ogbonna 1992). That 'greener' or more 'ethical' cultures can be developed also lacks empirical substantiation beyond accounts which are either brief and anecdotal (e.g. Smart 1992; Bernstein 1992) or self-reported (e.g. Chappell 1993). Accordingly, the use of culture management to improve corporate ethical and environmental behaviour has (belatedly) begun to be seriously questioned (Sinclair 1993; Dahler-Larsen 1994; Fineman 1996; Newton and Harte 1997). Sinclair (1993: 68) for example concludes that:

> The lessons from research are that you meddle with the organizational culture if you've got little choice, lots of resources, and lots of time – a combination of circumstances, some would argue, rare enough to render the approach irrelevant.

The issue of cultural uniformity being in itself undesirable has also been considered to some extent in the green and ethical business literatures and is clearly an important one (Sinclair 1993; Dahler-Larsen 1994; Fineman 1996). Dahler-Larsen (1994) for example argues that drives for cultural unity reward conformity rather than the very autonomy that is crucial for a sense of morality to exist. Fineman (1996) points to the possibility that attempts at cultural unity might railroad the green agenda according to managerial perspectives, thus driving out fundamental ecological principles of inclusion and democracy:

> If it is axiomatic that ethical environmentalism is built upon respect for others, it follows that any ethical developments in an organization's culture should acknowledge the range of values and feelings within that organization.
>
> Fineman (1996: 493)

Ultimately, both Fineman (1996) and Sinclair (1993) suggest that subcultural identities are perhaps the principal repositories of organizational moralities as well as potentially offering the best route for influencing or activating moralization. The proposition that subcultural values and norms act as both highly integrative organizational bonds and important influences on organizational micro-behaviour is well established in the organization studies literature (e.g. Martin and Siehl 1983; Van Maanen and Barley 1985; Martin 1992; Anthony 1994). It is possible that a positive moralization effect could thus be fostered by encouraging surveillance, dialogue and critique between these subcultural groups, prompting 'ethical discourse and dialectic as well as conflict' (Sinclair 1993: 69). Starkey (1998) reinforces this argument with the contention that moral development in organizations requires factionalism and dissent in order to promote learning. Hence the role of management becomes one of surfacing conflicting values, unleashing the moral commitment of subcultures, and from this forming synthesis and mutual coexistence rather than authoritarian ideological control (Sinclair 1993; Starkey 1998).

This non-unitary perspective certainly appears to relate strongly to the empirical evidence emerging from the organizational contexts studied here. Many of my informants' responses were informed by subcultural attachments and allegiances, and it was these as much as anything which seemed to shape their enacted moral frames of reference. Indeed, affective moralization of the environment was clearly bounded into certain subcultural arenas, suggesting significant potential for this approach. However, processes of amoralization were found to occur partly through the power differentials evident between these arenas and other subcultural factions. Therefore, whilst the prescriptions for moralization based on differentiation might be regarded as appropriate in terms of identifying the positive effect of embracing difference, encouraging moral dialogue and surfacing awareness of conflicting moral perspectives, what they lack is any explicit identification of the importance of the relative power of these subcultures. Indeed, this power appears to be critical in shaping the discourses in which these differences, dialogues, and perspectives can actually be articulated (Pfeffer 1981b; Phillips and Brown 1993). This is particularly true in the case of specific issues (the environment) and specific processes (the marketing of products) since these are likely to be strongly associated with certain occupational and/or subcultural groups that are perceived to hold guardianship over them.

Dahler-Larsen (1994) takes the criticism of organization cultures in relation to moralization yet further. For him, the failure is not just in the superficiality and authoritarianism of unitary cultures, but also in the substitution by culture of internal corporate attachments in the place of society as the 'sacred' moral realm. Hence, even feeling engagement through subcultural associations would be deficient for the establishment of true morality since 'nothing less than society itself is the source and objective of morality' (Dahler-Larsen 1994: 7). Starkey (1998) counters this by emphasizing both the fragmentation of broad societal identities and moralities, and the rise of corporate visions and missions that aspire towards social goals. In my analysis, such social aspirations in the sampled organizations appeared to transfer most significantly from 'out there' annoyances into the moral order of the organization when attached to powerful internal polities (such as the company's leadership). Without this internalization, social concerns tended to be regarded as customer, pressure group or media issues which needed to be 'managed' in line with profit interests rather than being any source, or subject, of morality in themselves (see also Jackall 1988; Bauman 1993).

Finally, a 'moralized' green marketing might also be expected to involve some formal communication of that sense of morality to internal and external audiences through marketing artefacts such as products and promotions. Products are in themselves important repositories of meaning, particularly in terms of brands, and as cultural artefacts in their own right can communicate key aspects of morality. This would account for some of the claims by the social mission company leaders that the mere existence of their products in the marketplace was a representation and legitimation of a certain social ideology. However, division of labour and employee specialization mean that internal constituencies often remain ignorant of the moral import of product offerings. This can be accentuated when communications intended for external audiences are seen by employees (as is often the case of advertising, labelling, etc.) and the values articulated are incongruent with those held or experienced internally (Gilly and Wolfinbarger 1998). Hence, whilst moralization might be expected to be accompanied by greener products and promotion, it is unlikely that these alone would be sufficient to prompt it.

Routes to moralization

Overall then, the evidence from this study suggests that any moralization of green marketing practice is likely to be significantly easier in companies with explicit social missions than in those without. Perhaps surprisingly, this does not however appear to be influenced too much by the centrality of the mission to the firm's marketing strategy. Indeed, of more importance than the mission *per se* seems to be the systems of structure, culture and power within the organization that influence the legitimacy of an *internal* moral discourse around greening. And in these particular organizations, such systems appeared to be reasonably supportive of intimations of moralization provided that the integrity of the leaders' convictions was (or was perceived to be) genuine (Fineman 1997), and that it did not conflict too much with existing perceptions of organizational values (Gilly and Wolfinbarger 1998) or expectations for personal cultural autonomy (Martin 1992). To the extent that the social mission companies in this study were apparently increasing their attention to culture management techniques, there is clearly a case for suggesting that moralization might become in this way more expansive than was in evidence at the time of fieldwork. This would indicate a subtle shift away from a focus solely on reforming external publics towards also seeking to convert internal subjects (Mintzberg 1989). Whether this would then impact negatively on the cultural and moral autonomy of employees would probably depend on the manner in which it was introduced, i.e. whether more attention was focused on opening up dialogue across existing subcultural divisions, selecting-in environmentally-concerned employees at the recruitment stage, or 'educating' all employees to internalize the company's (unitary) values. Given the previous discussion, it might be expected that this list represents decreasing potential for 'true' moralization.

In theory, the impact of external stakeholders on marketing practice, as in the case of CollabOrg, for example, might also appear to represent some possibility of moralization. Such interaction might be viewed as an opportunity for the introduction of new cultural knowledge into the marketing process in the form of vocabularies, stories and symbols with more explicit moral resonance. This can prompt organizational learning through the development of alternate 'frame-breaking' perspectives (Menon and Menon 1997). In practice, however, this effect was found to be limited, most notably because of the moderating effect of the subcultural buffer provided by environmental protagonists. This does not, however, mean that a more radical approach from pressure groups would be met with greater success in effecting moralization since firms have been shown to be generally unwilling or unable to accept the legitimacy of concerns raised by more aggressive green stakeholders (Fineman and Clarke 1996). Indeed, informants here emphasized the superior appeal of their particular NGO partner compared with, for example Greenpeace and Friends of the Earth, since the CollabOrg NGO was perceived and presented as run by 'nice people' who were more 'conservative', 'responsible' and 'willing to work with business' than the other 'fanatical' pressure groups. It remains then a fine balance for collaborative stakeholders to maintain in working with companies: too much overt moralizing and they will be rejected; too little, and companies are unlikely to be fundamentally challenged at a cultural level.

Finally, in the case of the conventional companies, the most promising potential route to moralization would be through one or more powerful senior executives adopting a crusading policy entrepreneur role either from within, or interacting with, marketing and related departments. Given sufficient political power and influence, and assuming that others perceived the stance as genuine, such a role could have substantial impact on organizational members' articulated green values, creating space for interpretations of green marketing outside purely instrumental and commercial discourses. However, there is clearly a delicate balance to be maintained here also. Too much personalization of the environmental agenda can disaffect other organizational members. This suggests that environmental protagonists might usefully adopt a more 'empowerment' type approach. Also, it would appear that this form of moralization would probably need to focus on developing within some kind of subcultural community (either new or existing) and at the same time ensuring that it wielded substantial power within the marketing organization. Still, whilst this represents a useful prescription for action, it is entirely contingent on requisite will being exercised from within – something which at present appears to be rather lacking.

Conclusion

In this chapter, I have attempted to develop further the findings relating to the three organizational approaches presented in Chapters 4, 5 and 6, and as integrated around aspects of green marketing and morality in Chapter 7. Two main themes – amoralization and moralization – have been set out and explored. Certainly it is true to say that prior to this, these themes have yet to be examined to any extent within the existing green marketing literature (nor even the broader marketing literature) and therefore I would suggest that the preceding discussion should be seen as an attempt to develop new and original 'grounded' theory in this respect. A number of important insights have been made. First, amoralization has been defined in the current context as the removal of moral meaning from the green marketing process, or from the objects of green marketing, i.e. it is the phenomenon whereby green marketing is rendered an amoral subject. Amoralization can be seen to be an important element in the green marketing process, and was in evidence in all three organizational approaches, albeit to varying degrees, and in different ways.

Second, amoralization was shown to be tied to the behaviour of certain individuals and groups within the organization – usually the principal environmental protagonists – and I have argued that these *agents of amoralization* effected this process in a number of ways. Amoralization could therefore be argued to emerge either deliberately or accidentally, consciously or unconsciously. To some extent this was seen to depend on the organizational, and wider institutional, context faced by these individuals and groups. Allied with these agents, the third principal insight concerns the four processes of amoralization seen to be associated with their activities. These to me captured the range of cultural dynamics contributing to amoralization in the three organizational types. These conceptual categories – *morality boundaries, appropriation of discourse, mobilization of narrative,* and *depersonalization* – should be regarded as important emergent variables in explaining the amoralization dynamic. In particular, they should help to illustrate how different approaches to issue selling and impression management on the part of 'green' champions within the marketing organization affect the moral meanings subsequently constructed and communicated within it.

Fourth, I located the roots of amoralization, and its different manifestations in the three organizational contexts, within the realms of structure, power, politics and culture. Whilst to some extent this might be regarded as simply reflecting the attempt to make some kind of cultural analysis in this study, the citing of these findings within important streams of organizational and management literature suggests at least that my findings are explainable and understandable within the extant literature. This not only adds some strength to the veracity of my analysis, but also contributes an important cross-disciplinary angle to the core literatures of this study. Indeed it could be argued that it is the failure of the mainstream literatures in marketing, business ethics and green business to take critical account of cultural and political dimensions that has to date weakened their theoretical insight and practical relevance (Gladwin 1993; Brownlie *et al.* 1994; Brigley 1995; Newton and Harte 1997).

Fifth, the consequences of amoralization were discussed during this chapter, and although it was argued that even extensive greening of the marketing process could potentially take place without strong moral engagement being widely shared throughout the organization, the degree of amoralization was shown to vary according to organizational type. A range of potentially negative consequences were also identified, such as the subsequent lack of support for radical green innovation, and the possibility of the process of amoralization extending into other stakeholder groups, thus conceivably limiting the potential for a pluralistic green agenda. Therefore, from a 'deep' green perspective, the consequences of amoralization would be regarded as profoundly negative, although from a 'shallow' green perspective this might not necessarily be the case. Indeed, the avowed necessity of amoralization in order to introduce green issues into the marketing process, as expressed by many respondents in this study, might suggest that the positive effects could outweigh the negative consequences.

Sixth, I also discussed the possibility of *moralization* of green marketing in the context of these findings. Moralization was defined as the phenomenon whereby green marketing was interpreted morally, subjected to moral reflection, or made morally relevant in some way. The potential for culture change to realize moralization was examined and found to be wanting due to factors such as the difficulty of managing deep layers of culture, the subsequent exclusion of moral autonomy and contrasting values, and the failure to focus morality outside the organization. An approach to culture management that encourages subcultural attachments and moralities to develop and flourish was identified as potentially more appropriate, although it was argued that the findings of this study suggest that power differentials between these factions might be a critical feature in determining the success of such approaches.

Finally, possible routes to moralization were examined for each of the three organizational approaches considered in this study. It was argued that this process was likely to be easiest in the social mission companies, and the potential for an expanded morality in such contexts was set out. The collaborative approach was shown to have some potential, although in practice this had not been extensively realized, at least in the case addressed here. Lastly, in the conventional companies the possibility for greater moralization was set out in terms of the political power and influence of policy entrepreneurs – where this was higher, the potential for moralization was argued to be greater.

These then represent some of the more important and profound findings of the study, and together with those identified in the previous chapter, form much of the core contribution of this book. In the final chapter, I will not only summarize and clarify this contribution, but also try to make some greater sense of it. Hence I will set these findings into a wider organizational, cultural and international context, and also set out how I see this work contributing to, and maintaining, an ongoing stream of research and theory development.

9 Conclusions

Introduction

Throughout this book I have been concerned with investigating morality in marketing, and situating this investigation in the context of one particular form of marketing, namely that broadly defined as 'green' marketing. The exploratory, qualitative, comparative empirical case study investigation which forms the core of this book was, as I have argued, aimed at providing theoretical and descriptive insights into contemporary green marketing practices; in so doing, I sought to reveal their moral dimensions. Utilizing a social constructionist perspective, the focus throughout has been on examining aspects of moral meaning as constructed, perceived, understood and communicated by organizational members and organizational communications of various forms. As I showed earlier in the book, this is a relatively unusual way to approach such questions in marketing, and represents an important omission in the existing literature.

In this, the final chapter, I shall discuss the extent to which I feel the empirical study achieved the aims I set out for it (see in particular Chapter 3), and perhaps more importantly, I will assess the overall significance and contribution of the study and its findings. To do this, I will show how the insights developed here provide important new understandings of marketing, morality and the natural environment. Moreover, by placing the study in a wider organizational, cultural and international context, I will show that whilst only a handful of organizations from a single country have been examined here, there are important implications to be gleaned for understanding similar phenomena in other organizations, other countries, and at other times. That is not to say that there are not problems associated with the approach adopted here, and as the chapter proceeds, a number of possible limitations will be identified. In addressing these limitations, though I shall elucidate how the literature might usefully be advanced so as to build upon the insights provided here, and indeed consolidate them into a more systematic and concrete stream of theory. Finally, I will advance some possible implications of a more practical nature for managers, policy entrepreneurs, green activists and the like, and in the very last section, to ensure that my essential message has not been missed, and at the very least to summarize the key contributions of the book, I shall provide a brief summary of my main findings.

Towards some conclusions

A number of important findings have emerged from this study, and I would suggest that these have important implications for theoretical development in the marketing, business ethics and green business literatures. In this section these conclusions are set out, and their implications discussed. Four main issues are addressed here, namely: marketing as a moral domain; green marketing theory and practice; cultural dynamics of green marketing; and moral meaning in marketing.

Marketing as a moral domain

We can conclude first, and perhaps fairly uncontroversially, that marketing is indeed in some respects a moral domain. For a start, as we saw in Chapter 2, marketing has been subjected to some very important moral critiques, and the extensions of marketing theory represented by the subsequent development of 'societal marketing', 'green marketing' and 'social marketing' among others, suggest that the goals of the marketing system are not *necessarily* purely economic in nature, or that moral questions can or should be altogether excluded from marketing theory and practice. Indeed, as made clear in Chapter 2, moral issues pervade the theory and practice of marketing from top to bottom and from beginning to end. From the point of view of practitioners, however, as we have seen, and as I shall clarify below, this does not as a consequence suggest that those involved in the marketing process are similarly aware of and/or concerned with these moral dimensions. None the less, descriptive studies of 'ethical decision making' in marketing have shown that marketing decisions are beset by moral considerations and criteria, and that marketing decision makers are indeed likely at times to proceed through some form of process of moral reasoning. Again, though, this may or may not be a conscious process, and the existing literature provides little insight either way. Indeed, the study presented here was specifically designed to begin in some way to address these deficiencies.

Even though it is possible to say then that marketing is a moral domain, it does not follow that it can also be said that marketing is necessarily either 'ethical' or even 'moral'. It is not necessarily 'ethical' because this is in itself a value judgement, and to say so would presuppose that marketing had been evaluated according to certain ethical rules, principles or criteria. This may indeed be the case, but it does not follow from the observation that marketing is a moral domain. It is also not necessarily 'moral' because, within the terminology of this book, to say so would suggest that those involved in the marketing process did so with an understanding of, feeling for and use of moral arguments, categories, vocabularies and sensibilities. The enquiry into whether indeed such moral meaning is a part of the marketing process is an empirical question, and is the principal one investigated during the course of this book.

Green marketing theory and practice

As I have said, in order to explore moral meaning in marketing, I decided to focus the main part of the study specifically on green marketing, i.e. marketing activities whereby some account had been taken of dimensions relating to the natural environment. Following empirical examination of three very different approaches to green marketing, it was found that few individuals in organizations saw environmental features as strong product augmentations, and there was widespread recognition that green marketing was experiencing some kind of backlash in the UK. This, as I argued in Chapter 7, has also been identified in many other countries during the 1990s. In response, green marketing strategies were found to vary, but most success in this context appeared to be in either muted or collaborative strategies. Passive and niche strategies were felt to present some benefits in certain markets, but would not be widely viable.

In the main then, I would suggest that environmental concerns were seen either in terms of maintaining legitimacy in the eyes of government and non-government organizations and the wider public, or else in terms of a personal goal or drive of internal constituencies, particularly those at the top of their organizations. Hence, I have suggested that, in practice, green marketing could be best understood as a process composed of a network of internal and external interactions. Critical internal interactions were observed to occur between those charged with the responsibility for introducing greening into the marketing process and other important marketing constituencies within the organization. Critical external interactions were observed to occur between the focus organization and its suppliers, competitors, customers, governmental and non-governmental organizations, other industry network members and other stakeholders. Accordingly, I have argued that green marketing could be modelled fairly successfully utilizing stakeholder theory and the networks model of marketing exchange, both of which defy any atomistic view of the individual firm. These are considered to be fruitful avenues for subsequent development of green marketing theory. Moreover, although these theoretical perspectives on green marketing might have little to say in themselves about morality, their basis in *relationships* makes possible a moral view of green marketing through their particular theoretical lenses.

Cultural dynamics of green marketing

The cultural dynamics of green marketing have been explored and analysed in some depth during this book, particularly to the extent that they reveal the moral terrain of the organization. In the main, these were traced through the impression management and issue selling tactics of green champions in the case organizations. Whilst these dynamics clearly varied according to the particular organizational context focused upon, common themes relating to the manipulation of language, symbols and images could be observed. These dynamics might be seen as important forces shaping the green marketing process. Moreover, and for the purposes of this book more importantly, these dynamics were also shown to support a process of *amoralization* in and around green marketing – i.e. a phenomenon whereby moral meaning was removed from the green marketing process. Accordingly, in Chapter 8 I set out a set of superordinate categories of those dynamics which I felt captured the essence of the amoralization phenomenon across organizational contexts. These were *morality boundaries, appropriation of discourse, mobilization of narrative* and *personalization.*

Clearly then, some form of cultural analysis of organizations can be a very effective means of identifying and examining important new dimensions of, and ways of seeing, morality in marketing. In the main, amoralization was shown to arise from the need or otherwise of environmental protagonists to exercise some control over the organizational meanings and shared frames of reference that attended green marketing projects and policies. The rationale for this was generally presented in terms of ensuring a relatively uncontested and uncontroversial introduction of new policy. Moreover, it was argued that fundamentally the existence or otherwise of this need depended on variables such as levels of organizational size and bureaucracy, the relative power resources of various organizational and extra-organizational actors and subcultures, and the perceived strength or 'stickiness' of the perceived extant culture. The addition of these structural, cultural and political dimensions to the study of morality can be seen then to be vital in terms of developing new insight based on the perceived 'realities' of organizational life. Clearly, this is an approach that demands further attention in the future. In this way, there might be considerable hope for marketing academics and organization theorists to provide for a more informed body of knowledge in relation to morality in marketing and in organizations more generally.

Moral meaning in marketing

Overall, for those actually engaged in the marketing process, moral meaning in marketing practice was found to be rather underdeveloped, both cognitively and affectively. Such a possibility was shown quite dramatically by this study, with the goals of marketing only rarely acknowledged as being morally meaningful by these individuals and groups. More commonly, the moral domain of marketing appeared to be focused on internal subjects, and in particular on role-related behavioural norms, codes of practice, and rules regarding organization members' personal and organizational success. This has important implications for how marketing might be conceptualized and theorized. In particular, the finding that the introduction of social and environmental goals into marketing practices does not necessarily follow from, or elicit, any form of moral transformation within the marketing organization, suggests that the revised forms of marketing discussed in Chapter 2 constitute, in practice, only very minor departures from the largely instrumental, technicist perspective of traditional marketing theory. Hence, the expansion of the goals of marketing to include social and environmental features does not necessarily constitute a new marketing paradigm, but merely an extension of the existing one.

Moreover, the possibility that marketing might actually be a territory for amoralization seems to be one that is rarely, if ever, confronted within the marketing literature. However, this is clearly an issue that is critical to an understanding of morality in marketing, and surely should not be overlooked in this way. Amoralization was shown to be a significant feature of green marketing in the organizational environments studied, albeit to varying degrees and in different ways. I would also suggest that it might be a significant feature of marketing generally. As Desmond (1998) has recently argued, the loss of moral impulse and feeling in organizations is exacerbated by marketing, for decisions in this area frequently involve people from agencies which are both internal and external to the organization, such as advertising, PR and through-the-line agencies. This imposition of psychic and moral distance between organizational actors, and from causes and consequences, has implications for the exercise of individual moral responsibility and action. Drawing on the work of Bauman (1993) Desmond argues that moral agency is easily 'floated' within such groupings where the individual is a mere cog in an enormous machine. Moreover, he suggests that where the individual within the organization experiences a conflict of interest, their loyalties and sympathies fall usually on the side of their colleagues and not with those who are perceived to be 'other' or external to the organization. Accordingly, issues such as the environment tend to be marginalized from a moral realm which is constructed and made meaningful by the internal relationships of the organization's moral community (Watson 1998).

Certainly if the marketing academy is serious about envisaging a 'moral', not least an 'ethical' marketing, then the true role and nature of moral meaning simply cannot be ignored, and it would be as well to begin with an understanding of the practical (a)moral marketing milieu as experienced by marketers and other organization members rather than idealistic prescriptions of how marketing 'should' be. Thus, the identification of marketing amoralization might be regarded not only as an important addition to the knowledge of marketing practice but also as a critical element to be incorporated into models and prescriptions of, for example, societal marketing and marketing ethics, as well as green marketing.

Marketing, morality and the natural environment in context

Whilst I would certainly argue that these findings provide important contributions to the literature, I also acknowledge that they come as a result of a study that was focused on a relatively small number of organizations, in a single country and at a particular point in time. Hence, notwithstanding the considerable epistemological potential of the inductive, case-study method adopted in the study, it is worthwhile examining to what extent these results appear to have some kind of relevance within a wider organizational, national, cultural and temporal context.

From the point of view of other organizations, it certainly cannot be said that the findings reported here are representative of business organizations *generally*, and there can be little argument that the conclusions reached can only truly claim validity with any certainty for the particular cases selected as the sample for this investigation. Indeed, I am sure that a completely different picture might emerge from a number of other organizations not sampled here. In particular, local government, charities and civil society organizations might present very different contexts for examining aspects of morality in relation to green marketing. However, by the same token, for business organizations, there is no reason to suggest that the results presented here are especially unique or unusual. Indeed, my efforts to develop a comparative case sample exhibiting substantial variation in organizational context suggests that many key findings will be relevant to some degree to many other organizational contexts. For example, similar results have emerged from other UK studies of business organizations with respect to the perceived green marketing backlash (Wong *et al.* 1996), the importance of environmental policy entrepreneurs in shaping and furthering the green agenda (Fineman 1997) and the 'rationality' and amorality attending greening (Fineman 1996, 1998). This, combined with the subsequent development of theoretical propositions and constructs to a degree of abstraction sufficient to encompass the contextual variations of the sample, suggests to me at least that it is possible to have considerable confidence in the wider applicability of these findings. Moreover, it is the depth of insight gained through qualitative, interpretive research that is its major strength, particularly in exploratory research, and it is inevitable that some level of breadth has to be compromised to achieve this, given the bounded conditions of any study. However, to enhance confidence in the representativeness of the findings, and to develop improved generalizability, further cases certainly could and should be investigated in the future.

Whilst different organizations may be reasonably likely to yield broadly similar findings (at least in some respects), if we think of these organizations as located in different national and cultural contexts, there might be other questions to deal with. In the US for example, there is a suggestion from Drumwright's (1994) study of green purchasing that organization members are likely to be more prone to construct their interpretations and understandings of greening in explicit and personal moral terms. This is supported by the highly moralized, if not exactly impartial, accounts of 'new age' entrepreneurs in the US such as Tom Chappell, Ben Cohen and others who speak of empowered and morally expressive managers and employees in 'boutique' social responsibility firms (see Nichols 1994). Moreover, recent US studies (e.g. Mitroff and Denton 1999) have even pointed to corporate employees stressing the need for some kind of spirituality and spiritual meaning in the workplace – an issue not as yet even on the research agenda in the UK. Hence, we might see that in some respects the US could offer a somewhat different cultural milieu in which to explore issues of organizational morality, although this is not certain given earlier studies (e.g. Jackall 1988; Bird and Waters 1989) offering considerable evidence to the contrary. Whilst there is less empirical data in this respect relating to other countries, one might expect greater moral engagement in countries regarded as traditionally concerned with environmental issues, such as in Northern Europe and Scandinavia, and less so in those often thought of as generally unconcerned such as in Eastern Europe and Asia.

This suggests of course that other concerns of this book are also likely to vary across national boundaries. In particular, for green marketing, and for green management generally, some countries clearly have more advanced practices and processes. Whilst few comparative studies have been made, again firms in countries such as Germany and the US have been found to operate in stricter regulatory environments than in the UK, with markets more open to green concerns, and with more advanced green programmes (see for example Steger 1993; Peattie and Ringler 1994; Menon and Menon 1997). Countries in Asia meanwhile have in the past been faced with far less overt pressure than in the UK and elsewhere to develop such programmes, but evidence suggests that this is changing (see for example, Steadman *et al.* 1995; Butler and Kraisornsuthasinee 1999). Evidence suggests however that the broad context of a 'backlash' against green marketing, as referred to in this book, appears to be one in evidence in a number of countries such as the US (Carlson *et al.* 1993; Kangun and Polonsky 1995; Schrum *et al.* 1995; Ackerstein and Lemon 1999) and Australia (Kangun and Polonsky 1995; Mendleson and Polonsky 1995).

Finally, I must also acknowledge the temporal context of the study. Fieldwork was conducted between 1995 and 1996, and analysis primarily between 1995 and 1998 (although some further analysis was conducted during the preparation of this book in 1999). At this time, the posited 'backlash' was seen to be in full swing, firms were very much in a period of experimentation with managing environmental issues, and the regulatory environment was in flux. Whilst 'ethical' issues in general were also at this time beginning to receive increased attention from business in the UK and elsewhere, this was very much a time of restructuring, downsizing and increasing job insecurity. I am sure that were I to have conducted this work at another time, there would have been certain differences in the responses that were forthcoming from respondents, given the likelihood of a different business environment being in place. In particular, the context, practices and perceptions of green marketing would almost certainly differ through time. However, I strongly feel that for the main area of my findings – i.e. those pertaining to moral meaning – any differences would be ones of degree rather than substance. After all, the amorality embedded in organizational life has been referred to at least since the time of Max Weber, and such discussions very much still continue today (see for example Parker 1998).

Limits and limitations

If these issues of context specificity raise certain questions over the limits of the study's relevance, then it is appropriate to think of them in terms of a broader discussion of the potential limitations of the study. No piece of research can be completely perfect, and certainly will fail to be all things to all people. Clearly there are certain limitations with the particular approach adopted here, and with the way in which it has subsequently been applied. None the less, this is only to be expected – there is, as I argued in Chapter 3, no one 'true' and 'right' method; what is important though is that the limitations of that which has been used are made explicit, and in this way readers can judge for themselves the veracity and usefulness of the resulting theory.

Perhaps the strongest and most common objection to any kind of case study work (and particularly that which utilizes a relatively small number of cases) is that the findings are too contextually specific, and thus limited in their generalizability to other cases and circumstances. This I have already discussed, and whilst I acknowledge it as an issue, I do not feel it detracts significantly from the contribution my work makes. However, there are also questions of generalizability in relation to my attempt to study morality in marketing by focusing specifically on green marketing. In this sense, there must be certain reservations over the extent to which the findings relating to green marketing can be readily assumed to have implications for other forms of marketing, and for marketing more generally. It is important to recognize therefore that at this early stage in theory development, such implications can only be suggested rather than confirmed in any way. Nonetheless, although these results are grounded in the substantive data of green marketing, they again have been developed to a level of abstraction that makes them potentially applicable to situations and contexts which might occur in other areas within the field of marketing and morality. Hence, the intention has been to generate substantive theory as a 'strategic link' in the formulation of formal theory from data (Glaser and Strauss 1967). In order to strengthen this link though, other substantive areas such as societal marketing and social marketing should be explored in the future, and even more conventional marketing processes such as new product development, market research and communications should provide fertile sources of substantive data.

Although these issues of generalizability probably represent for many people the major limitations of the study, there are a number of more minor concerns. First, the main form of data collected during the fieldwork stage consisted of respondents' own impressions, thoughts and arguments. There is no guarantee that these were their 'real' opinions and although some degree of triangulation with other data sources was attempted where possible, and considerable attention was paid to reducing 'desirability bias' (see Chapter 3), the results reported should be viewed in the context that they represent only the *espoused* convictions and insights of informants. However, possibly the major concern in this respect – that informants would overly exaggerate the responsibility and integrity of their organizations – does not seem to have been a significant problem given the degrees of amorality identified here. Another possible concern, however, is that although some account has been made of the historical context of the sampled organizations, and although data collection was performed over a sixteen-month period, this study does represent to some extent something of a snapshot of the field of study. Whilst I have already discussed the limits of temporal context, this also brings up the question of analysing what are in fact mainly processes of organizational life through a largely static research method. In a sense then, the study relied on respondents' retrospective accounts and impressions of earlier stages in these processes. Whilst a longitudinal design may therefore be ultimately desirable, the exploratory nature of this research precluded such an approach.

Nevertheless, a number of studies of similar phenomena have adopted and endorsed retrospective data collection designs (see Bourgeois and Eisenhardt 1988; Eisenhardt and Schoonhoven 1990). Indeed, Miller *et al.* (1997) suggest that when conducted carefully, retrospective analyses of organizational phenomena are a valid and reliable means of gaining insights into organizational change (cf. Golden 1997).

Finally, it should be remembered that the findings I have presented and the conclusions I have reached should not be assumed to constitute a concrete or highly 'objective' reality. Rather, it is hoped that they constitute for the reader a credible and convincing version of reality, but certainly a version that I have mediated and shaped through rigorous, and to some extent creative, analysis. Indeed, this is very much an exploratory study, and should not be regarded as the definitive account of the research field. Avenues for further research which might build upon and consolidate this work are however apparent, and these I will discuss next.

Directions for further research

There are a number of ways in which this work could, and to my mind should, act as a foundation for further research. First, given possible concerns over the limited generalizability of the conclusions reached, the most obvious direction for further research to take is in replicating the study in other organizations, within different contexts, and for forms of marketing other than green marketing. Ideally, longitudinal designs could also be used. In this way, the concepts and constructs which have emerged from this study could be honed and sharpened into a more complete and rounded theory of moral meaning in marketing.

Second, I have argued at a number of points in the book that stakeholder theory and the networks model of marketing exchange appeared to provide theoretical structure to the green marketing dynamics revealed in the study. This observation, though, requires further investigation before any definitive theory of green marketing could be developed. Moreover, I have argued that these models principally provide descriptive and explanatory insight into green marketing. Their potential for normative or prescriptive power might also therefore be usefully explored.

Third, much of the discussion in the previous chapter also opens up a number of potentially fruitful avenues for future research. This could include more systematic empirical examination of the forces shaping amoralization, as well as longitudinal research investigating in more detail the outcomes of differing degrees and forms of moralization and amoralization. Moreover, although I discussed possible routes to moralization in some detail, I made no attempt to explicitly track and test the viability of these routes during this study. Hence, some exploration of their relative plausibility and potential for success would aid substantially in generating theory concerned with moral meaning in marketing, as well as in developing further recommendations and insights for practitioners.

Finally, although this study has attempted to draw together some of the disparate elements of the marketing and morality area such as the SMC and ethical decision making, further research is required in order to integrate these better. For example, how do amoralization and moralization fit into Hunt and Vitell's (1986, 1993) model of ethical decision making? Is it possible to predict different approaches to the SMC based on the cultural dynamics of the organization? These questions, and many others of a similar nature, could be valuably explored in further work. Clearly then, there is still much work to do before the area of marketing and morality is fully understood and conceptualized. Indeed, Glaser and Strauss (1967: 40) argue that in developing inductive theory grounded in data there can be no last word, and that ultimately, 'the published word is not the final one, but only a pause in the never-ending process of generating theory'. It is hoped then that this pause has at least been interesting, plausible, useful and as far as possible a meaningful one.

Implications for managers, green champions and others

In the light of my aspirations to have achieved some kind of understanding that might in some respect be 'useful', and since much of the discussion in the book is of a theoretical nature, it is worthwhile me briefly making explicit how the findings presented in the book could be of practical import. But what lessons and insights, if any, do the results of this study provide for managers and employees involved in green marketing, or for those otherwise interested in rendering the marketing process more 'moralized', more 'green' or more 'ethical' in its execution?

First, it can be argued that successful green marketing programmes need to take account not simply of the individual firm but of the network of internal and external interactions which might potentially impact upon any given programme. Accordingly, the role of the green marketing protagonist is likely to be in some sense political, suggesting that a high degree of interpersonal and political skills might be required for successful achievement of the project's goals. From an organizational point of view, the alliance approach to green marketing might be seen to provide a suitable framework in which to manage these various relationships more successfully. Moreover, alliances with stakeholders and network members appear to offer substantial potential for marketing solutions which can take account of 'deep ecology' principles of mutuality, interdependence and reciprocity. Critical in this respect appears to be the level of attention accorded to managing the cultural variations between collaborating organizations and the congruity of bonds between the actors, resources and activities linked by the project.

Second, for managers wishing to introduce greening into relatively unsympathetic, even hostile marketing contexts, the evidence from this study suggests that some degree of management of the moral meanings attending greening may be necessary. Whist there must clearly be doubts as to the long-term advisability of completely amoralizing the greening process, it cannot be doubted that some degree of amoralization appears to be useful in facilitating the introduction of greening initiatives into the organization. The way to do this, it appears, is to focus on the realms of language and symbolism, thus necessitating some considerable dexterity with symbols on the part of environmental protagonists. Again, those elements identified as the processes of amoralization, as well as the contextually-specific cultural dynamics detailed in Chapters 4, 5 and 6 might be consulted for guidance on possible avenues for achieving this.

However, from an environment point of view, such amoralization might be seen as potentially harmful to the green agenda, and certainly in terms of 'deep' greening, should probably be avoided. In order to introduce more fundamental and lasting greening initiatives then, a more 'moralized' process would be recommended. By the same token, though, the scope and potential for individuals to manage morality – and especially to enhance moralization – appears to be largely pre-determined, not so much by their own ability, but by existing organizational characteristics. The third main implication then relates to the rather limited possibilities for morality to be injected meaningfully into the marketing landscape. Basic structural factors such as organizational type, owner-ship, governance, size and degree of bureaucratization might have considerable impact on the potential in this respect. Hence, managers wishing to introduce greater moralization into a large, highly bureaucratized, joint stock company governed by professional directors and owned by institutional shareholders are likely to be faced with far more extensive obstacles than those confronted with the same task in a small, entrepreneurial, social mission co-operative. This is not to say that the former will necessarily be less 'ethical' than the latter, only that moral awareness and communication in general is likely to be lower. Moreover, levels of amoralization and moralization appear to be highly contingent on the cultural and political context in which the marketing process is enacted, and it is highly likely that only by grasping the cultural and political dynamics at play in any given situation can the manager begin to effect any kind of meaningful moral transformation of marketing.

This is not to suggest that the manager can, or even should, attempt to change the culture of the organization. The discussion in the previous chapter suggests that this might be not only extremely difficult, but possibly even counter-productive for the objectives intended. Clearly, attempts at cultural homogeneity and unity have less potential for moralization than those which recognize the existence of subcultural differences and their attendant power differentials. My fourth, and final, implication then is that managerial knowledge of the prevailing political and cultural landscape of the organization rather than of an ideal 'ethical culture' is critical for developing insight into which dynamics might be fruitfully employed either to introduce green or social projects in a relatively uncontested fashion, or – somewhat more challengingly – to introduce a more moralized version of these projects. In the final analysis, the move towards a form of market-ing more meaningful in a moral sense, and more open and sensitive to green sensibilities remains a long way off, and will not be reached without enormous effort, insight and commitment.

Summary of main contributions

A number of important insights have been presented throughout this book. However, I would suggest that the main contributions of the study reported here can be summarized in terms of the following four points:

1 The book has provided an in-depth empirically-based examination of green marketing – an area which previously had not been subjected to a great deal of empirical enquiry. The study not only attempted to formulate a moral dimension to green marketing, but also explored the practice of green marketing across a range of different organizational contexts, as well as providing new insight into process as well as content issues. This can be seen to be a valuable addition to an emerging, but previously rather unconvincing, area of literature.

2 The inductive, qualitative, case study research method applied in the study is one that has been shown to be well-suited to the types of question under examination, but which has also been significantly under-utilized in the marketing, business ethics, and green business fields to date. As a result, it has been possible to develop unique and important insights into the area of marketing and morality, particularly in relation to the cultural dynamics of green marketing and the phenomenon of amoralization. The comparative case method applied here has allowed for understandings of amoralization to be refined in terms of specific contexts. The use of an interpretive approach to produce important findings has also contributed to some extent to a redressing of the existing, and epistemologically prohibitive, imbalance towards positivist, quantitative methods in the extant literature.

3 The study has also made an important step towards developing a more rigorous utilization of the concept of organizational culture to marketing, business ethics and green business. The more common utilization of culture in these areas – i.e. as a managerial variable – has been largely discredited in the organization studies and organizational behaviour fields. Hence, the use here of culture as a means of analysing meaning within the organization reflects a move towards establishing a more informed conceptual understanding of morality within the marketing process.

4 Finally, and perhaps most importantly, by focusing on moral meaning, the book has addressed an aspect of marketing and morality which, although critically important, had not been previously subjected to any significant degree of scholarly investigation. Accordingly, new knowledge has emerged regarding how organization members experience, think, feel and communicate about morality in the organization. This has led to the development of important concepts and constructs which contribute to our understanding of this area – such as amoralization and moralization – and examination of their nature and impact in different organizational contexts. If these findings succeed in providing insight or illumination to fellow academics or to practitioners – and there is every reason to believe that they will – then the ambition of this book will have been realized.

Notes

1 Introduction

1 The term 'marketing' is used in its broadest sense here to describe any of a number of related activities associated with the facilitation and securing of exchanges between an organization and its customers. To use a distinction more often used in the strategy literature, marketing is viewed here as comprising not only content (what marketing decisions are made and which marketing activities are undertaken) but also process (how those decisions are reached and how those activities come to take place) and context (the situation in which those decisions are made). Indeed, in the light of the work of leading strategy writers such as Pettigrew (e.g. 1973, 1979, 1985) and Mintzberg (e.g. 1989, 1990, 1991), and the exhortations of critical marketing theorists, such as Brownlie *et al.* (1994), much of the focus in this book is on the process of marketing, such as to discover how marketing *is* conducted rather than how it *should be* conducted.

2 The term green marketing is used here as an umbrella term for the diverse literature which goes under the varied headings of 'ecological marketing', 'green consumerism', 'sustainable marketing', etc. Whilst it is recognized that these terms can in themselves impute particular theoretical and ideological positions (van Dam and Apeldoorn 1996), the intention here is not to imply a particular position by the use of the green marketing label; it is simply a shorthand for identifying literature which relates marketing to the natural environment.

3 Definitions of what constitutes 'natural', 'environmental', 'ecology', 'greening' and related concepts are highly complex and continue to occupy scholars in environmental ethics, politics, sociology, organization studies and various other areas of enquiry (e.g. Gorz 1980; Naess 1989; Gladwin 1993; Shrivastava 1994; Macnaghten and Urry 1995). In this book, the definition employed for the natural environment has remained deliberately non-specific, in order to more effectively elicit the meanings applied by organization members. This is important from a moral perspective since different meanings reflect different ethical positions and assumptions (Naess 1989; Shrivastava 1993). Accordingly, the range of terms relating to the natural environment are used fairly indiscriminately, unless a more precise definition is necessary to develop a particular point, or to reflect the meaning intended by an interviewee or author.

4 For a fuller discussion of moral relativism, see Beauchamp and Bowie (1997: 8–12); De George (1999: 33–55).

2 Marketing and morality: perspectives and issues

1 It is beyond the scope of this book to examine in any detail the morality of capitalism. Although related, it is a different question to that which refers to the morality of

marketing. For the purpose of the study, 'marketing' is intended to mean marketing in a capitalist economy. Hence, capitalist objectives can be seen to be a constraint on the moral possibilities of marketing (Robin and Reidenbach 1993).

2 Dates given refer to translated works. It is worth mentioning that at the time Baudrillard produced the original French language versions (in 1972 and 1970 respectively) he employed Marxian and structuralist techniques of analysis, indicating a largely modernist perspective; this stands in marked contrast to his later, postmodernist/post-structuralist work (Kellner 1989; Ritzer 1997).

3 For more in-depth discussion regarding depictions of the consumer as an identity seeker, chooser or victim (and others), see Gabriel and Lang (1995).

4 This is symptomatic of a more widespread failure of mainstream marketing literature to develop a critical perspective on consumption and consumer culture. This debate has taken place largely in the cultural studies and critical theory literature rather than in marketing journals.

5 Deontology is essentially an ethic of duty whereby morality is determined by looking at the motive for action. Utilitarianism is an ethic of consequences which basically stresses the assessment of relative social costs and benefits. Virtue ethics considers the moral character of individuals within their communities. For more extensive discussion, see Chryssides and Kaler (1993), Beauchamp and Bowie (1997), De George (1999).

6 This is certainly the case with all of Kotler's texts. The appearance of the SMC elsewhere is to some extent due to the sizeable impact that Kotler and his texts have had on mainstream marketing thought.

7 This basically says that different levels of the product can be identified. These are: the core product, which is the fundamental benefit sought by consumers; the expected (or actual) product, which is the basic physical product which delivers those benefits; and the augmented product, which is the addition of unsolicited extras which provide additional benefit to the consumer.

8 See Crane (2000) for more in-depth and extended analysis of 'ethical' product concepts.

9 For example, Vandermerwe and Oliff (1990: 10–11), Peattie (1995: 59), Schlegelmilch *et al.* (1996: 35) and Menon and Menon (1997: 51) all present the growth of green consumerism as inevitable and perpetual. Smith (1990) and Strong (1996: 5–6) among others argue similarly for ethical consumerism.

10 Indeed, there is a swathe of survey evidence of this kind which reveals a cynicism amongst managers concerning the ethics of superiors and peer groups (Treviño 1986), with the work by Ferrell and colleagues (Ferrell and Weaver 1978; Krugman and Ferrell 1981) illustrating this most explicitly in the marketing field.

3 Exploring moral meaning in green marketing

1 Interested readers can find a whole host of excellent treatments of this subject. For a good, basic introduction to the general issues in relation to management research see Easterby-Smith *et al.* (1991) or for a discussion specific to qualitative research, I recommend, among others, Morgan and Smircich (1980) and the special issue on qualitative methods in the *Journal of Management Studies* (20/3, 1983). My own position is set out more fully in Crane (1999).

2 A recent special edition of the *European Journal of Marketing* on marketing and social responsibility (30/5, 1996) also provides a good example of the balance of research in the literature. Of six papers published, only two were based on original empirical work carried out by the authors – and both were surveys.

3 Excellent discussions on sample sizes in qualitative research can be found in Mintzberg (1979), Eisenhardt (1989, 1991), and Dyer and Wilkins (1991).

4 The formulation, impact and implications of the original Rochdale principles have been discussed at length elsewhere (see in particular, Bonner 1961).

4 Conventional companies

1 It should be noted that these assertions from executives tended to be based either on secondary research (such as Mintel reports) or anecdotal evidence. To my knowledge, the company itself had conducted no market research at all on environmental issues.

2 Such concern with its environmental reputation was almost certainly intensified by RetailCo's recurrent problems with animal rights activists. Hence, one senior executive confided to me that, 'where we've been hammered in the past is animal testing'. This had involved various protest activities through the 1980s and 1990s such as store picketing and disruption of the corporate parent's AGM.

3 Drumwright (1994) in fact regards an ethical motivation as intrinsic to the definition of a policy entrepreneur. This stricter definition is not utilized here.

4 Whilst definitions of sustainability can vary immensely (Dobson 1996), the definition of 'sustainable development' from the Brundtland Report (World Commission on Environment and Development 1987) is probably the most widely cited. It defines sustainable development as follows: 'Development that meets the needs of the present without compromising the ability of future generations to meet their own needs.'

5 To preserve anonymity, 'concern' is a substitute term (although similar) for the actual termed used by RetailCo.

5 Social mission companies

1 This is not so say that these firms have been without their critics in terms of their social programmes. See for example, Entine (1994) and Cowe and Entine (1996).

2 At the time of the fieldwork, this was a very new development and amounted to only a single experimental store, the success of which could not at the time be determined with any certainty.

3 Given the size of RetailSoc, other policy entrepreneurs may also have been present elsewhere in the organization. However, these were not identified during quite extensive fieldwork at the organization, and so cannot be included in this discussion.

4 Size was certainly an important issue here. Equally, it should be remembered that at the time of the fieldwork, MarketingSoc employed only voluntary staff in addition to its two directors.

5 The only exception to this was at MarketingSoc where managers claimed that any future employees would have to be environmentally motivated individuals. However, at the time of fieldwork only voluntary staff were employed at MarketingSoc.

6 Business–NGO collaboration

1 CollabOrg was established to continue the work of a virtually identical predecessor. This first alliance had been formed in December 1991, but with a set termination in 1995. Since all of the original group members became members of CollabOrg at the group's termination in 1995, they were, for the purpose of this study, regarded as a single organization.

2 See Lamming and Hampson (1996) for a discussion of the relative merits of vendor questionnaires and other forms of environmental management through supply chains.

3 In CollabOrg as a whole, out of seventy-three executives identified as the main representatives for their companies in the group, only six were dedicated procurement staff.

4 It is important to note that at the time of data collection, few certified products were yet on the market, and managers were generally very cautious in their estimations of the potential appeal to consumers.

5 Drumwright (1994) also attests to the low profile of top management in successful green

purchasing initiatives. This conflicts with much of the existing prescriptive green business literature (e.g. Elkington and Burke 1989; Welford and Gouldson 1993).

6 Unlike the commercial partners, there was not a complete avoidance of 'sustainability' terms on the part of their NGO partner, either by NGO respondents themselves, or in communications to other audiences. It is also important to note that the accreditation organization used by CollabOrg had also decided to utilize 'well-managed' in defining its principles of forest management.

7 Green marketing and morality: evidence from three approaches

1 This refers only to conventional and social mission companies – packaging was not directly included in the CollabOrg initiative.

2 Donaldson and Preston (1995) argue that there are two other conceptions of stakeholder theory in addition to its descriptive form, i.e. as a normative model of how organizations should behave, and as an instrumental model of how organizations can improve their performance. Whilst it is not the intention to explore these dimensions here, they certainly demand further attention in the future in order to develop a more complete theory of green marketing.

3 For more detail on the 'shallow'–'deep' distinction as it pertains to management and marketing, see Gray (1992), Shrivastava (1994), Kilbourne (1995) and Welford (1995).

8 Amoralization, moralization, marketing and the natural environment

1 Asking respondents directly would of course have been one solution. This, however, was not deemed appropriate in many instances due to the fact that interviews were deliberately focused on environmental rather than ethical issues, as discussed in Chapter 3. Only where respondents themselves had already brought up questions of morality was this approach taken. In other situations, more elliptical reference was made to the amoralization process. This could help to gain insight without unduly steering respondents, or otherwise prompting desirability bias.

References

Abratt, R. and Sacks, D. (1988), 'The Marketing Challenge: Towards Being Profitable and Socially Responsible', *Journal of Business Ethics*, vol. 7, pp. 497–507.

Abratt, R. and Sacks, D. (1989), 'Perceptions of the Societal Marketing Concept', *European Journal of Marketing*, vol. 23 (6), pp. 25–33.

Ackerstein, D.S. and Lemon, K.A. (1999), 'Greening the Brand: Environmental Marketing Strategies and the American Consumer', in M. Charter and M.J. Polonsky (eds), *Greener Marketing: A Global Perspective on Greening Marketing Practice*, Sheffield: Greenleaf.

Advertising Association (1993), 'Speaking Up for Advertising', in G.C. Chryssides and J.H. Kaler, *An Introduction to Business Ethics*, London: Chapman and Hall.

Akaah, I.P. and Riordan, E.A. (1989), 'Judgements of Marketing Professionals About Ethical Issues in Marketing Research: A Replication and Extension', *Journal of Marketing Research*, vol. 26, February, pp. 112–120.

Aldag, R.J. and Bartol, K.M. (1978), 'Empirical Studies of Corporate Social Performance and Policy: A Survey of Problems and Results', in L.E. Preston (ed.), *Research in Corporate Social Performance and Policy (vol. 1)*, Greenwich, CT: JAI Press.

Anderson, J.C., Hakansson, H. and Johanson, J. (1994), 'Dyadic Business Relationships Within a Business Network Context', *Journal of Marketing*, vol. 58, pp. 1–15.

Anderson, W.T. and Cunningham, W.H. (1972), 'The Socially Conscious Consumer', *Journal of Marketing*, vol. 36 (3), pp. 23–31.

Anthony, P. (1994), *Managing Culture*, Buckingham: Open University Press.

Arnold, M.J. and Fisher, J.E. (1996), 'Counterculture, Criticisms, and Crisis: Assessing the Effect of the Sixties on Marketing Thought', *Journal of Macromarketing*, vol. 16 (1), pp. 118–133.

Ashford, S.J., Rothbard, N.P., Piderit, S.K. and Dutton, J.E. (1998), 'Out on a Limb: the Role of Context and Impression Management in Selling Gender-Equity Issues', *Administrative Science Quarterly*, vol. 43, pp. 23–57.

Ashley, W.J. (1912), 'Preface', in E. Cadbury, *Experiments in Industrial Organization*, London: Longman Green.

Assael, H. (1995), *Consumer Behaviour and Marketing Action*, 5th edn, Cincinnati, OH: South-Western College.

Aupperle, K., Carroll, A. and Hatfield, J. (1985), 'An Empirical Examination of the Relationship Between Corporate Social Responsibility and Profitability', *Academy of Management Journal*, vol. 28 (2), pp. 446–463.

Bailey, J. (1955), *The British Co-operative Movement*, London: Hutchinson.

Banerjee, S., Gulas, C.S. and Iyer, E. (1995), 'Shades of Green: A Multidimensional Analysis of Environmental Advertising', *Journal of Advertising*, vol. 24 (2), pp. 21–31.

Bartels, R. (1967), 'A Model for Ethics in Marketing', *Journal of Marketing*, vol. 31 (1), January, pp. 20–26.

Barthes, R. (1973), *Mythologies*, Paladin.

Bate, P. (1984), 'The Impact of Organizational Culture on Approaches to Organizational Problem Solving', *Organization Studies*, vol. 5 (1), pp. 43–66.

Baudrillard, J. (1981), *For a Critique of the Political Economy of the Sign*, St. Louis, MO: Telos Press.

Baudrillard, J. (1983), *Simulations*, trans. P. Foss, P. Patton and P. Beitchman, New York: Semiotext(e).

Baudrillard, J. (1997), *The Consumer Society: Myths and Structures*, London: Sage.

Bauman, Z. (1989), *Modernity and the Holocaust*, Oxford: Polity Press.

Bauman, Z. (1993), *Postmodern Ethics*, Oxford: Blackwell.

Baumhart, R.C. (1961), 'How Ethical Are Businesses?', *Harvard Business Review*, July–August, p. 6.

Beauchamp, T.L. (1989), *Case Studies in Business, Society and Ethics*, Englewood Cliffs, NJ: Prentice Hall.

Beauchamp, T.L. and Bowie, N.E. (1997), *Ethical Theory and Business*, 5th edn, Englewood Cliffs, NJ: Prentice Hall.

Bebbington, J. and Gray, R. (1992), 'Greener Pricing', in M. Charter (ed.), *Greener Marketing*, Sheffield: Greenleaf.

Berger, P.L. and Luckmann, T. (1966), *The Social Construction of Reality*, London: Penguin.

Bernstein, D. (1992), *In the Company of Green*, London: ISBA Publications.

Birchall, J. (1994), *Co-op: The People's Business*, Manchester: Manchester University Press.

Bird, F.B. and Waters, J.A. (1989), 'The Moral Muteness of Managers', *California Management Review*, vol. 32 (1), pp. 73–88.

Boje, D.M. (1991), 'The Storytelling Organization: a Study of Story Performance in an Office-Supply Firm', *Administrative Science Quarterly*, vol. 36, pp. 106–126.

Boje, D.M., Fedor, D.B. and Rowland, K.M. (1982), 'Myth Making: A Qualitative Step in OD Interventions', *The Journal of Applied Behavioural Science*, vol. 18 (1), pp. 17–28.

Bone, P.F. and Corey, R.J. (1998), 'Moral Reflections in Marketing', *Journal of Macromarketing*, vol. 18 (2), pp. 104–114.

Bonner, A. (1961), *British Co-operation*, Stockport: Co-operative Union Ltd.

Bonoma, T.V. (1985), 'Case Research in Marketing: Opportunities, Problems, and a Process', *Journal of Marketing Research*, vol. XXII, May, pp. 199–208.

Bourgeois, L.J. and Eisenhardt, K.M. (1988), 'Strategic Decision Processes in High Velocity Environments: Four Cases in the Microcomputer Industry', *Management Science*, vol. 34 (7), pp. 816–835.

Bowie, N. (1991), 'New Directions in Corporate Social Responsibility', *Business Horizons*, July–August, pp. 56–65.

Boyce, M.E. (1995), 'Collective Centring and Collective Sensemaking in the Stories and Storytelling of One Organization', *Organization Studies*, vol. 16 (1), pp. 107–137.

Brigley, S. (1995), 'Business Ethics Research: A Cultural Perspective', *Business Ethics: A European Review*, vol. 4 (1), pp. 17–23.

Brown, A.D. (1994), 'Politics, Symbolic Action and Myth Making in Pursuit of Legitimacy', *Organization Studies*, vol. 15 (6), pp. 861–878.

Brown, A.D. (1995a), *Organizational Culture*, London: Pitman.

Brown, A.D. (1995b), 'Managing Understandings: Politics, Symbolism, Niche Marketing and the Quest for Legitimacy in IT Implementation', *Organization Studies*, vol. 16 (6), pp. 951–969.

Brown, A.D. and Ennew, C.T. (1995), 'Market Research and the Politics of New Product Development', *Journal of Marketing Management*, vol. 11 (4), pp. 339–353.

Brownlie, D., Saren, M., Whittington, R. and Wensley, R. (1994), 'The New Marketing Myopia: Critical Perspectives on Theory and Research in Marketing – Introduction', *European Journal of Marketing*, vol. 28 (3), pp. 6–12.

Bucklin, L.P. and Sengupta, S. (1993), 'Organizing Successful Co-Marketing Alliances', *Journal of Marketing*, vol. 57 (2), April, pp. 32–46.

Burke, L. and Logsdon, J.M. (1996), 'How Corporate Social Responsibility Pays Off', *Long Range Planning*, vol. 29 (4), pp. 495–502.

Butcher, M. (1996), 'The Co-operative Movement: Business Relic or a Model for the Future?', *Business Studies*, December, pp. 25–28.

Butler, J. E. and Kraisornsuthasinee, S. (1999), 'Green Strategies in Developing Economies: A South–East Asian Perspective', in M. Charter and M.J. Polonsky (eds), *Greener Marketing: A Global Perspective on Greening Marketing Practice*, Sheffield: Greenleaf.

Carlson, L., Grove, S.J. and Kangun, N. (1993), 'A Content Analysis of Environmental Advertising Claims: A Matrix Method Approach', *Journal of Advertising*, vol. 22 (3), pp. 27–39.

Carroll, A.B. (1979), 'A Three-Dimensional Conceptual Model of Corporate Performance', *Academy of Management Review*, vol. 4 (4), pp. 497–505.

Carr-Saunders, A.M., Florence, P.S. and Peers, R. (1938), *Consumers' Co-operation in Great Britain*, London: George Allen & Unwin.

Chakrabarti, A.K. (1974), 'The Role of the Champion in Product Innovation', *California Management Review*, vol. 27 (2), pp. 58–62.

Chappell, T. (1993), *The Soul of a Business: Managing for Profit and the Common Good*, New York: Bantam Books.

Charter, M. (1992), *Greener Marketing*, Sheffield: Greenleaf.

Chen, A.Y.S., Sawyers, R.B. and Williams, P.F. (1997), 'Reinforcing Ethical Decision Making Through Corporate Culture', *Journal of Business Ethics*, vol. 16, pp. 855–865.

Chonko, L.B. and Hunt, S.D. (1985), 'Ethics and Marketing Management: An Empirical Investigation', *Journal of Business Research*, vol. 19, pp. 339–359.

Christensen, L.T. (1995), 'Buffering Organizational Identity in the Marketing Culture', *Organization Studies*, vol. 16 (4), pp. 651–672.

Chryssides, G.C. and Kaler, J.H. (1993), *An Introduction to Business Ethics*, London: Chapman & Hall.

Chryssides, G.C. and Kaler, J.H. (1996), *Essentials of Business Ethics*, London: McGraw-Hill.

Churchill, D. (1986), 'The Rochdale Pioneering Spirit Adrift Among the High Street Store Groups', *Financial Times*, 24 May 1986, p. 5.

Clutterbuck, D., Dearlove, D. and Snow, D. (1992), *Actions Speak Louder*, 2nd edn, London: Kogan Page.

Collins, J.W. and Ganotis, C.G. (1973), 'Is Social Responsibility Sabotaged by the Rank and File?', *Business and Society Review / Innovation*, Autumn, pp. 82–88.

Cooper, G. (1998), 'Women Consumers "More Ethical Than Men"', *The Independent*, 12 January 1998, p. 2.

Corey, E.R. (1993), 'Marketing Managers: Caught in the Middle', in N.C. Smith and J.A. Quelch (eds), *Ethics in Marketing*, Homewood, IL: Irwin.

Cowe, R. and Entine, J. (1996), 'Fair Enough?', *Guardian*, Weekend, 14 December 1996, pp. 30–35.

Cramer, J. and Schot, J. (1993), 'Environmental Comakership Among Firms as a Cornerstone in the Striving for Sustainable Development', in K. Fischer and J. Schot (eds), *Environmental Strategies for Industry*, Washington, DC: Island Press.

Crane, A. (1999), 'Are You Ethical? Please Tick Yes ☐ or No ☐: On Researching Ethics in Business Organizations', *Journal of Business Ethics*, vol. 20 (3), pp. 237–248.

Crane, A. (2000), 'Unpacking the Ethical Product', *Journal of Business Ethics*, forthcoming.

CWS (1995), *Responsible Retailing*, Manchester: CWS Ltd.

Dahler-Larsen, P. (1994), 'Corporate Culture and Morality: Durkheim-Inspired Reflections on the Limits of Corporate Culture', *Journal of Management Studies*, vol. 31 (1), pp. 1–18.

David, F.R. (1989), 'How Companies Define Their Mission', *Long Range Planning*, vol. 22 (1), pp. 90–97.

Davidson, M. (1992), *The Consumerist Manifesto*, London: Routledge.

Davis, J.J. (1992), 'Ethics and Environmental Marketing', *Journal of Business Ethics*, vol. 11, pp. 81–87.

De George, R.T. (1990), *Business Ethics*, 3rd edn, New York: Macmillan.

De George, R.T. (1999), *Business Ethics*, 5th edn, Upper Saddle River, NJ: Prentice Hall.

Deal, T.E. and Kennedy, A.A. (1982), *Corporate Cultures*, Reading, MA: Addison Wesley.

Desmond, J. (1998), 'Marketing and Moral Indifference', in M. Parker (ed.), *Ethics and Organizations*, London: Sage.

Devlin, J.F., Ennew, C.T., Hull, A. and Sherman, L.A. (1996), 'Ethics and the Church: Should God be Sold or Found?', in M. Baker (ed.), *2021 – A Vision for the Next 25 Years*, Proceedings of the 1996 Annual Marketing Education Group Conference, University of Strathclyde, Glasgow.

Diacon, S.D. and Ennew, C.T. (1996), 'Can Business Ethics Enhance Corporate Governance? Evidence from a Survey of UK Insurance Executives', *Journal of Business Ethics*, vol. 15 (6), pp. 623–634.

Dibb, S., Simkin, L., Pride, W.M. and Ferrell, O.C. (1994), *Marketing: Concepts and Strategies*, 2nd edn, Boston, MA: Houghton Mifflin.

Dillon, P.S. and Fischer, K. (1992), *Environmental Management in Corporations: Methods and Motivations*, Medford, MA: CEM.

Dixon, D.F. (1992), 'Consumer Sovereignty, Democracy, and the Marketing Concept: A Macromarketing Perspective', *Canadian Journal of Administrative Sciences*, vol. 9 (2), pp. 116–125.

Dobson, A. (1996), 'Environmental Sustainabilities: An Analysis and Typology', *Environmental Politics*, vol. 5 (3), pp. 401–428.

Donaldson, T. and Preston, L.E. (1995), 'The Stakeholder Theory of the Corporation: Concepts, Evidence and Implications', *Academy of Management Review*, vol. 20 (1), pp. 65–91.

Dooley, R.S. and Lerner, L.D. (1994), 'Pollution, Profits, and Stakeholders: The Constraining Effect of Economic Performance on CEO Concern with Stakeholder Expectations', *Journal of Business Ethics*, vol. 13, pp. 701–711.

Drumwright, M. (1994), 'Socially Responsible Organizational Buying: Environmental Concern as a Noneconomic Buying Criterion', *Journal of Marketing*, vol. 58 (3), July, pp. 1–19.

Drumwright, M. (1996), 'Company Advertising With a Social Dimension: The Role of Noneconomic Criteria', *Journal of Marketing*, vol. 60 (4), pp. 71–87.

Du Gay, P. and Salaman, G. (1992), 'The Cult(ure) of the Customer', *Journal of Management Studies*, vol. 29 (5), pp. 615–633.

Dutton, J.E. and Ashford, S.J. (1993), 'Selling Issues to Top Management', *Academy of Management Review*, vol. 18 (3), pp. 397–428.

Dyer, W.G. and Wilkins, A.L. (1991), 'Better Stories, Not Better Constructs to Generate

Better Theory: A Rejoinder to Eisenhardt', *Academy of Management Review*, vol. 16 (3), pp. 613–619.

Easterby-Smith, M., Thorpe, R. and Lowe, A. (1991), *Management Research*, London: Sage Publications.

Easton, G. (1992), 'Industrial Networks: A Review', in B. Axelsson and G. Easton (eds), *Industrial Networks: A New View of Reality*, London: Routledge.

Eisenhardt, K.M. (1989), 'Building Theories from Case Study Research', *Academy of Management Review*, vol. 14 (4), pp. 532–550.

Eisenhardt, K.M. (1991), 'Better Stories and Better Constructs: The Case for Rigor and Comparative Logic', *Academy of Management Review*, vol. 16 (3), pp. 620–627.

Eisenhardt, K.M. and Schoonhoven, C.B. (1990), 'Organizational Growth: Linking Founding Team, Strategy, Environment, and Growth among U.S. Semiconductor Ventures, 1978–1988', *Administrative Science Quarterly*, vol. 35, pp. 504–529.

Elkington, J. (1997), 'Foreword', in D.F. Murphy, and J. Bendell, *In the Company of Partners: Business, Environmental Groups and Sustainable Development Post-Rio*, Bristol: Policy Press.

Elkington, J. and Burke, T. (1989), *The Green Capitalists*, London: Victor Gollancz.

Elsbach, K.D. (1994), 'Managing Organizational Legitimacy in the California Cattle Industry: the Construction and Effectiveness of Verbal Accounts', *Administrative Science Quarterly*, vol. 39, pp. 57–88.

Elsbach, K.D. and Sutton, R.I. (1992), 'Acquiring Organizational Legitimacy Through Illegitimate Actions: a Marriage of Institutional and Impression Management Theories', *Academy of Management Journal*, vol. 35 (4), pp. 699–738.

Entine, J. (1994), 'Shattered Image', *Business Ethics*, vol. 8 (5), pp. 23–28.

Evered, R and Louis, M.R. (1981), 'Alternative Perspectives in the Organizational Sciences', *Academy of Management Review*, vol. 6 (3), pp. 385–395.

Farmer, R.N. (1967), 'Would You Let Your Daughter Marry a Marketing Man?', *Journal of Marketing*, vol. 31, January, pp. 1–3.

Featherstone, M. (1991), *Consumer Culture and Postmodernism*, London: Sage.

Ferrell, O.C. and Weaver, K.M. (1978), 'Ethical Beliefs of Marketing Managers', *Journal of Marketing*, vol. 42 (4), pp. 69–73.

Ferrell, O.C., Gresham, L.G. and Fraedrich, J. (1989), 'A Synthesis of Ethical Decision Models for Marketing', *Journal of Macromarketing*, vol. 9 (2), pp. 55–64.

Fineman, S. (1995), 'Moral Meanings and Green Organizational Change', paper presented at the Academy of Management Meeting, Vancouver.

Fineman, S. (1996), 'Emotional Subtexts in Corporate Greening', *Organization Studies*, vol. 17 (3), pp. 479–500.

Fineman, S. (1997), 'Constructing the Green Manager', *British Journal of Management*, vol. 8 (1), pp. 31–38.

Fineman, S. (1998), 'The Natural Environment, Organization and Ethics', in M. Parker (ed.), *Ethics and Organizations*, London: Sage.

Fineman, S. and Clarke, K. (1996), 'Green Stakeholders: Industry Interpretations and Response', *Journal of Management Studies*, vol. 33 (6), pp. 715–730.

Fineman, S. and Mangham, I. (1983), 'Data, Meanings and Creativity: A Preface', *Journal of Management Studies*, vol. 20 (3), pp. 295–300.

Fisk, G. (1973), 'Criteria for a Theory of Responsible Consumption', *Journal of Marketing*, vol. 37 (2), April, pp. 24–31.

Fisk, G. (1974), *Marketing and the Ecological Crisis*, New York: Harper and Row.

Ford, D. (1980), 'The Development of Buyer–Seller Relationships in Industrial Markets', *European Journal of Marketing*, vol. 14 (5/6), pp. 339–353.

Fox, K.A. and Kotler, P. (1980), 'The Marketing of Social Causes: The First Ten Years', *Journal of Marketing*, vol. 44 (4), Fall, pp. 24–33.

Frances, J. and Garnsey, E. (1996), 'Supermarkets and Suppliers in the United Kingdom: System Integration, Information and Control', *Accounting, Organizations and Society*, vol. 21(6), pp. 591–610.

Freeman, R.E. (1984), *Strategic Management: A Stakeholder Approach*, Boston, MA: Pitman.

Freeman, R.E. and Gilbert, D.R. (1988), *Corporate Strategy and the Search for Ethics*, Englewood Cliffs, NJ: Prentice Hall.

Friedman, M. (1970), 'The Social Responsibility of Business is to Increase its Profits', *New York Times Magazine*, 13 September 1970.

Fuller, D.A. (1999), *Sustainable Marketing: Managerial–Ecological Issues*, Thousand Oaks, CA: Sage.

Gabriel, Y. and Lang, T. (1995), *The Unmanageable Consumer: Contemporary Consumption and its Fragmentation*, London: Sage.

Galbraith, J.K. (1972), *The New Industrial State*, 2nd edn, Harmondsworth: Penguin.

Galbraith, J.K. (1977), *The Affluent Society*, 3rd rev. edn, Harmondsworth: Penguin.

Gardner, W.L. and Martinko, M.J. (1988), 'Impression Management: an Observational Study Linking Audience Characteristics with Verbal Self-presentations', *Academy of Management Journal*, vol. 31 (1), pp. 42–65.

Gaski, F. (1985), 'Dangerous Territory: the Societal Marketing Concept Revisited', *Business Horizons*, vol. 28, pp. 42–7.

Geertz, C. (1973), *The Interpretation of Cultures*, New York: Basic Books.

Gilly, M.C. and Wolfinbarger, M. (1998), 'Advertising's Internal Audience', *Journal of Marketing*, vol. 62 (1), January, pp. 69–88.

Gladwin, T.N. (1993), 'The Meaning of Greening: A Plea for Organizational Theory', in K. Fischer and J. Schot (eds), *Environmental Strategies for Industry*, Washington, DC: Island Press.

Glaser, B.G. and Strauss, A.L. (1967), *The Discovery of Grounded Theory*, New York: Aldine.

Golden, B.R. (1997), 'Further Remarks on Retrospective Accounts in Organizational and Strategic Management Research', *Academy of Management Journal*, vol. 40 (5), pp. 1243–1252.

Gorz, A. (1980), *Ecology as Politics*, trans. P. Vigderman and J. Cloud, London: Pluto.

Gorz, A. (1989), *Critique of Economic Reason*, trans. G. Handyside and C. Turner, London: Verso.

Gray, R.H. (1992), 'Accounting and Environmentalism: An Exploration of the Challenge of Gently Accounting for Accountability, Transparency and Sustainability', *Accounting, Organizations and Society*, vol. 17 (5), pp. 399–426.

Gray, R.H., Bebbington, K.J. and Waters, D. (1993), *Accounting for the Environment: The Greening of Accountancy Part II*, London: Paul Chapman.

Gray, R.H., Kouhy, R. and Lavers, S. (1995), 'Corporate Social and Environmental Reporting: A Review of the Literature and a Longitudinal Study of UK Disclosure', *Accounting, Auditing and Accountability Journal*, vol. 8 (2), pp. 46–77.

Greyser, S.A. (1972), 'Advertising: Attacks and Counters', *Harvard Business Review*, vol. 50 (2), March–April, pp. 1–9.

Gummesson, E. (1987), 'The New Marketing – Developing Long-Term Interactive Relationships', *Long Range Planning*, vol. 20 (4), pp. 10–20.

Gummesson, E. (1991), *Qualitative Methods in Management Research*, London: Sage.

Hakansson, H. and Snehota, I. (1997a), 'No Business is an Island: The Network Concept of Business Strategy', in D. Ford (ed.), *Understanding Business Markets*, 2nd edn, London: Dryden Press.

Hakansson, H. and Snehota, I. (1997b), 'Analysing Business Relationships', in D. Ford (ed.), *Understanding Business Markets*, 2nd edn, London: Dryden Press.

Hamel, G. and Prahalad, C.K. (1991), 'Corporate Imagination and Expeditionary Marketing', *Harvard Business Review*, July–August, pp. 81–92.

Hamel, G. and Prahalad, C.K. (1994), 'Seeing the Future First', *Fortune*, 5 September 1994, pp. 64–68.

Hamel, G., Doz, Y.L. and Prahalad, C.K. (1989), 'Collaborate With Your Competitors – and Win', *Harvard Business Review*, January–February, pp. 133–139.

Hartman, C.L. and Stafford, E.R. (1997), 'Green Alliances: Building New Business with Environmental Groups', *Long Range Planning*, vol. 30 (2), pp. 184–196.

Hartman, C.L. and Stafford, E.R. (1998), 'Crafting "Enviropreneurial" Value Chain Strategies Through Green Alliances', *Business Horizons*, March–April, pp. 62–72.

Harvey, B., Smith, S. and Wilkinson, B. (1984), *Managers and Corporate Social Policy*, London: Macmillan Press.

Hassard, J. (1993), *Sociology and Organization Theory*, Cambridge: Cambridge University Press.

Herzberg, F. (1968), 'One More Time: How Do You Motivate Employees?', *Harvard Business Review*, vol. 46 (1), pp. 53–62.

Hoffman, A.J. (1993), 'The Importance of Fit Between Individual Values and Organizational Culture in the Greening of Industry', *Business Strategy and the Environment*, vol. 2 (4), pp. 10–18.

Hunt, S.D. and Vitell, S.J. (1986), 'A General Theory of Marketing Ethics', *Journal of Macromarketing*, vol. 6, Spring, pp. 5–16.

Hunt, S.D. and Vitell, S.J. (1993), 'The General Theory of Marketing Ethics: A Retrospective and Revision', in N.C. Smith and J.A. Quelch (eds), *Ethics in Marketing*, Homewood, IL: Irwin.

Hunt, S.D., Wood, V.R. and Chonko, L.B. (1989), 'Corporate Ethical Values and Organizational Commitment in Marketing', *Journal of Marketing*, vol. 53 (3), July, pp. 79–90.

Irvine, S. and Ponton, A. (1988), *A Green Manifesto*, London: Macdonald Optima.

Iyer, E. and Banerjee, B. (1993), 'Anatomy of Green Advertising', *Advances in Consumer Research*, vol. 20, Chicago: Association for Consumer Research, pp. 494–501.

Iyer, E., Banerjee, B. and Gulas, C. (1994), 'An Exposé on Green Television Ads', *Advances in Consumer Research*, vol. 21, Chicago: Association for Consumer Research.

Jackall, R. (1988), *Moral Mazes*, New York: Oxford University Press.

Jarillo, J.C. and Stevenson, H.H. (1991), 'Co-operative Strategies – the Payoffs and the Pitfalls', *Long Range Planning*, vol. 24 (1), pp. 64–70.

Jennings, P.D. and Zandgergen, P.A. (1995). 'Ecologically Sustainable Organizations: An Institutional Approach', *Academy of Management Review*, vol. 20 (4), pp. 1015–1052.

Johnson, G. and Scholes, K. (1997), *Exploring Corporate Strategy: Text and Cases*, 4th edn, Hemel Hempstead: Prentice Hall.

Jones, D.G.B. and Monieson, D.D. (1990), 'Early Developments in the Philosophy of Marketing Thought', *Journal of Marketing*, vol. 54, January, pp. 102–113.

Jones, T.M. (1991), 'Ethical Decision Making by Individuals in Organizations: An Issue-Contingent Model', *Academy of Management Review*, vol. 16 (2), April, pp. 366–395.

Kangun, N. (1972), *Society and Marketing*, New York: Harper & Row.

Kangun, N. and Polonsky, M.J. (1995), 'Regulation of Environmental Marketing Claims: A Comparative Perspective', *International Journal of Advertising*, vol. 14 (1), pp. 1–24.

Kellner, D. (1989), *Jean Baudrillard: From Marxism to Postmodernism and Beyond*, Cambridge: Polity Press.

Kilbourne, W. (1995), 'Green Advertising: Salvation or Oxymoron?', *Journal of Advertising*, vol. 24 (2), pp. 7–19.

Kilbourne, W., McDonagh, P. and Prothero, A. (1997), 'Sustainable Consumption and the Quality of Life: A Macromarketing Challenge to the Dominant Social Paradigm', *Journal of Macromarketing*, vol. 17 (1), pp. 4–24.

Kinnear, T.C., Taylor, J.R. and Ahmed, S.A. (1974), 'Ecologically Concerned Consumers: Who Are They?', *Journal of Marketing*, vol. 38 (2), April, pp. 20–24.

Knights, D. and Morgan, G. (1991), 'Corporate Strategy, Organizations, and Subjectivity: A Critique', *Organization Studies*, vol. 12 (2), pp. 251–273.

Knights, D., Sturdy, A. and Morgan, G. (1994), 'The Consumer Rules? An Examination of the Rhetoric and "Reality" of Marketing in Financial Services', *European Journal of Marketing*, vol. 28 (3), pp. 42–54.

Kohlberg, L. (1969), 'Stage and Sequence: The Cognitive Development Approach to Socialization', in D.A. Goslin (ed.), *Handbook of Socialization Theory and Research*, Chicago: Rand McNally.

Kotha, S. (1995), 'Mass Customization: Implementing the Emerging Paradigm for Competitive Advantage', *Strategic Management Journal*, vol. 16 (special issue), pp. 21–42.

Kotler, P. (1972), 'What Consumerism Means for Marketers', *Harvard Business Review*, vol. 50, May–June, pp. 48–57.

Kotler, P. and Levy, S.J. (1969), 'Broadening the Concept of Marketing', *Journal of Marketing*, vol. 33 (1), January, pp. 10–15.

Kotler, P. and Roberto, E.L. (1989), *Social Marketing: Strategies for Changing Public Behaviour*, New York: Free Press.

Kotler, P. and Zaltman, G. (1971), 'Social Marketing: An Approach to Planned Social Change', *Journal of Marketing*, vol. 35 (3) July, pp. 3–12.

Kotler, P., Armstrong, G., Saunders, J. and Wong, V. (1996), *Principles of Marketing* (European edn), Hemel Hempstead: Prentice Hall.

Krugman, D.M. and Ferrell, O.C. (1981), 'The Organizational Ethics of Advertising: Corporate and Agency Views', *Journal of Advertising*, vol. 10 (1), pp. 21–30.

Laczniak, G.R. (1993), 'Marketing Ethics: Onward Toward Greater Expectations', *Journal of Public Policy and Marketing*, vol. 12 (1), pp. 91–96.

Laczniak, G.R. and Murphy, P.E. (1993), *Ethical Marketing Decisions: The Higher Road*, Boston, MA: Allyn & Bacon.

Laczniak, G.R., Lusch, R.F. and Murphy, P.E. (1979), 'Social Marketing: Its Ethical Dimensions', *Journal of Marketing*, vol. 43 (2), Spring, pp. 29–36.

Lager, F. (1994), *Ben and Jerry's: The Inside Scoop*, New York: Crown Publishers Inc.

Lamming, R. and Hampson, J. (1996), 'The Environment as a Supply Chain Management Issue', *British Journal of Management*, vol. 7 (special issue), pp. S45–S62.

Lazer, W. and Kelley, E.J. (1973), *Social Marketing: Perspectives and Viewpoints*, Homewood, IL: Irwin.

Letiche, H. (1998), 'Business Ethics: (In-)Justice and (Anti-)Law – Reflections on Derrida, Bauman and Lipovetsky', in M. Parker (ed.), *Ethics and Organizations*, London: Sage.

Levitt, T. (1958), 'The Dangers of Being Socially Responsible', *Harvard Business Review*, September–October, pp. 41–50.

Levitt, T. (1972), 'The Morality(?) of Advertising', in N. Kangun (ed.), *Society and Marketing*, New York: Harper & Row.

Levitt, T. (1980), 'Marketing Success Through Differentiation – Of Anything', *Harvard Business Review*, January–February, pp. 83–91.

Levy, S.J. and Zaltman, G. (1975), *Marketing, Society, and Conflict*, Englewood Cliffs, NJ: Prentice Hall.

Lill, D., Gross, C. and Peterson, R. (1986), 'The Inclusion of Social Responsibility Themes by Magazine Advertisers: A Longitudinal Study', *Journal of Advertising*, vol. 15 (2), pp. 35–41.

McDonagh, P. (1996), 'Relationship Marketing: Death from Natural Causes!', paper presented at the Department of Marketing Research Seminar, University of Stirling, 22 October 1996.

McDonagh, P. (1998), 'Towards a Theory of Sustainable Communication in Risk Society: Relating Issues of Sustainability to Marketing Communications', *Journal of Marketing Management*, vol. 14 (6), pp. 591–622.

McGuire, J.B., Sundgren, A. and Schneeweis, T. (1988), 'Corporate Social Responsibility and Firm Financial Performance', *Academy of Management Journal*, vol. 31 (4), pp. 854–872.

Macnaghten, P. and Urry, J. (1995), 'Towards a Sociology of Nature', *Sociology*, vol. 29 (2), pp. 203–220.

Martin, J. (1985), 'Can Organizational Culture Be Managed?', in P.J. Frost, L.F. Moore, M.R. Louis, C. Lundberg and J. Martin (eds), *Organizational Culture*, Newbury Park, CA: Sage.

Martin, J. (1992), *Cultures in Organizations: Three Perspectives*, New York: Oxford University Press.

Martin, J. (1995), 'Ignore Your Customer', *Fortune*, 1 May 1995, pp. 83–86.

Martin, J. and Siehl, C. (1983), 'Organizational Culture and Counterculture: An Uneasy Symbiosis', *Organizational Dynamics*, vol. 12 (2), pp. 52–64.

Martin, J., Feldman, M.S., Hatch, M.J. and Sitkin, S.B. (1983), 'The Uniqueness Paradox in Organizational Stories', *Administrative Science Quarterly*, vol. 28, pp. 438–453.

Martin, P.Y. and Turner, B.A. (1986), 'Grounded Theory and Organizational Research', *The Journal of Applied Behavioral Science*, vol. 22 (2), pp. 141–157.

Mendleson, N. and Polonsky, M.J. (1995), 'Using Strategic Alliances to Develop Credible Green Marketing', *Journal of Consumer Marketing*, vol. 12 (2), pp. 4–18.

Menon, A. and Menon, A. (1997), 'Enviropreneurial Marketing Strategy: The Emergence of Corporate Environmentalism as Market Strategy', *Journal of Marketing*, vol. 61 (1), January, pp. 51–67.

Meyerson, D.E. and Scully, M.A. (1995), 'Tempered Radicalism and the Politics of Ambivalence and Change', *Organization Science*, vol. 6, pp. 585–600.

Miles, M.B. and Huberman, A.M. (1994), *Qualitative Data Analysis*, 2nd edn, Thousand Oaks, CA: Sage.

Miller, C.C., Cardinal, L.B. and Glick, W.H. (1997), 'Retrospective Reports in Organizational Research: A Re-examination of Recent Evidence', *Academy of Management Journal*, vol. 40 (1), pp. 189–204.

Milne, G.R., Iyer, E.S., and Gooding-Williams, S. (1996), 'Environmental Organization Alliance Relationships Within and Across Non-profit, Business, and Government Sectors', *Journal of Public Policy and Marketing*, vol. 15 (2), pp. 203–215.

Mintzberg, H. (1979), 'An Emerging Strategy of "Direct" Research', *Administrative Science Quarterly*, vol. 24, December, pp. 582–589.

Mintzberg, H. (1983), 'The Case For Corporate Social Responsibility', *Journal of Business Strategy*, vol. 4 (2), pp. 3–15.

Mintzberg, H. (1989), *Mintzberg on Management*, New York: Free Press.

Mintzberg, H. (1990), 'The Design School: Reconsidering the Basic Premises of Strategic Management', *Strategic Management Journal*, vol. 11 (6), pp. 171–195.

Mintzberg, H. (1991), 'Learning 1, Planning 0: Reply to Igor Ansoff', *Strategic Management Journal*, vol. 12 (6), pp. 463–466.

Mitroff, I.I. and Denton, E.A. (1999), 'A Study of Spirituality in the Workplace', *Sloan Management Review*, vol. 40 (4), pp. 83–92.

Morgan, G. (1983), 'Research as Engagement: A Personal View', in G. Morgan (ed.), *Beyond Method: Strategies for Social Research*, Newbury Park, CA: Sage.

Morgan, G. and Smircich, L. (1980), 'The Case for Qualitative Research', *Academy of Management Review*, vol. 5 (4), pp. 491–500.

Murphy, D.F. (1996a), 'In the Company of Partners. Business, NGOs and Sustainable Development: Towards a Global Perspective', in R. Aspinwall and J. Smith (eds), *Environmentalist and Business Partnerships: A Sustainable Model? A Critical Assessment of the Impact of the WWF UK 1995 Group*, Cambridge: White Horse Press.

Murphy, D.F. (1996b), 'DIY–WWF Alliance: Doing it Together for the World's Forests', School for Policy Studies/New Consumer Working Paper, University of Bristol.

Murphy, D.F. and Bendell, J. (1997), *In the Company of Partners: Business, Environmental Groups and Sustainable Development Post-Rio*, Bristol: Policy Press.

Murphy, P.E. and Laczniak, G.R. (1981), 'Marketing Ethics: A Review With Implications for Managers, Educators and Researchers', in B.M Enis and K.J. Roering (eds), *Review of Marketing*, Chicago: American Marketing Association.

Nadel, M.V. (1971), *The Politics of Consumer Protection*, Indianapolis, IN: Bobbs-Merrill.

Naess, A. (1989), *Ecology, Community and Lifestyle*, trans. and rev. D. Rothenberg, Cambridge: Cambridge University Press.

National Consumer Council (1996), *Green Claims: A Consumer Investigation into Marketing Claims About the Environment*, London: National Consumer Council.

Newton, T.J. and Harte, G. (1997), 'Green Business: Technicist Kitsch?', *Journal of Management Studies*, vol. 34 (1), pp. 75–98.

Nichols, M. (1994), 'Does New Age Business Have a Message for Managers?', *Harvard Business Review*, March–April, pp. 52–60.

Nord, W.R. (1985), 'Can Organizational Culture Be Managed? A Synthesis', in P.J. Frost, L.F. Moore, M.R. Louis, C. Lundberg and J. Martin (eds), *Organizational Culture*, Newbury Park, CA: Sage.

Nwachukwu, S.L.S. and Vitell, S.J. (1997), 'The Influence of Corporate Culture on Managerial Ethical Judgements', *Journal of Business Ethics*, vol. 16, pp. 757–776.

O'Shaughnessy, N.J. (1990), 'High Priesthood, Low Priestcraft: The Role of Political Consultants', *European Journal of Marketing*, vol. 24 (2), pp. 7–23.

Ogbonna, E. (1992), 'Managing Organizational Culture: Fantasy or Reality?', *Human Resource Management Journal*, vol. 3 (2), pp. 42–54.

Ogbonna, E. and Harris, L.C. (1998). 'Managing Organizational Culture: Compliance or Genuine Change?', *British Journal of Management*, vol. 9, pp. 273–288.

Ostergaard, G.N. and Halsey, A.H. (1965), *Power in Co-operatives: A Study of the Internal Politics of British Retail Societies*, Oxford: Basil Blackwell.

Ottman, J.A. (1993), *Green Marketing: Challenges & Opportunities*, Lincolnwood, IL: NTC Business Books.

Owen, C.L. and Scherer, R.F. (1993), 'Social Responsibility and Market Share', *Review of Business*, vol. 15 (1), pp. 11–16.

Packard, V. (1957), *The Hidden Persuaders*, New York: Pocket Books (Cardinal Edition).

Parker, M. (1997), 'Business Ethics and Social Theory: Against Ethics', paper presented at the 1997 British Academy of Management Annual Conference, London Business School, September.

Parker, M. (ed.) (1998), *Ethics and Organizations*, London: Sage.

Patten, D.M. (1992), 'Intra-Industry Environmental Disclosures in Response to the Alaskan Oil Spill: A Note on Legitimacy Theory', *Accounting, Organizations and Society*, vol. 17 (5), pp. 471–476.

Peattie, K. (1992), *Green Marketing*, London: Pitman.

Peattie, K. (1995), *Environmental Marketing Management*, London: Pitman.

Peattie, K. (1999), 'Trappings Versus Substance in the Greening of Marketing Planning', *Journal of Strategic Marketing*, vol. 7, pp. 131–148.

Peattie, K. and Charter, M. (1994), 'Green Marketing' in M.J. Baker (ed.), *The Marketing Book*, 3rd edn, Oxford: Butterworth-Heinemann.

Peattie, K. and Ratnayaka, M. (1992), 'Responding to the Green Movement', *Industrial Marketing Management*, vol. 21 (2), pp. 103–110.

Peattie, K. and Ringler, A. (1994), 'Management and the Environment: A Comparison Between the U.K. and Germany', *European Management Journal*, vol. 12 (2), pp. 216–225.

Peters, T.J. and Waterman, R.H. (1982), *In Search of Excellence*, London: Harper & Row.

Pettigrew, A.M. (1973), *The Politics of Organizational Decision-Making*, London: Tavistock.

Pettigrew, A.M. (1979), 'On Studying Organizational Cultures', *Administrative Science Quarterly*, vol. 24, December, pp. 570–581.

Pettigrew, A.M. (1985), *The Awakening Giant*, Oxford: Blackwell.

Pfeffer, J. (1981a), 'Management as Symbolic Action: the Creation and Maintenance of Organizational Paradigms', *Research in Organizational Behaviour*, vol. 3, pp. 1–52.

Pfeffer, J. (1981b), *Power in Organizations*, Marshfield, MA: Pitman.

Pfeffer, J. and Salancik, G.R. (1978), The External Control of Organizations: A Resource Dependence Perspective, New York: Harper & Row.

Phillips, B.J. (1997), 'In Defence of Advertising: A Social Perspective', *Journal of Business Ethics*, vol. 16, pp. 109–118.

Phillips, N. (1991), 'The Sociology of Knowledge: Towards an Existential View of Business Ethics', *Journal of Business Ethics*, vol. 10, pp. 787–795.

Phillips, N. and Brown, J.L. (1993), 'Analyzing Communications In and Around Organizations: A Critical Hermeneutic Approach', *Academy of Management Journal*, vol. 36 (6), pp. 1547–1576.

Pollay, R.W. (1986), 'The Distorted Mirror: Reflections on the Unintended Consequences of Advertising', *Journal of Marketing*, vol. 50 (2), April, pp. 18–36.

Polonsky, M.J. and Ottman, J.A. (1998), 'Stakeholders' Contribution to the Green New Product Development Process', *Journal of Marketing Management*, vol. 14 (6), pp. 533–558.

Posner, B.Z. and Schmidt, W.H. (1984), 'Values and the American Manager: An Update', *California Management Review*, vol. 26 (3), Spring, pp. 202–216.

Posner, B.Z. and Schmidt, W.H. (1992), 'Values and the American Manager: An Update Updated', *California Management Review*, vol. 34 (3), Spring, pp. 80–94.

Prothero, A. (1990), 'Green Consumerism and the Societal Marketing Concept: Marketing Strategies for the 1990s', *Journal of Marketing Management*, vol. 6 (2), pp. 87–103.

Prothero, A. and McDonagh, P. (1992), 'Producing Environmentally Acceptable Cosmetics? The Impact of Environmentalism on the United Kingdom Cosmetics and Toiletries Industry', *Journal of Marketing Management*, vol. 8 (2), pp. 147–166.

Prothero, A., McDonagh, P. and Peattie, K. (1994), 'Green Marketing Communications – Dressing Windows or Opening Doors?', in J. Bell *et al.* (eds), *Marketing: Unity in Diversity*, Proceedings of the 1994 Marketing Education Group Annual Conference, University of Ulster, vol. II, pp. 766–776.

Puxty, A.G. (1986), 'Social Accounting as Immanent Legitimation: A Critique of Technist Ideology', *Advances in Public Interest Accounting*, vol. 1, pp. 95–112.

Randall, D.M. and Gibson, A.M. (1990), 'Methodology in Business Ethics Research: A Review and Critical Assessment', *Journal of Business Ethics*, vol. 9 (6), pp. 457–471.

Rittenburg, T.L. and Parthasarathy, M. (1997), 'Ethical Implications of Target Market Selection', *Journal of Macromarketing*, vol. 17 (2), pp. 49–64.

Ritzer, G. (1997), 'Introduction', in J. Baudrillard, *The Consumer Society: Myths and Structures* (English trans.), London: Sage.

Robertson, D.C. and Nicholson, N. (1996), 'Expressions of Corporate Social Responsibility in UK Firms', *Journal of Business Ethics*, vol. 15, pp. 1095–1106.

Robin, D.P. and Reidenbach, R.E. (1987), 'Social Responsibility, Ethics and Marketing Strategy: Closing the Gap Between Concept and Application', *Journal of Marketing*, vol. 51 (1), January, pp. 44–58.

Robin, D.P. and Reidenbach, R.E. (1993), 'Searching for a Place to Stand: Toward a Workable Ethical Philosophy for Marketing', *Journal of Public Policy and Marketing*, vol. 12 (1), Spring, pp. 97–105.

Roddick, A. (1992), *Body and Soul*, London: Vermillion.

Rogers, D. (1998), 'Ethical Tactics Arouse Public Doubt', *Marketing*, 6 August 1998, pp. 12–13.

Rowlinson, M. and Hassard, J. (1993), 'The Invention of Corporate Culture: A History of the Histories of Cadbury', *Human Relations*, vol. 46 (3), pp. 299–326.

Sagoff, M. (1986), 'At the Shrine of Our Lady of Fatima, or Why Political Questions Are Not All Economic', in D. VanDeVeer and C. Pierce (eds), *People, Penguins, And Plastic Trees: Basic Issues in Environmental Ethics*, Belmont, CA: Wadsworth.

Salancik, G.R. and Pfeffer, J. (1977), 'Who Gets Power – And How They Hold On To It: A Strategic Contingency Model of Power', *Organization Dynamics*, vol. 5, pp. 3–21.

Schein, E.H. (1992), *Organizational Culture and Leadership*, 2nd edn, San Francisco: Jossey-Bass.

Schlegelmilch, B.B. (1988), 'Targeting of Fund-raising Appeals – How to Identify Donors', *European Journal of Marketing*, vol. 22 (1), pp. 31–40.

Schlegelmilch, B.B. and Houston, J.E. (1989), 'Corporate Codes of Ethics in Large UK Companies: An Empirical Investigation of Use, Content and Attitudes', *European Journal of Marketing*, vol. 23 (6), pp. 7–24.

Schlegelmilch, B.B., Bohlen, G. and Diamantopoulos, A. (1996), 'The Link Between Green Purchasing Decisions and Measures of Environmental Consciousness', *European Journal of Marketing*, vol. 30 (5), pp. 35–55.

Schot, J. (1992), 'Credibility and Markets as Greening Forces for the Chemical Industry', *Business Strategy and the Environment*, vol. 1 (1), pp. 35–44.

Schot, J. and Fischer, K. (1993), 'The Greening of the Industrial Firm', in K. Fischer and J. Schot (eds), *Environmental Strategies for Industry*, Washington, DC: Island Press.

Schrum, L.J., McCarty, J.A. and Lowrey, T.M. (1995), 'Buyer Characteristics of the Green Consumer and their Implications for Advertising Strategy', *Journal of Advertising*, vol. 24 (2), pp. 71–82.

Schumacher, E.F. (1974), *Small is Beautiful*, London: Abacus.

Sethi, S.P. (1979), 'A Conceptual Framework for Environmental Analysis of Social Issues and Evaluation of Business Response Patterns', *Academy of Management Review*, vol. 4 (1), pp. 63–74.

Sharp Paine, L. (1993), 'Children as Consumers: The Ethics of Children's Television Advertising', in N.C. Smith and J.A. Quelch (eds), *Ethics in Marketing*, Homewood, IL: Irwin.

Sharp Paine, L. (1994), 'Managing for Organizational Integrity', *Harvard Business Review*, March–April, pp. 106–117.

Shrivastava, P. (1993), 'The Greening of Business', in D. Smith (ed.), *Business and the Environment: Implications of the New Environmentalism*, London: Paul Chapman.

Shrivastava, P. (1994), 'CASTRATED Environment: GREENING Organizational Studies', *Organizational Studies*, vol. 15 (5), pp. 705–726.

Shrivastava, P. (1995a), 'Ecocentric Management for a Risk Society', *Academy of Management Review*, vol. 20 (1), pp. 118–137.

Shrivastava, P. (1995b), 'Environmental Technologies and Competitive Advantage', *Strategic Management Journal*, vol. 16 (special issue), Summer, pp. 183–200.

Siehl, C. (1985), 'After the Founder: An Opportunity to Manage Culture', in P.J. Frost, L.F. Moore, M.R. Louis, C. Lundberg and J. Martin (eds), *Organizational Culture*, Newbury Park, CA: Sage.

Simintiras, A.C., Schlegelmilch, B.B. and Diamantopoulos, A. (1997), 'Greening the Marketing Mix: A Review of the Literature and an Agenda for Future Research', in P. McDonagh and A. Prothero (eds) *Green Management: A Reader*, London: Dryden Press.

Simmons, P. and Wynne, B. (1993), 'Responsible Care: Trust, Credibility, and Environmental Management', in K. Fischer and J. Schot (eds), *Environmental Strategies for Industry*, Washington, DC: Island Press.

Simms, C. (1992), 'Green Issues and Strategic Management in the Grocery Retail Sector', *International Journal of Retail and Distribution Management*, vol. 20 (1), pp. 32–42.

Simonian, H. (1995), 'Pitfalls of Eco-Shopping', *Financial Times*, 5 January 1995, p. 14.

Sinclair, A. (1993), 'Approaches to Organizational Culture and Ethics', *Journal of Business Ethics*, vol. 12, pp. 63–73.

Smart, B. (1992), *Beyond Compliance: A New Industry View of the Environment*, Washington, DC: World Resources Institute.

Smircich, L. (1983), 'Concepts of Culture and Organizational Analysis', *Administrative Science Quarterly*, vol. 28, September, pp. 339–358.

Smith, N.C. (1990), *Morality and the Market: Consumer Pressure for Corporate Accountability*, London: Routledge.

Smith, N.C. (1995), 'Marketing Ethics for the Ethics Era', *Sloan Management Review*, vol. 36 (4), pp. 85–97.

Smith, N.C. and Cooper-Martin, E. (1997), 'Ethics and Target Marketing: The Role of Product Harm and Consumer Vulnerability', *Journal of Marketing*, vol. 61, July, pp. 1–20.

Smith, N.C. and Quelch, J.A. (1993), *Ethics in Marketing*, Homewood, IL: Irwin.

Sparks, J.R. and Hunt, S.D. (1998), 'Marketing Researcher Ethical Sensitivity: Conceptualization, Measurement, and Exploratory Investigation', *Journal of Marketing*, vol. 62, April, pp. 92–109.

Starkey, K. (1998), 'Durkheim and the Limits of Corporate Culture: Whose Culture? Which Durkheim?', *Journal of Management Studies*, vol. 35 (2), pp. 125–136.

Stead, W.E. and Stead, J.G. (1992), *Management for a Small Planet: Strategic Decision Making and the Environment*, Newbury Park, CA: Sage.

Steadman, M.E., Zimmerer, T.W. and Green, R.F. (1995), 'Pressures from Stakeholders Hit Japanese Companies', *Long Range Planning*, vol. 28 (6), pp. 29–37.

Steger, U. (1993), 'The Greening of the Boardroom: How German Companies are Dealing with Environmental Issues', in K. Fischer and J. Schot (eds), *Environmental Strategies for Industry*, Washington, DC: Island Press.

Stephenson, T.E. (1963), *Management in Co-operative Societies*, London: Heineman.

Strauss, A. and Corbin, J. (1990), *Basics of Qualitative Research: Grounded Theory Procedures and Techniques*, Newbury Park, CA: Sage.

Strong, C. (1996), 'Features Contributing to the Growth of Ethical Consumerism – A Preliminary Investigation', *Marketing Intelligence & Planning*, vol. 14 (5), pp. 5–13.

Stroup, M.A. and Neubert, R.L. (1987), 'The Evolution of Social Responsibility', *Business Horizons*, March–April, pp. 22–24.

Taylor, G. and Welford, R. (1994), 'Environmental Strategies of Leading UK Supermarket Chains', in R. Welford (ed.), *Cases in Environmental Management and Business Strategy*, London: Pitman.

ten Bos, R. (1997), 'Business Ethics and Bauman Ethics', *Organization Studies*, vol. 18 (6), pp. 997–1014.

Thompson, C.J. (1995), 'A Contextualist Proposal for the Conceptualisation and Study of Marketing', *Public Policy and Marketing*, vol. 14 (2), pp. 177–191.

Thornhill, J. (1992), 'Balancing Profit and Principle', *Financial Times*, 22 June 1992, p. 5.

Tombs, S. (1993), 'The Chemical Industry and Environmental Issues', in D. Smith (ed.), *Business and the Environment: Implications of the New Environmentalism*, London: Paul Chapman.

Treviño, L.K. (1986), 'Ethical Decision Making in Organizations: A Person–Situation Interactionist Model', *Academy of Management Review*, vol. 11 (3), pp. 601–617.

Treviño, L.K. and Nelson, K.A. (1995), *Managing Business Ethics: Straight Talk About How To Do It Right*, New York: John Wiley.

Treviño, L.K., Butterfield, K.D. and McCabe, D.L. (1998), 'The Ethical Context in Organizations: Influences on Employee Attitudes and Behaviours', *Business Ethics Quarterly*, vol. 8 (3), pp. 447–476.

Tsalikis, J. and Fritzsche, D.J. (1989), 'Business Ethics: A Literature Review with a Focus on Marketing Ethics', *Journal of Business Ethics*, vol. 8, September, pp. 695–743.

Turner, B. (1971), *Exploring the Industrial Subculture*, London: Macmillan.

Turner, B.A. (1983), 'The Use of Grounded Theory for the Qualitative Analysis of Organizational Behaviour', *Journal of Management Studies*, vol. 20 (3), pp. 333–348.

Unsworth, B. (1992), *Sacred Hunger*, London: Hamish Hamilton.

van Dam, Y. and Apeldoorn, P. (1996), 'Sustainable Marketing', *Journal of Macromarketing*, vol. 16 (2), pp. 45–56.

Van Maanen, J. (1973), 'Observations on the Making of Policemen', *Human Organization*, vol. 32 (4), pp. 407–418.

Van Maanen, J. (1979), 'Reclaiming Qualitative Methods for Organizational Research: A Preface', *Administrative Science Quarterly*, vol. 24, December, pp. 520–526.

Van Maanen, J. (1991), 'The Smile Factory: Work at Disneyland', in P.J. Frost, L.F. Moore, M.R. Louis, C.C. Lundberg and J. Martin (eds), *Reframing Organizational Culture*, Newbury Park, CA: Sage.

Van Maanen, J. and Barley, S.R. (1985), 'Fragments of a Theory', in P.J. Frost, L.F. Moore, M.R. Louis, C. Lundberg and J. Martin (eds), *Organizational Culture*, Newbury Park, CA: Sage.

Vandermerwe, S. and Oliff, M.D. (1990), 'Customers Drive Corporations Green', *Long Range Planning*, vol. 23 (6), pp. 10–16.

Varadarajan, P.R. and Rajaratnam, D. (1986), 'Symbiotic Marketing Revisited', *Journal of Marketing*, vol. 50 (1), January, pp. 7–17.

Vitell, S.J., Rallapalli, K.C. and Singhapakdi, A. (1993), 'Marketing Norms: The Influence of Personal Moral Philosophies and Organizational Ethical Culture', *Journal of the Academy of Management Science*, vol. 21 (4), pp. 331–337.

Walley, N. and Whitehead, B. (1994), 'It's Not Easy Being Green', *Harvard Business Review*, May–June, pp. 46–52.

Wasik, J.F. (1996), *Green Marketing and Management: A Global Perspective*, Cambridge, MA: Blackwell.

Waters, J.A. and Bird, F. (1987), 'The Moral Dimension of Organizational Culture', *Journal of Business Ethics*, vol. 6, pp. 15–22.

Watson, T.J. (1994a), *In Search of Management: Culture, Chaos and Control in Managerial Work*, London: Routledge.

Watson, T.J. (1994b), 'Managing, Crafting and Researching: Words, Skill and Imagination in Shaping Management Research', *British Journal of Management*, vol. 5 (special issue), S77–S87.

Watson, T.J. (1998), 'Ethical Codes and Moral Communities: the Gunlaw Temptation, the Simon Solution and the David Dilemma', in M. Parker (ed.), *Ethics and Organizations*, London: Sage.

Weber, M. (1947), *The Theory of Social and Economic Organization*, trans. A.M. Henderson and T. Parsons, Oxford: Oxford University Press.

Weick, K.E. (1989), 'Theory Construction as Disciplined Imagination', *Academy of Management Review*, vol. 14 (4), pp. 516–531.

Weick, K.E. (1995), *Sensemaking in Organizations*, Thousand Oaks, CA: Sage.

Welford, R. (1995), *Environmental Strategy and Sustainable Development*, London: Routledge.

Welford, R. and Gouldson, A. (1993), *Environmental Management and Business Strategy*, London: Pitman.

Werhane, P.H. (1998), 'Moral Imagination and the Search for Ethical Decision-Making in Management', *Business Ethics Quarterly*, The Ruffin Series (1), pp. 75–98.

Westley, F. and Vredenburg, H. (1991), 'Strategic Bridging: The Collaboration Between Environmentalists and Business in the Marketing of Green Products', *Journal of Applied Behavioural Science*, vol. 27 (1), pp. 65–90.

Wilkins, A.W. (1983), 'Organizational Stories as Symbols Which Control the Organization', in L.R. Pondy, P.J. Frost, G. Morgan, and T.C. Dandridge (eds), *Organizational Symbolism*, Greenwich, CT: JAI Press.

Williamson, J. (1978), *Decoding Advertisements*, London: Marion Boyars.

Williamson, J. (1986), *Consuming Passions*, London: Marion Boyars.

Wong, V., Turner, W. and Stoneman, P. (1996), 'Marketing Strategies and Market Prospects for Environmentally-Friendly Consumer Products', *British Journal of Management*, vol. 7 (3), pp. 263–281.

World Commission on Environment and Development (1987), *Our Common Future*, Oxford: Oxford University Press.

Yeo, S. (1995), *Who Was J.T.W. Mitchell?*, Manchester: CWS Membership Services.

Yin, R. (1989), *Case Study Research: Design and Methods*, rev. edn, Newbury Park, CA: Sage.

Index